RE-VISION
ESSAYS IN FEMINIST FILM CRITICISM

 The American Film Institute

The American Film Institute Monograph Series

Ann Martin
Supervising Editor

RE-VISION

ESSAYS IN FEMINIST FILM CRITICISM

Edited by

Mary Ann Doane,
Patricia Mellencamp
and
Linda Williams

University Publications of America, Inc.

Copyright © The American Film Institute 1984

LCCCN 83-23366
ISBN 0-89093-585-8

The American Film Institute *Monograph* Series is published by University Publications of America, Inc., Frederick, MD, in association with The American Film Institute.

The American Film Institute
2021 North Western Avenue
P.O. Box 27999
Los Angeles, California 90027

Library of Congress Cataloging in Publication Data

Re-vision : essays in feminist film criticism.
    (American Film Institute monograph series; v. 3)
    1. Feminism and motion pictures—Addresses, essays, lectures. 2. Feminist motion pictures—History and criticism—Addresses, essays, lectures. I. Doane, Mary Ann. II. Mellencamp, Patricia. III. Williams, Linda, 1946-   . IV. Series.
PN1995.9.W6R4   1984   792'.01'5   83-23366
ISBN 0-89093-585-8

Table of Contents

Preface

In their introduction, the editors of *Re-vision* observe that during the seventies and early eighties, women's work in film—the making of feminist documentaries, the organizing of women's film festivals, the writing of criticism and theory—was remarkable for its high degree of cooperation and collaboration. It is fitting, then, that this volume of thoughtful, provocative essays of feminist film criticism is the result of their collective work as well as the collaboration of the Center for the Humanities at the University of Southern California and the Center for Twentieth Century Studies at the University of Wisconsin-Milwaukee.

In 1975-76, the Center for Twentieth Century Studies, then under the imaginative direction of the late Michel Benamou, began its pioneering work in film theory with the help of the good counsel of its Senior Fellow, Ronald Gottesman, a man of rare generosity in all spheres. Every year after that, conferences on film theory were held in Milwaukee until 1981, when the Center for the Humanities, with Ronald Gottesman as its director, sponsored "Cinema Histories, Cinema Practices I." Organized by Ronald Gottesman and the University of Wisconsin-Milwaukee's Patricia Mellencamp, "Cinema Histories, Cinema Practices I," the impetus for this volume, focused on the reexamination of the premises of cinema histories—the history of cinema, history in cinema, and cinema as history. Within this framework, a critical concern was the reconsideration and development—the re-visioning—of theoretical models provided by the feminist critique of cinema's institutions and both written and filmic texts. It remained for the Center for Twentieth Century Studies to help with some of the practical details of seeing the present volume into print and to host "Cinema Histories, Cinema Practices II" in the fall of 1982.

On behalf of Mary Ann Doane, Patricia Mellencamp and Linda Williams, I should like to express our appreciation to the splendid staff of the Center for Twentieth Century Studies, especially Naomi Galbreath, Jean Lile and

Virginia Schauble. Without the generous and faithful help of the National Endowment of the Arts, for which we are most grateful, this volume would not have been possible. And lastly, I should like to thank Ann Martin, the supervising editor for the new American Film Institute Monograph Series, for her imagination and resourcefulness in implementing this important series as well as for her meticulous attention to this volume.

Kathleen Woodward, Director
Center for Twentieth Century Studies

Contributors

TERESA DE LAURETIS is Professor of Italian and Coordinator of the Film Major at the University of Wisconsin-Milwaukee. She has written for *Film Quarterly, Screen, Ciné-Tracts, Discourse, Medianalyses*, etc., and is co-editor, with Stephen Heath, of *The Cinematic Apparatus* (St. Martin's Press, 1980). Her forthcoming book *Alice Doesn't: Feminism, Semiotics, Cinema* will be published by Indiana University Press.

MARY ANN DOANE is Assistant Professor in the Semiotics Program at Brown University. She has written on sound and the cinema, identification and feminist criticism, and is currently working on a book on the "woman's film" of the 1940s.

CHRISTINE GLEDHILL job-shares a post in the Education Department of the British Film Institute, and writes and lectures on a freelance basis. She contributed a two-part essay on *Klute* and feminist film criticism to *Women in Film Noir* (British Film Institute, 1980), and is currently preparing an anthology on melodrama and the woman's film for BFI publishing.

JUDITH MAYNE is Associate Professor of French at Ohio State University. She has written on film and the novel, Soviet cinema, and feminist criticism.

PATRICIA MELLENCAMP teaches in the Art History Department of the University of Wisconsin-Milwaukee. She is co-editor, with Stephen Heath, of *Cinema and Language* (AFI Monograph I, 1983), and has edited two issues of *Ciné-Tracts*, on "Identification" and "The Film Body."

B. RUBY RICH is Director of the Film Program at the New York State Council on the Arts. She is an Associate Editor of *Jump Cut* and has published in the *Village Voice, Heresies, Radical America, Chrysalis* and *Feminist Review.*

KAJA SILVERMAN is Associate Professor of Film at Simon Fraser University. She is the author of *The Subject of Semiotics* (Oxford University Press, 1983), and of several articles on masochism and marginal male subjectivity.

LINDA WILLIAMS teaches English and Film at the University of Illinois at Chicago. *Figures of Desire*, her book on Surrealist film, has been published by the University of Illinois Press. She is also an Associate Editor of *Jump Cut*.

Acknowledgments

Christine Gledhill's article "Recent Developments in Feminist Film Criticism" first appeared in *Quarterly Review of Film Studies*, vol. 3, no. 4 (1978). PO Box 67, South Salem, NY 10590.

Judith Mayne's article "The Woman at the Keyhole: Women's Cinema and Feminist Criticism" first appeared in *New German Critique* 23 (Spring/Summer, 1981). The University of Wisconsin-Milwaukee, Department of German, Box 413, Milwaukee, WI 53201.

B. Ruby Rich's article "From Repressive Tolerance to Erotic Liberation: *Maedchen in Uniform*" first appeared in *Jump Cut* 24/25 (March, 1981). 2620 No. Richmond, Chicago, IL 60647.

Feminist Film Criticism: An Introduction

Mary Ann Doane
Patricia Mellencamp
Linda Williams

> *Re-vision—the act of looking back, of seeing with fresh eyes, of entering an old text from a new critical direction—is for women more than a chapter in cultural history: it is an act of survival.*
>
> —Adrienne Rich[1]

In the last decade feminist film criticism, growing out of the energy of the women's movement, has become an academic field, a series of approaches, perched somewhat uneasily between the already marginally legitimate areas of film and women's studies programs in this country. Yet despite, or perhaps because of, this marginality, it has become a vital area of research and debate. In the last five years alone, several anthologies on women and film have been published; several journals dealing extensively with important aspects of women and film continue to publish highly significant work; and other journals have devoted special issues to the topic. This essay will sketch a brief critical history of these works and their theoretical lineage.

The strategy of feminist film criticism coincides with, while relocating, contemporary theories of the text. Roland Barthes, for example, writing of the multiplicity of meaning in texts, suggests that multiplicity may also be a way of denying the rigid constraints of sexual duality. "The opposition of the sexes must not be a law of Nature...both the meanings and the sexes must be pluralized."[2] Another strategy—both exhortation and struggle within Adrienne Rich's poetry and essays—is that of "revision," learning to see "with fresh eyes," entering old texts from new critical directions. This essay will proceed from and expand these two arguments.

*One fictions history starting from a political reality that
renders it true; one fictions a politics that doesn't as yet
exist starting from a historical truth.*

—Michel Foucault[3]

To fiction "history starting from a political reality that renders it true,"
we must begin with the present "politics," the context behind this volume.
The conference "Cinema Histories, Cinema Practices I" was held in California in May 1981. There was no special session for the topic "women and film"
within the conference format. Although there are many situations in which
such a forum is desirable, in this case conference organizers viewed feminism
as an integral part of any historical and theoretical critique of representation.
As the conference description stated:

> Critical to *all* the topic areas is the impetus toward reexamination and
> the positing of new theoretical models provided by feminist critiques of
> cinema's institutions and written and filmed texts. This project will
> analyze women's essentially erased places... these stories are rarely
> told, barely remembered.[4]

That a remarkable body of feminist papers did grow out of the full range
of the conference program, rather than from a ghettoized women's segment
of it, attests to the centrality of the issues with which feminists are concerned
and to the many successes of the feminist struggle over the past decade.

During the four day event, it became apparent that feminist discourses
did not adhere to the traditional demarcations of film scholarship. The papers
were not undisciplined, they were merely at odds with traditional empirical
views of film history; in many cases they did not address history at all. Because
feminist discourse on film can only be written as a counter-history, or
re-vision, of the more orthodox canon and because there is still so much
re-vision to be done before a genuine women's history can emerge, we
thought it appropriate to separate these essays from the more general
conference debate on history and practice, placing them within another,
emerging context.[5] The papers by de Lauretis, Doane, Silverman and Williams were presented at the conference (and subsequently revised). The
essays by Gledhill, Mayne and Rich have been previously published and were
chosen for inclusion in this volume because they are particularly compatible
with the concerns of the conference.

Since the various anthologies of women and film published in recent
years have not paused to examine what feminist re-vision has accomplished
in film studies over the last decade, it seems timely to do so now. The
following chronology of events, major publications and (some) films is
adapted and updated from that outlined by B. Ruby Rich in her article "In the
Name of Feminist Film Criticism."[6] Bracketed entries are our additions and
updates; we have also provided all entries after 1978. The chronology is

offered as a brief way of indicating some of the achievements, trends, and diverse directions within which the ongoing work of feminist film criticism must be situated. The reader is forewarned that it is selective and incomplete.

1971   Release of *Growing Up Female, Janie's Janie, Three Lives* and *The Woman's Film*—first generation of feminist documentaries.

1972   First New York International Festival of Women's Films and the Women's Event at Edinburgh Film Festival. First issue of *Women and Film* magazine; special issues on women and film in *Take One, Film Library Quarterly* and *The Velvet Light Trap*; filmography of women directors in *Film Comment*. [John Berger's *Ways of Seeing*.]

1973   Toronto Women and Film Festival, Washington Women's Film Festival, season of women's cinema at National Film Theatre in London and Buffalo women's film conference. Marjorie Rosen's *Popcorn Venus* (first book on women in film) and *Notes on Women's Cinema*, edited by Claire Johnston for British Film Institute (first anthology of feminist film theory).

1974   Chicago Films by Women Festival. First issue of *Jump Cut* (quarterly on contemporary film emphasizing feminist perspective); two books on images of women in film: Molly Haskell's *From Reverence to Rape* and Joan Mellen's *Women and Their Sexuality in the New Film*.

1975   Conference of Feminists in the Media, New York and Los Angeles. *Women and Film* ceases publication; *The Work of Dorothy Arzner* (BFI monograph edited by Johnston), and Sharon Smith's *Women Who Make Movies* (guide to women filmmakers). [Laura Mulvey's "Visual Pleasure and Narrative Cinema" (*Screen*, Autumn, 1975). Release of Chantal Akerman's *Jeanne Dielman, 23 Quai de Commerce, 1080 Bruxelles* in Europe.]

1976   Second New York International Festival of Women's Films (smaller, noncollective, less successful than first) and Womanscene, a section of women's films in Toronto's Festival of Festivals (smaller, noncollective, but comparable in choices to 1973).

1977   First issue of *Camera Obscura* (journal of film theory founded largely by former *Women and Film* members, initially in opposition to it); Karyn Kay and Gerald Peary's *Women and the Cinema* (first anthology of criticism on women and film). [Release of Laura Mulvey and Peter Wollen's *Riddles of the Sphinx*.]

1978   *Women in Film Noir* (BFI anthology edited by E. Ann Kaplan); special feminist issues of *Quarterly Review of Film Studies* and *New German Critique*. Brandon French's *On the Verge of Revolt: Women in American Films of the Fifties*, [and Sumiko Higashi's *Virgins, Vamps, and Flappers: the American Silent Movie Heroine*—both studies of images of women. *m/f: A Feminist Journal* from Great Britain, contains frequent articles on women in film and media, from Marxist, feminist and psychoanalytic perspectives].

1979 Alternative Cinema Conference, bringing together over 100 feminists in the media for screenings, caucuses and strategizing within the left; Feminism and Cinema event at Edinburgh Film Festival, assessing the decade's filmmaking and theory, and debating over what might come next. Patricia Eren's *Sexual Stratagems: The World of Women in Film* (anthology on women and cinema). First issue of *Discourse: Berkeley Journal for Theoretical Studies in Media and Culture.* Release of Sally Potter's *Thriller,* and the collectively produced *Sigmund Freud's Dora: A Case of Mistaken Identity.*

1980 *Take Back the Night: Women on Pornography* (an anthology of feminist articles on the ideology of pornography edited by Laura Lederer); *Millennium Film Journal* (part of the Spring, 1980 issue devoted to feminism and film); *Ciné-Tracts* 11 and 12 publish feminist essays from "Conditions of Presence" Milwaukee conference, in issues on Identification and the Film Body.

1981 *Jump Cut* 24/25 publishes a special section on Lesbians and Film.

1982 *Film Reader* 5 publishes an issue on feminist film criticism made up of papers from the Lolita Raclin Rodgers Memorial Conference on Feminist Film Criticism at Northwestern University. *Wide Angle*, vol. 5, no. 2 issue on "Sexual Difference." Annette Kuhn, *Women's Pictures: Feminism and Cinema.*

Out of the above compilation, admittedly incomplete, several broad outlines emerge: the initial feminist documentaries and women's film festivals which were an integral part of the activism and consciousness-raising of the woman's movement; beginning scholarship on the "image of woman" in male-authored cinema (paralleled in literary and art history studies by similar "image of woman" investigations of stereotyping); the discovery of a previously lost history of women filmmakers, writers, editors, animators and documentarians; the introduction of new critical theories and methodologies of semiology and psychoanalysis by British feminists; and finally, the rise of feminist film criticism as an academic field that has already begun to produce a generation of feminist film scholars.[7]

As Ruby Rich observes, the overall tendency has been "a growing acceptance of feminist film as an area of study rather than a sphere of action."[8] Clearly this loss of activism is regrettable. Yet if feminist work on film has grown increasingly theoretical, less oriented towards political action, this does not necessarily mean that theory itself is counter-productive to the cause of feminism, nor that the institutional form of the debates within feminism have simply reproduced a male model of academic competition. In all the major activities listed in the chronology—filmmaking, festival organizing, scholarship—there has been a remarkable degree of cooperation and collaboration. Feminists sharing similar concerns collaborate in joint authorship and editorships, cooperative filmmaking and distribution arrangements.

Thus, many of the political aspirations of the women's movement form an integral part of the very structure of feminist work in and on film.

Nevertheless, the dangers attached to the assimilation of feminism within an institution such as the university or within the realm of academic discourses remain. For institutions, as Michel Foucault has so frequently reminded us, have their own very subtle forms of discursive coercion and ideological recuperation. Thus the very marginality of the feminist discourse in relation to traditional institutions has constituted much of its force. Our aim is not to simply gain entrance to what Kaja Silverman, borrowing from Foucault, refers to as male "discursive fellowships," but to unsettle and dislocate the modes of the production of knowledge which have traditionally maintained a hierarchy along the lines of sexual and class differences. Given the length of the history of this rationalization of sexual oppression disguised as epistemology, change would seem to entail nothing less than a massive reorganization of the disciplines which purport to territorialize and guard knowledge. Feminist film theory, given the "illegality"—by the standards of traditional academic discourse—of its two components (feminism and film studies) is in a unique position to pose precisely these challenges.

The chronology above clearly traces, at the very least, an increasing insistence on the crucial nature of a feminist analysis of filmic representation. What, if anything, can the chronology teach us? It is tempting to view the past eleven years as a steady progression towards a more sophisticated understanding of the problem of women's representation in film. But, as Christine Gledhill goes to some pains to illustrate in the first article of this volume, the matter is not so simple. Issues which at one time seemed solved—the complicity of a realist aesthetic with a patriarchal way of seeing—have often come back to haunt us, occasioning a more thorough understanding of the problems.

The pioneering essays and reviews published in *Women and Film*, the popular surveys of female images in film in Marjorie Rosen's and Molly Haskell's books, all criticized the failure of films to capture the complex realities of women's lives. Rosen and Haskell chronicled the decade-by-decade misrepresentation and stereotypes of women, occasionally locating, as in Haskell's chapter on "The Woman's Film," exceptional glimpses into more "authentic" expressions of women's experience.

Because woman's sexual difference had so often in the past been used to oppress her, the first response of these critics (and of a great many feminists at the time) was to de-emphasize difference. Thus Haskell and Rosen, writing at a time when "buddy films" had nearly pushed women off the screen altogether, looked back nostalgically at the exceptional women, the Rosalind Russells and Katharine Hepburns, who had once held their own with the men.

For these and other reasons the "image of" tradition of feminist film criticism has been recently criticized for revolving around fairly simple notions of realist representation. Yet it is important to recognize the value of such studies, both as a point of departure for students first encountering the subject and for historians and sociologists who seek more detailed information about the relation of stereotypical images to the epochs that produce them. If feminist film critics have rejected this tradition with increasing vehemence—in a way that many feminist literary critics, exercising a greater pragmatism and pluralism, have not—it is for reasons inherent in the film medium.

Two factors converge to limit the value of analyzing the image of women in film against existing or historical "realities": first, the limit in the variety of the images themselves in a relatively short film tradition that has, in Hollywood at least, privileged action-packed narratives and relegated women (in most of the major genres) to decorous objects of exchange; and second, the literal, as opposed to the metaphorical literary, nature of the term "image" in film. The strength of the term "image" in literary criticism lies precisely in its metaphoricity—its ability to designate, rather vaguely, a cluster of attributes or semantic values attached to the signifier "woman." In film even the most blatant stereotype is naturalized by a medium that presents a convincing illusion of a flesh and blood woman. It is here that the ontology of the sign becomes crucial for feminist criticism. For the cinematic sign, to use Peirce's terminology, is primarily iconic and indexical, while the literary sign is primarily symbolic. The idea that the gap between sign and referent is smaller in the cinema (an idea which acts as a foundation for the signifying strategies of the classical realist film) works to naturalize cinematic "femininity" and to bind filmic images more closely to "lived reality," i.e., the ideology of men's and women's daily lives. Hence, the very process of imaging becomes problematic for feminist analyses of film. Because the very notion of "woman" in a patriarchal society is a narcissistic construct, because the female always exists in some sense *to be seen*, the term "image" must be taken literally in feminist film theory. Thus the very crucial displacement observable in this anthology from "images of" to the axis of vision itself—to the modes of organizing vision and hearing which result in the production of that "image."

In literature, however, the signifying material is linguistic, permitting at least the illusion of a certain free play of the signifier divorced from the demands of naturalization. Furthermore, the very length of the novelistic tradition provides a greater variety of instanciations of the female. Feminist literary critics have had more *of* women to study in male-authored works than feminist film critics have had in the works of male auteurs. What is more, once they had explored the limitations of male-authored representations of women, feminist literary critics were able to turn to a comparatively substantial canon of works by women writers. In so doing they began, in Elizabeth Abel's words, "to reconceptualize sexual difference to women's advantage." Feminist literary critics began to emphasize not women's similarity to men, but the "distinctive features of female texts," to trace "lines of influence connecting women in a fertile and partially autonomous tradition."[9] Here the feminist film critic has reason to be envious. For where in the classic cinema do we encounter anything like an "autonomous tradition," with "distinctive features" and "lines of influence"? And if, with some difficulty, we can conceive of Lois Weber and Dorothy Arzner as the Jane Austen and George Eliot of Hollywood, to whom do they trace their own influences? In other words, it became possible for feminist literary critics, working within an image of woman tradition, to arrive at a validation of female difference through the study of women writers.

By comparison, in the relative absence of a realist tradition of women film artists working both within and against a dominant male tradition, it is not surprising that feminist film critics soon seized upon methodologies that could account for the absence of "woman as woman."[10] They began to interrogate the assumptions behind a cinematic language of representation which promoted the concept of "realism" and its effects on the construction and maintenance of sexual difference along patriarchal lines. This investigation necessitated a resort to more elaborate and complex theories of signification and subjectivity.

Thus feminist film critics, first in Britain, then increasingly in the United States, began to embrace semiotic and psychoanalytic theories that seemed capable of accounting for the ways in which patriarchal ideology has elided the representation of women. Similarly, in formulating filmmaking practices, they began to conceive of radical avant-garde alternatives (initially formulated along a modernist, Godardian model) to traditional forms of representation. A key work was Claire Johnston's 1973 pamphlet, *Notes on Women's Cinema* with her essay, "Woman's Cinema as Counter-Cinema," which proposed that only a filmmaking practice that questioned and countered the dominant cinema of realist representation could begin to speak for women.

In formulating a notion of a feminist "counter-cinema" that would counter not only the stereotypes but also the very language of patriarchy, the British feminists[11] rejected the cinema vérité practices of the first generation of feminist documentary films. Earlier U.S. feminist documentaries— *Growing Up Female, Janie's Janie, The Woman's Film*, and *Antonia, Portrait of a Woman*—had aimed at creating more truthful, unstereotyped images of women in their particular social, racial and class contexts. These works, and those which have continued in this tradition, are enormously important organizing and educational tools. Yet the British feminists criticized them on the basis of their acceptance of realistic documentary modes of representation associated with patriarchy.[12] This theoretical work was also buttressed by a growing number of feminist avant-garde films which explicitly dealt with issues of representation, language, voyeurism, desire and the image—e.g., *Riddles of the Sphinx*, and more recently, *Thriller* and *Sigmund Freud's Dora*.

It had become clear by the mid-70s that two divergent traditions of feminist film theory and practice had emerged: those critics and filmmakers (often U.S., often coming out of sociological, phenomenological or journalistic traditions) committed to portraying women characters, women's "truth," on the screen even if the form of that truth was similar (though perhaps not identical) to the dominant forms of representation under patriarchy; and those critics and filmmakers (often British, often coming out of semiotic, psychoanalytic traditions) who were convinced that women's "truth" demanded radically new forms of representation if it was to emerge at all.

Yet such a dichotomy oversimplifies the many points in between, the ongoing arguments concerning what constitutes the dominant forms of representation under patriarchy. The polarization also places the two positions in an inaccurate adversary relation to one another, while suggesting that the U.S. sociological position is incapable of theorizing and that the British adoption of French linguistic and psychoanalytic theories ignores social, political and economic contexts and problems. Both implications distort the efforts of a great many feminist film scholars who do not fit such a simple, territorial mold.[13] One thing, however, is clear: in the relative absence of works by women (except for the explicitly feminist works produced by the women's movement itself), feminist critics have become increasingly adept at "reading against the grain" of the classical cinematic text. In this kind of reading, the critic is less concerned with the truth or falsity of the image of woman than with gaining an understanding of the textual contradictions that are symptomatic of the repression of women in patriarchal culture. This tendency in feminist film criticism has been enormously fruitful—expanding our understanding not only of the strategies of filmic texts which work to support and sustain patriarchal constructions but also of the weak spots, the failings of those constructions.

There is a certain strength, and even an unassailability, which seems to characterize the above position. By continually outlining the contours of the absence or repression of femininity, we can avoid linking it with an unmovable identity or essence, one which inevitably, it would seem, has been foreseen and incorporated within the incessant elaboration of sexual difference. In other words, we can avoid charges of essentialism by negating all potential feminine identities, revealing their complicity with a patriarchal ideology.

The problem with this approach—a problem which has been brought into particularly sharp focus in recent debate—is that it leaves the feminist analyst nowhere to stand. The notion of "identity," temporary as it might be, would appear to be crucial to the development of any politics, even a politics of signification. The feminist theorist is thus confronted with something of a double bind: she can continue to analyze and interpret various instances of the repression of woman, of her radical absence in the discourses of men—a pose which necessitates remaining within that very problematic herself, repeating its terms; or she can attempt to delineate a feminine specificity, always risking a recapitulation of patriarchal constructions and a naturalization of "woman." The choice appears to be a not very attractive one between a continual repetition of the same gesture of demystification (itself perhaps mystified as to its methodological heritage) and a possible regression to ideas of feminine identity which threaten to constitute a veritable re-mystification.

Such a dilemma forms a part of the broader context within which the essays in this volume must be placed. It is a dilemma which is reflected, for instance, in Christine Gledhill's attempts to retain the concepts of identification and recognition while acknowledging the problems with traditional ideas of realism. Gledhill is thus faced with the epistemological assumptions behind the notion of a "self" who could identify. It is a dilemma also embodied in a film like *Riddles of the Sphinx*, which deploys psychoanalytic categories and narratives in order to dismantle patriarchal modes of thought at the same time that it often appears to resuscitate a long-buried femininity associated with the unconscious and a hitherto indecipherable language.

In many of the essays in this volume, the quandary assumes the form of an almost aggressive use of the possessive, delineated as specifically female, laced with more hesitant refusals of a static definition. Teresa de Lauretis takes up Milena's question in *Bad Timing*—"What about *my* time?"—and, transforming it, proposes as the crucial question of contemporary feminist film theory, "... what about my time and place in the apparatus of look and identification, in the nexus of image, sound and narrative temporality?" Mary Ann Doane and Ruby Rich, in rather different ways, reinvestigate and in some sense attempt to reclaim genres which have been attributed to the female—the "woman's film" and the female boarding school genre. Kaja Silverman, although situating her discourse within the context of dispossession (of body and voice) rather than possession, links strategies of disjunction between sound and image to a specifically feminist practice, if not a specifically feminine one. Linda Williams initiates her analysis by asking what happens when a woman looks, or fails to look, in the horror film—when she either appropriates or relinquishes possession of the look. However, because the horror film's project is a condemnation of the desire and curiosity of the woman's look, and because it demands that the woman both fear and recognize herself in the form of the monster, the very issue of female possession in relation to structures of vision is at stake.

Obviously, in the realm of the cinematic image, it is particularly crucial to isolate and define the woman's relation to the act of looking. And, as Judith Mayne points out in her essay, "an equally important and vital aspect of women's cinema...concerns the construction of narrative space." Because narrative, as Mayne defines it, involves a kind of negotiation between private and public spheres, it is complicit with an articulation of space along the existing lines of sexual difference, linking the woman with a domestic space which has always been "proper" to her, and the man with spheres of action and power. For Mayne it is vital to dissociate the voyeuristic look from its space and, simultaneously, to attempt to trace and understand women's traditional relation to the categories of space and time. Thus, she affirms the ambiguity of the term "woman's cinema"—its links to both a type of cinema where woman is the masochistic construct of a discourse produced by males and a type of cinema produced by female, if not necessarily feminist, filmmakers.

The concern with the possessive, with outlining the terms of what might be a "woman's cinema," is thus particularly strong in this group of essays. To claim a temporality, a space, a subjectivity or a look as proper to the female is a way of attempting to reclaim a territory and to de-marginalize women. If sexuality is, as Serge Leclaire points out, a "fact of discourse,"[14] this is above all a discursive strategy.

Nevertheless, we must also acknowledge the difficulties inherent in a resort to the possessive and the limitations of this way of conceptualizing the problem. For a feminist use of the concept of the possessive, even a militant one, cannot effect a separation of the term from its connotations of ownership, individualism, and a capitalist economy ultimately based on patriarchal models of exchange. Such a strategy is far removed from what Luce Irigaray envisages as another, specifically feminist, kind of trade:

> Exchange without identifiable terms of trade, without accounts, without end....Where nature would spend itself without exhaustion, trade without labor, give of itself—protected from masculine transactions— for nothing: there would be free enjoyment, well-being without suffering, pleasure without possession.[15]

Despite the utopian strains of her discourse, Irigaray points to a very real tendency in much contemporary feminist theory—a tendency to deconstruct and disavow all notions of identity, ownership, possession. The demand for the delineation of a female specificity is countered by the refusal to espouse an identity, any identity. It is not by chance, then, that what is "specifically feminine" turns out to be a continual process of negation, disruption, denial.

Julia Kristeva presents this idea most emphatically in an interview cited by de Lauretis: ". . . the category woman is even that which does not fit into *being*. From there, women's practice can only be negative, in opposition to that which exists, to say that 'this is not it' and 'it is not yet.' "[16] And in de Lauretis' own analysis, the time and place of feminine desire—so crucial to the feminist interrogation—are ultimately "now" and "nowhere" (the "now" always in "nowhere") and "can only be stated as negativity, as borders."

But this negativity is not entirely negative and the borders are, in a way, central. To understand this movement from a seemingly optimistic affirmation of female subjectivity to what appears to be the reinvocation of metaphors of absence, lack and negativity, it is necessary to trace the historical vicissitudes of the concept of sexual difference. Initially, as noted above, the goal was quite clearly to annihilate sexual difference in the interests of an obliteration of any idea of hierachy between the sexes. For the very notion of irrevocable sexual differences, linked directly to an unchangeable nature, is the foundation of a patriarchal order, its most dependable guarantee. Under the pretense of honoring womanhood and its uniqueness, a masculine discourse could use difference to validate its own formulations (*vive la différence!*). Feminist analysis thus posited as its most important task the denial of difference and an exposure of the discursive strategies which locate and characterize woman as absence, lack, or destructive negativity. However, these terms are negative or derogatory only within the bounds of a classical philosophy of identity, within what has come to be called the logocentric enclosure.[17] It was a very short step from a recognition of the woman's forced association with difference, lack and absence to the corollary recognition that these terms are the valorized ones (as opposed to sameness, identity, unity, presence, etc.) within modern theories of signification. Hence, the consequence Gledhill refers to as "the attractiveness of equating the feminine with difference itself, a motive force keeping everything in process, refusing the sedimentation into fixed positions of the masculine and the feminine."

In this way, femininity became the underside, the repressed, of a classical or rational/conceptual discourse. It was aligned with the heterogeneity which always threatens to disrupt systems of signification. Woman's proverbial alliance with the powers of destruction was transformed into a positive quality—for it was the rigidity, constraint and monosemic nature of traditional signifying systems which were at fault. Feminism thus allied itself with the avant-garde or with any signifying practice which challenged existing discursive structures. Kristeva is the name most frequently associated with such a position but it is shared by others as well—Irigaray, Hélène Cixous, Xavière Gauthier, Mary Daly, Susan Griffin. The notions of woman's speech, woman's writing, and a female discourse have all been defined in relation to this work against a dominant phallogocentric grammar and syntax, a work performed always from a site outside or in the gaps of the existing symbolic order. Josette Feral, in an essay entitled "The Powers of Difference," quotes Michel de Certeau's assertion, "theorizing always needs a Savage," and claims that the Savage in Western philosophy has always been woman: "His [man's] Savage, the Woman, is here, very close, present, and speechless, to take upon herself the full weight of the violence that inhabits such structures as can only exist through her repression."[18] The recent theoretical alliance between femininity and heterogeneity is symptomatic of a willingness to affirm the status of woman as Savage and her potential for the destruction of traditional modes of knowing. This is one of the more explicit ways in which feminism refuses to be confined to an epistemological ghetto, demanding an interrogation of the very disciplines and institutions which formulate and coordinate knowledge and power.

One can thus trace a marked movement within feminist theory over the past decade from an analysis of difference as oppressive to a delineation and specification of difference as liberating, as offering the only possibility of radical change. However, the dangers of such a valorization of femininity as difference or heterogeneity are clear. For the gesture involves an alignment of the feminine with a signifying—or better, asignifying—principle which is unknowable except outside the boundaries of the classical logocentric discourse we all inhabit. This yoking of the female once again to the attributes of inaccessibility and unknowability can only work to further dematerialize and de-realize "woman." But it also exhibits a failure to recognize and explore the implications of the ideological positioning of woman as a conservative force, as the support of traditional social structures. What is perhaps most crucial to understand is the way in which patriarchy manages to define and locate woman in relation to contradictory properties—she is simultaneously associated with a conservative stability and a disruptive and threatening radicalism.

Hence, the theoretical shift outlined above entails an acknowledgment of feminine specificity, but only in a curiously antithetical way—one which labors against a static definition and, in fact, the very idea of ontology. For what is at stake is not "being" but a position within discourse. As Alice Jardine points out, feminist theory has felt the effects of a larger historical shift away from the question, "Who am I?" and toward "that fundamentally twentieth-century question, 'Who is speaking?'."[19] Ontology gives way to discourse theory and linguistics becomes a dominant science. And linguistics tells us that language is highly regulated in its distribution of places, of "I's" and "you's," "he's" and particularly "she's." Symptomatic of the limitation and exclusions involved in the woman's relation to language is the image of the "old wives' tale." A discourse which is marked as the possession of the woman is simultaneously marked as seriously deficient in its relation to knowledge and truth. In this context, when Barthes states, with reference to an "old-wives' remark"—"... let us imagine a language in which the set of grammatical categories would sometimes force the subject to speak in the aspect of an old woman"[20]—the reader can only view such a statement as ironic, such a language as ridiculous. Yet, this reaction is indicative of the strength of the network of checks, restraints and constructs which language places upon subjectivity.

Discourse theory has thus assumed a prominent role in feminist theory in general. Perhaps this explains the frequency and the insistence of references to the work of Foucault in the essays in this volume (Silverman, de Lauretis, Doane). For Foucault has not only consistently attempted to conceptualize the relation between discourse and power (and, most recently, sexuality), he has also forged a link between a certain kind of discourse theory and an analysis of the collaboration between power and the gaze. This aspect of his work makes it particularly relevant to an understanding of the cinema and its representation of the woman with respect to processes of looking. In his analysis of discourse, Foucault frequently uses terms borrowed from optics: dispersion, diffusion, diffraction.[21] His terminology points toward an arduous (and inevitably futile) struggle to comprehend language on a level at which it and its effects may be *seen*. In the process, Foucault eschews interpretation (language has no depth, only a surface) and argues against the notion of repression. Power works to positively construct and deploy subjective positions and sexualities, not to negate or repress them. And the historical notion of an ever-present Gaze, regulating all images and self-images, is crucial to such an understanding of discursive networks of power. For example, the importance of vision as a construct is evident in *The Birth of the Clinic*, where Foucault defines the clinician as granting an epistemological privilege to the surface gaze and clinical thought itself as a kind of conflation of a "pure Gaze" with "pure Language"—"a speaking eye."[22]

But this emphasis upon vision is perhaps most insistent in his utilization of Jeremy Bentham's plan of the Panopticon in *Discipline and Punish*. The Panopticon is a design for a penitentiary in which the prisoners, unable to see each other or the authority in the central tower who watches them, are never quite sure whether they are being looked at and are thus always potential objects of the Gaze.

> Visibility is a trap.... He [the prisoner] is seen, but he does not see; he is the object of information, never a subject in communication.... Hence the major effect of the Panopticon: to induce in the inmate a state of conscious and permanent visibility that assures the automatic functioning of power....The Panopticon is a machine for dissociating the see/being seen dyad: in the peripheric ring, one is totally seen, without ever seeing; in the central tower, one sees everything without ever being seen.[23]

The dissociation of the see/being seen dyad and the sense of permanent visibility seem to perfectly describe the condition not only of the inmate in Bentham's prison but of the woman as well. For, defined in terms of visibility, she carries her own Panopticon with her wherever she goes, her self-image a function of her being for another. In the realm of the cinema, the effects of this attribution of "to-be-looked-at-ness" to the woman have been well defined and analyzed. Many of the essays here attempt to take this analysis a step further by investigating the other side of the dyad, that of the woman's active relation to processes of seeing (Williams, Doane, Mayne). The subjectivity assigned to femininity within patriarchal systems is inevitably bound up with the structure of the look and the localization of the eye as authority.

And, as if the strength of such an oppression were not enough, the woman's experience of subjugation to the ever-present eye of the Other comes back to haunt her. For the mirror which is delegated to her as the special locus of female subjectivity reflects back to her as she is in the process of theorizing her own, untenable situation under patriarchy. The dilemma of difference is assigned to the woman by a patriarchal system—it is a double bind which serves to "keep her in her place." Hence the temptation to avoid the problem altogether by relinquishing not only her place, her identity but *any* place, *any* identity, and instead espousing process, movement. And, in order to do this most effectively, it might be better, as Barthes suggests, neither to destroy difference nor to valorize it, but to multiply and disperse differences, to move toward a world where difference would not be synonymous with exclusion.

> According to Freud (in the book about Moses), one touch of difference leads to racism. But a great deal of difference leads away from it, irremediably. To equalize, democratize, homogenize—all such efforts will never manage to expel "the tiniest difference," seed of racial intolerance. For that one must pluralize, refine, continuously.[24]

And similarly, Feral claims, "The task of woman remains, however, to inscribe in the social body not so much difference in itself as a multiplicity of differences."[25]

The essays in this volume will, hopefully, contribute to that inscription in the social body of "a multiplicity of differences." Ranging over a wide variety of films and topics, the essays here also provide a number of different entries and suggestions for breaking the hold of a monolithic construction of sexual difference. The "re-vision," of the title is designed to imply not only the sense of a rewriting of earlier feminist formulations but also the sense of recovering, reclaiming vision—in short, both seeing differently and wrenching the "look" (and the "voice") from their previous structures. And chief among these goals must be that of seeing difference differently, re-vising the old apprehension of sexual difference and making it possible to multiply differences, to move away from homogeneity, away from the same, redesigning the architecture of the woman's Panopticon.

NOTES

1. Adrienne Rich, "When We Dead Awaken: Writing as Re-Vision," in *On Lies, Secrets and Silence* (New York: W.W. Norton, 1979), p. 35.

2. Roland Barthes, *Roland Barthes*, trans. Richard Howard (New York: Hill and Wang, 1977), p. 69.

3. Michel Foucault, *Power/Knowledge: Selected Interviews and Other Writings, 1972-1977*, ed. Colin Gordon (New York: Pantheon Books, 1980), p. 193.

4. See *Cinema Histories, Cinema Practices*, ed. Patricia Mellencamp and Philip Rosen, The American Film Institute Monograph No. 4 (Los Angeles, CA: The American Film Institute, 1983). The introduction to the volume includes the description of the Cinema Histories, Cinema Practices I Conference, which derived its historical position from the writings of Michel Foucault.

5. The essays concerned with this debate are being published as the fourth in The American Film Institute Monograph Series: *Cinema Histories, Cinema Practices*.

6. B. Ruby Rich, "In the Name of Feminist Film Criticism," *Heresies* 9 (Spring 1980), pp. 74-81. An earlier version of this article was published as "The Crisis of Naming in Feminist Film Criticism," *Jump Cut*, no. 19 (December 1978), pp. 9-12.

7. For example, dissertations have been written by Diane Waldman on gothic films of female paranoia of the 40s; Serafina Bathrick on the reestablishment of the women's sphere in post-World War II culture; Sandy Flitterman on French cinema of the 20s; Ellen Seiter on recent women's film and soap opera; Tania Modleski on soap opera and Harlequin romances.

8. Rich, p. 76.

9. "Editor's Introduction," *Critical Inquiry*, vol. 8, no. 2 (Winter 1981), p. 173.

10. Claire Johnston, "Women's Cinema as Counter-Cinema," in *Notes on Women's Cinema*, Screen Pamphlet no. 2 (March 1973), p. 24.

11. Claire Johnston, Pamela Cook and Laura Mulvey.

12. Just how exclusively patriarchal these modes of representation are, and whether female audiences experience them the same way male audiences do, remains open to question (see Mayne's article in this volume). So too is the issue of whether the feminist documentaries have really patterned themselves on the model of cinema vérité. Julia Lesage has shown, for example, that many of the early feminist documentaries developed an aesthetics in keeping with the personal, non-hierarchical, supportive and task-oriented goals of the woman's movement ("The Political Aesthetic of the Feminist Documentary Film," *Quarterly Review of Film Studies*, vol. 3, no. 4 [Fall 1978], pp. 507-523).

13. For example, the early American journal, *Women and Film*, is usually taken as an example of the so-called U.S. sociological approach. Yet, perusing back issues, one finds a large number of articles employing semiological methods to explain the way in which women are codified in films.

14. Serge Leclaire, "Sexuality: A Fact of Discourse," in *Homosexualities and French Literature*, ed. George Stambolian and Elaine Marks (Ithaca, NY: Cornell University Press, 1979), pp. 42-55.

15. Luce Irigaray, "When the goods get together," (from *Ce sexe qui n'en est pas un* [Paris: Minuit, 1977] in *New French Feminisms*, ed. Elaine Marks and Isabelle de Courtivron (Amherst, MA: University of Massachusetts Press, 1980), p. 110.

16. Julia Kristeva, "Interview—1974: Julia Kristeva and *Psychanalyse et Politique*," trans. Claire Pajaczkowska, *m/f* 5/6 (1981), p. 166. (Reprinted in *Polylogue* [Paris: Seuil, 1977].)

17. See the work of Jacques Derrida, in particular *L'écriture et la différence* (*Writing and Difference*, trans. Alan Bass [Chicago, IL: University of Chicago Press, 1978]) and *De la grammatologie* (*Of Grammatology*, trans. Gayatri Chakravorty Spivak [Baltimore, MD: Johns Hopkins University Press, 1974]).

18. Josette Feral, "The Powers of Difference," in *The Future of Difference*, ed. Hester Eisenstein and Alice Jardine (Boston, MA: G.K. Hall, 1980), p. 88.

19. Alice Jardine, "Prelude: The Future of Difference," in *The Future of Difference*, p. xxvii.

20. Barthes, p. 176.

21. See especially *The Archaeology of Knowledge*, trans. A.M. Sheridan-Smith (New York: Pantheon Books, 1972).

22. Michel Foucault, *The Birth of the Clinic: An Archaeology of Medical Perception*, trans. A.M. Sheridan-Smith (New York: Vintage Books, 1975), pp. 114-115.

23. Michel Foucault, *Discipline and Punish: The Birth of the Prison*, trans. Alan Sheridan (New York: Vintage Books, 1979), pp. 200-202.

24. Barthes, p. 69.

25. Feral, p. 93.

Developments in Feminist Film Criticism

Christine Gledhill

Introduction

The following article was written in 1978 for the *Quarterly Review of Film Studies*. At that time it was clear that a considerable shift had taken place since the early days of "women and film," which had seen a mushrooming of festivals, conferences, articles and courses devoted to the "image of women." In the intervening period, feminist work around the representation of women had met with the neo-Marxist, semiotic and poststructuralist work of Althusser, Barthes and Lacan, and had begun appropriating the tools offered by patriarchy for its own analysis—especially those represented by psychoanalysis. I wrote this article as a critical attempt to come to grips with this meeting. In particular I wanted to explore the theoretical underpinnings of this work as taken over by feminist writers. It seemed to me important to do so because these theories were often assumed rather than explained. The theoretical framework which feminist film criticism was constructing seemed to me then and now restrictive in the kinds of questions it asks of cinema and the range of film practices it makes available for feminist development.

This article is reproduced here in a somewhat shortened and slightly revised form and with the addition of a few tentative, generalized afterthoughts. I have not "updated" the piece in detail. Although the work that has been produced in the intervening four years seems to me to have considerably deepened our understanding of the original positions, the general framework has not changed and neither has my earlier critique.

A crucial issue for feminist film criticism is the argument that "women as women" are not represented in the cinema, that they do not have a voice, that the female point of view is not heard. Agreement on this unites all attempts at a feminist critique of the cinema. Early work on images of women explained this lack in terms of the dominance of stereotypes or the construction of woman as male "other." Sharon Smith, in the first issue of *Women and Film*, writes:

> Women, in any fully human form, have almost completely been left out of film. . . . That is, from its very beginning they were present, but not in characterizations any self-respecting person could identify with.[1]

Claire Johnston's seminal "Women's Cinema as Counter-Cinema" introduced the notion of fetishism into the argument, suggesting that even those stars or characters who seemed to escape Hollywood's general negativity—for instance Mae West or the independent woman stereotype of the 30s and 40s—were simply phallic substitutes. The psychoanalytic implications here were to be uncompromisingly developed by Johnston and others to the point that the founding issue, the lack of recognizable female heroines, was often dismissed as representing an impossible, even misguided, quest.

The guiding questions, then, for the following inquiry are: why "women as women" are not represented in the media; whether this is the case for all cinematic representation; if so, how it is that fictional constructions portrayed by women actors come to signify male discourse; and, finally, for whom this signification works—the male audience, or men *and* women? Recent feminist work on film seeks to break with the dominant assumptions of the literary tradition. Concentration on characters and stereotypes has been displaced by the semiotic/structuralist concern with "textual production," on the grounds that we cannot understand or change sexist images of women for progressive ones without considering how the operations of narrative, genre, lighting, *mise-en-scène*, etc., work to construct such images and their meanings. This critical shift from interpretation of meaning to an investigation of the means of its production locates the identification of ideology in aesthetic structures and filmmaking practices themselves, which as organizing principles produce their own ideological effect in the material they organize.

The value of this semiotic redefinition of film as text for feminist analysis is that it enables us to escape the simple enumeration of sexist stereotypes (to which there is a limit) and the analysis of characters as to the degrees of liberation they represent, which often depends more on the critic's personal point of view than anything that can be determined by a reading of the film.[2] We avoid the trap of regarding films as reflections, faithful or distorted, of society. However, there is a danger that, once the object of feminist criticism is defined solely in terms of the cinematic production of meaning, we lose the ability to deal with its relationship to women as defined in other social practices.

Although it is necessary to shift the emphasis from women in society in order to grapple with the social and aesthetic specificity of cinematic practices, the concern with how meaning is produced frequently stops at readings of films that are illuminating to feminist film theorists, or at a filmmaking practice whose first aim is to produce knowledge of its own production. The problem facing feminist work on the cinema now is how this knowledge can shape a practice of making, distributing, exhibiting and writing about films that will enable them to play a cultural and political role outside a self-reflexive theoretical discourse. What is at issue then, is the possibility of radical representation for women's cinema.

Feminist film theory must inevitably confront the hybrid phenomenon of realism as a dominant expectation of cultural production in the late nineteenth and twentieth centuries, which embraces both hegemonic and radical aspirations. Theoretical discussion of realism uses a wide range of terms with different shades of reference and indicating different relations to ideology. For instance, in Johnston's "Women's Cinema as Counter-Cinema," different concepts employed include: Barthes' notion of myth as a process of naturalization (describing a mechanism specific to bourgeois ideology); representation (a cultural activity not necessarily tied to realism, e.g., medieval painting); the laws of verisimilitude (implying consonance with what is generally accepted by a particular society to be true, as opposed to what a "progressive" realism might want to reveal); the camera developed "to safeguard the bourgeois notion of realism" (a construct belonging to an antirealist position) and which grasps only "the natural world of the dominant ideology" (referring to the world of phenomenal forms it is the aim of naturalism, as distinct from realism, to reflect). To this array of terms the first issue of *Camera Obscura* (Fall 1976) adds a view of mainstream cinema as "illusionist," thereby introducing a modernist inflection which rescues the materials and processes of art production from vulgar, bourgeois utilitarian ends. By reprinting the piece by Jean-Louis Baudry on the cinematic apparatus, the *Camera Obscura* collective shifts the meaning of realism from the deployment of a specific set of aesthetic techniques with more or less ideological effects to the capacity of a technological apparatus to reproduce in the subject the psychoanalytic structure, the "reality effect."

Much is at stake here, not simply questions of aesthetic technique. Before a proper mode of representation or aesthetic relation to the "real" can be established, we have to have some idea of where the "real" itself is located, and how, if at all, we can derive knowledge of it. At issue then is the status of "lived experience," of phenomenal appearances, their relation to underlying structures, the determining role of "signification" in the production of the real, and the place of "consciousness" in this production. Politically the issue is very important: an assertion of realism is the first recourse of any oppressed group wishing to combat the ideology promulgated by the media in the interests of hegemonic power. Once an oppressed group becomes aware of its cultural as well as political oppression, and identifies oppressive myths and stereotypes—and in the case of women, female images that simply express male fantasies—it becomes the concern of that group to expose the oppression of such images and replace their falsity, lies and escapist illusions with reality and the truth. However, feminist appropriation of recent film theory has shown that such a strategy must confront a number of problems.

The first has to do with defining the "reality" of women and the fact that it is not self-evidently given. There clearly will be contradictions between what the condition of women is, what their struggles for change aim to achieve, and how these realities are recognized and understood by feminists on the one hand, and non-feminists on the other. So while it is certainly possible to point to what is absent from media screens—women at work, home as a workplace, struggles to change legal and economic structures, the issues of sexual politics, expressions of women's sexuality and so on—there is no simple alternative reality to fill the gap and displace the stereotypes which will be instantly recognized and accepted by women generally. On the one hand, feminists would argue that the reality of women can only be satisfactorily understood through some form of feminist analysis, all the terms of which are not immediately apparent in everyday living. On the other, the mass media produce their own definitions of women which also have a concrete existence and determining effect on social reality. Stereotypes do not vanish with the production of images of real women, or of feminist aspiration. They are materialized in the way society is structured and the way we live our lives; they are part of our reality. Clearly then, as Roman Jakobson pointed out long ago, the claim to realism can be invoked by forces seeking to preserve or to challenge the status quo.[3] This means feminist cultural analysis needs to examine the nature of recognition.

The second problem is that a recourse to reality as a counter to stereotyping ignores the need to engage with the multiple function of the cinema as entertainment/ritual/art/fiction. Hans Magnus Enzensberger has suggested that mass consumerism invokes real needs and desires which capitalism orchestrates commercially in order to exploit.[4] And Johnston argues the inherent puritanism of narrowly realist attitudes, suggesting the necessity of engaging the "collective fantasies of women" in a feminist cinema.[5] Women are crucially located in this consumerist culture and its utopian elaboration in entertainment, both in terms of their social-economic role and in terms of their image, which is used to materialize its appeal. Realism narrowly defined in terms of actuality is not a powerful enough weapon to disengage women's fantasy from its imbrication in consumerist structures; the relation of propaganda and consciousness-raising films to the utopian, consumerist thrust of entertainment has yet to be worked through.[6]

A final problem, and one more specific to film, is that in turning to "realistic" filmmaking as a political strategy against stereotyping, the oppressed are in danger of unwittingly adopting a mode of realism which functions to preserve rather than to challenge the status quo. This is the case in much television or film documentary. In such works a naturalistic ideology proposes that reality equals what we can see, that perception equals cognition, and that the camera offers a window on the world, therefore cannot lie. By constituting the whole of cinematic production in the visual image, naturalism not only ignores the filmmaking apparatus but also the fact that the iconic sign is caught up in other signifying systems—linguistic, aesthetic, social, fictional, etc.—which together structure the film. The view generated by the media of their own practices reproduces this ideology. It is important to show how the media strive to perpetuate it. However, I think it highly questionable whether a theory of realism should equate all varieties of realist practice with the goal of naturalism and so with the operation of bourgeois ideology. It is equally questionable whether a theory of realism should equate the socioeconomic conditions of the production of a technology with the ultimate aesthetic/ideological effect it produces in the audience who inhabits a different set of conditions. To take this argument further, however, requires looking in more detail at the different positions used against realism. These arguments turn about the epistemological status of reality itself, of the representation of reality in aesthetic discourse, and of signification as the production of meaning.

In "Myth Today," Barthes describes how bourgeois ideology inserts itself into modern semiotic cultural phenomena.[7] His concern is with how the fabric of bourgeois cultural life divests reality of its material, historical specificity and returns it to an eternal, unchanging world of nature which reflects the world of bourgeois values but disguises its name. In "The Rhetoric of the Image," he concentrates on how this happens specifically in the photographic image, which has an existential relation to the person or object it represents in a way that the word does not.[8] For a totally hypothetical and, in practice, unrealizable instant, he suggests the photographic image is purely denotative—it is what it means and means what it is. Similarly, the social world is full of objects which have a purely utilitarian function—clothes exist to be worn, food to be eaten, houses to protect us from the weather and so on. The issue for Barthes is what happens when these objects or photographic images are caught up in a semiotic system and enter the processes of signification.

At this point in bourgeois culture, the denotative image ceases to have as its referent the person, object, or function as these exist materially and historically. The denotative sign becomes a signifier in the second order of signification—connotation. Within bourgeois culture this process constitutes a kind of semiotic vampirism. The connotative signifier drains the original purely denotative sign of its historical and material reference—what Barthes suspectly calls its meaning—and turns it into a support for a new bourgeois signifier, the naturalized concept of eternal truths or the "human condition."

I am at the barber's, and a copy of *Paris-Match* is offered to me. On the cover, a young Negro in a French uniform is saluting, with his eyes uplifted, probably fixed on a fold of the tricolour. All this is the *meaning* of the picture. But, whether naively or not, I see very well what it signifies to me: that France is a great Empire, that all her sons, without colour discrimination, faithfully serve under her flag, and that there is no better answer to the detractors of an alleged colonialism than the zeal shown by this Negro in serving his so-called oppressors.

As meaning, the signifier already postulates a reading, I grasp it through my eyes, it has a sensory reality...there is a richness in it...it belongs to history, that of the...Negro: in the meaning, a signification is already built...it postulates a kind of knowledge, a past, a memory, a comparative order of facts, ideas, decisions.

When it becomes form, the meaning leaves its contingency behind; it empties itself, it becomes impoverished, history evaporates, only the letter remains.[9]

For feminism this theoretical construct has a great attraction.

It has long been a commonplace of feminist analysis that women are culturally located outside history—the world that is made and remade by the activity of real material men—and placed in an idealist sphere of nature and eternal values. It is also commonplace that women exist in cultural production as "the other," or the "eternal feminine," the necessary complement to the male, the opposite against which men struggle for self-definition and manhood.

Eileen McGarry, in a polemical article, used a Barthesian approach to intervene in the predominantly ciné-vérité practice of feminist film-makers.[10] She took up Barthes' analysis of cultural objects and practices—such as clothing, eating, etc.—as having first a pure function and then a semiotic signification, to elaborate the theory that reality itself is coded, and that within a patriarchal social structure everything to do with women is coded in a sexist way. In a film these social codes are overlaid with the codes of appearance for the actress or film star. She makes a convincing critique of Wiseman's *High School* in terms of the way he photographs and organizes the image of an elderly schoolteacher according to the stereotype "crabby old spinster," just as if he were organizing an actress in a role. What the audience recognizes as real is not an unmediated reality but the product of socially formed codes.

For McGarry, as for many other feminist film theorists, the insights of semiotic analysis have led into an antirealist polemic, which insists that, since representation is tied to cultural codes, the goal of feminist practice should be the deconstruction of these codes in order to demonstrate that patriarchal ideology inhabits the very tools of meaning production. The problem here is whether reality is as monolithically coded in terms of bourgeois and sexist ideology as Barthes and McGarry suggest. The argument as McGarry presents it does not exclude the codings of dress, appearance and gesture that connote, for instance, women's liberation (*The Woman's Film*), the oppression of women (*Women of the Rhondda*), or the struggle of women (*Women Against the Bill*).[11] Yet her view of the coding of reality appears to leave no room for the contradictions in the social formation which make Marxist-Feminist analysis and struggle possible.

At issue here is the early Barthes' nostalgia for a hypothesized and fleeting moment of pure denotation and a consequent false separation of reality and signification which eliminates their dialectic. The call to "semiotic guerrilla warfare," or a "struggle between representations" is fine, as long as we recognize that the base of such struggle is the material practice of real women. In McGarry's example, for instance, we need to understand the stereotype "crabby old spinster" not simply as an ideological construct but in terms of the economic and social relations within which an elderly single woman comes to fulfill or struggle against such typification. We are not dealing here with a struggle simply at the level of representations, but with the material contradictions embodied in such representations which inform women's daily lives.[12] For this reason it does not seem to me a foregone conclusion that practices of signification cannot represent, or produce new recognition of, those very struggles. Any capacity of artistic practices to achieve this will depend partly on how the audience is situated politically and ideologically. Elizabeth Cowie has argued that:

> Sexism in an image cannot be designated materially as a content in the way that denotative elements such as colours or objects in the image can be pointed to. Rather it is the development of new or different definitions and understandings of what men and women are and their roles in society which produces readings of images as sexist; the political perspective of feminism produces a further level of connotative reading.[13]

This argument suggests that the fact that we are able to see the schoolteacher in Wiseman's *High School* as a sexist stereotype is not because sexism resides in the image itself, but because the Women's Liberation Movement has produced a feminist perspective which enables us to read the connotation of the teacher in other than naturalized patriarchal terms. In this respect no artistic practice, realist or otherwise, can ensure either a conservative or radical reading on the part of the audience.

The above appeal to experience introduces a different strand in the antirealist position which turns on the problematic relation of individual consciousness and experience to reality, and derives from a theory of ideology propounded by Louis Althusser. How far can the acts of recognition performed in the practical activity of women and men be informed by or produce an understanding of the nature of the social process in which they are caught?

Whereas many Marxists—for instance Lukács and Brecht, two major and often opposed exponents of Marxist aesthetics—have sought to develop the terms of a realist practice capable of producing an understanding of the real world in its social practices and historical production, the Althusserian position claims that the attempt to represent the social formation can produce only "the natural world of the dominant ideology."[14] Behind this view lie two crucial concepts developed by Althusser: first, "ideology in general," and second, the ideological category of the subject. Althusser proposes a distinction between "ideology in general," which is necessary to the functioning of any society, and specific ideologies belonging to particular social formations at particular points in their history—bourgeois ideology, for instance. "Ideology in general" is theorized as a material force rather than merely a set of false ideas circulating in people's heads that should by now have been changed by socialist teaching and example. It acts as a material support for specific ideologies, and is a structure providing the necesary mediation between the forces and relations of production, the social institutions they give rise to, and the individuals who have to live through them. Ideology enables men and women to make sense of their world and feel in control of it. However, it is in their practical activity rather than in their ideas that ideology materializes itself; in fact it provides the terms of such activity.

> Ideology is indeed a system of representations, but in the majority of cases these representations have nothing to do with "consciousness": they are usually images, and occasionally concepts, but it is above all as *structures* that they impose on the vast majority of men [sic], not via their "consciousness." They are perceived-accepted-suffered cultural objects and they act functionally on men [sic] via a process that escapes them. Men [sic] "live" their ideologies...as their "world" itself...the "lived" relation between men [sic] and the world, including History (in political action or inaction), passes through ideology, or better, is ideology itself.[15]

As such, ideology is a necessary component of human society.

Ideology is able to materialize itself in the activities of women and men precisely because they operate under the illusion of being discrete individuals at the center of, and to a measure initiating, their lived experience, because they perform the daily acts of recognition which maintain and perpetuate the structures and institutions of the social formation. Althusser theorizes the ideological nature of identity and recognition through the psychoanalytic category of the subject developed by Lacan:

> You and I are *always already* subjects, and as such constantly practice the rituals of ideological recognition, which guarantee for us that we are indeed concrete, individual, distinguishable and (naturally) irreplaceable subjects.... All ideology hails or interpellates concrete individuals as concrete subjects, by the functioning of the category of the subject.[16]

This attack on the dominant discourse of Western philosophy since the Renaissance, aimed at irrevocably shifting humanist Man from the scene of history and women and men from the scene of their daily lives, also puts the "real" back a stage, not simply placing it beyond the reach of phenomenal appearances, but making it inaccessible to the conscious social practice of men and women. Everyday life and its struggles can only be experienced in ideological terms; knowledge about the causes and nature of these struggles is produced only by theoretical practice:

> Ideology... is identical with the "lived" experience of human existence itself. This "lived" experience is not a given, given by a pure "reality," but the spontaneous "lived experience of the ideology in its peculiar relationship to the real."[17]

This position clearly has grave consequences for an artistic practice seeking to represent reality. The problem is compounded by the fact that in capitalism it is bourgeois ideology that uses "ideology in general" for a material support. For the work of bourgeois ideology is understood to be aimed at dissolving class membership with its resulting contradiction$ into individuals, producing and maintaining them in the illusion of their non-contradictory discreteness, autonomy, freedom and centrality. To do this it has to reorganize sociality into forms that obscure the fact of society as a historical social production and an interrelated totality grounded in contradiction. This requires the masking, displacing, or imaginary unifying of contradiction in terms of such myths as "nature" or the unchangeable "human condition." Thus in bourgeois ideology the members of the social formation find themselves isolated individuals, who confront over and against them society as a preconstituted given appearing to derive from nature.[18]

In these terms the recognition and identification required by "ideology in general" for the formation of any subject reappear as the specific mechanisms for the production of the bourgeois individual. Recognition would appear to provide a sound support system for identification in the inaccessibility to conscious experience of "the real" and in the formation of the subject. Thus in analyses of realist aesthetics, this distinction between "ideology in general" and "bourgeois ideology" often appears to get lost, so that bourgeois ideology becomes monolithic and inescapable to the point that the room for maneuver available to social practices such as artistic production is very limited.

For feminist cultural practice this position constitutes a serious problem. The Women's Liberation Movement, for instance, has set great store on the interrogation of personal experience and consciousness-raising as a form of work aimed at uncovering the political in the personal. This work has created new identifications for individual women where the recognition of a gender position in terms of the category women—as opposed to the patriarchal abstractions "woman," the "eternal feminine"—is precisely to leave behind an individual identification and begin to recast the self in terms of a group membership. The first issue of *Camera Obscura* can be seen as attempting to responding demands of feminist filmmaking, and the antirepresentational emphasis of recent film theory. Stating their allegiance to neo-Marxist structural theory developed in terms of feminism by Johnston, Pamela Cook, Laura Mulvey and others, the collective claims a break with the classic (Hollywood) text and the dominant "realist" mode of film production. Accounting for their interest in the avant-garde work of Yvonne Rainer, they state:

> We felt that the Feminist problematic—the complex and ambiguous permutations of male dominance/female submission—could not be presented as a political, and therefore changeable, problem using the conventional modes of representation.[19]

In consequence, *Camera Obscura* rejects "identification" as a mechanism in the classic text or documentary for making a political intervention. This means taking a distance from much of the early filmmaking of the Women's Liberation Movement. The problem with *Janie's Janie*, for instance, is that "we can rather easily imagine not identifying with Janie, the subject." In Yvonne Rainer's films, on the other hand, "formal construction . . . forces the audience to analyze the problems which the films demonstrate." Thus *Camera Obscura* adopts the notion of counter-cinema as the only political filmmaking practice possible and implicitly links the Marxist concern to oppose idealism with materialism, the linguistic/semiotic demonstration of the materiality of language and textuality, and the modernist avant-garde's concern with the materials of their medium. Rainer's films, for instance, are said to "provide a link between radical formalism in the arts and radical political concerns." Nevertheless, *Camera Obscura* struggles with the needs of the movement to use the media as a means of exploring and understanding feminist problematics. From their accounts of the films it is this concern that is part of the attraction of Jackie Raynal's and Yvonne Rainer's work, Raynal investigating the issue of woman as spectacle and Rainer the problems of female subjectivity. Thus, for Rainer's films, the collective tries to rework the notion of identification:

> What we felt we needed was not a person to identify with but situations in which we could imagine ourselves, within a structure of distanciation which insures room for critical analysis. . . .[20]

> Because the narrative point of view is that of a generalized "she," the female viewer, already active as she recombines elements. . . can easily substitute herself into the picture. . . . This kind of substitution is radically different from the usual emotional identification with fictional characters. . . . One recognizes *as oneself*, not as a stand-in for a fictional character, the similarities between "she" and oneself. Substitution here is on the basis of conscious, recognized sameness, rather than emotional identification.[21]

Camera Obscura's attempt to reconcile antirealist cinema with the needs of the women's movement points to the crucial place of the audience in cultural production. This problem is compounded in that the women's movement does not in itself define a set of united interests but intersects with other forces, such as class struggle. Thus the movement produces very different needs of filmmaking—for films exploring feminist problematics, for those that speak to and win over women outside the movement who are caught up in other struggles, and so on. In this respect the problem of whether we identify with Janie or not surely has as much to do with where we are positioned in relation to feminism or class or filmmaking. Similarly, if we have a certain freedom not to identify with Janie, it is unclear how Rainer's films can "force" an audience into an appropriate analytical activity.[22] Rather, it seems likely that the audience will be as contradictory in its utilization of media products as any other aspect of society.

Disproving the epistemological claims of a particular medium or artistic practice is a different thing from analyzing its ideological effects in a particular conjuncture. Thus, I would argue that *Camera Obscura*'s rejection of early women's filmmaking is both right and wrong:

> We feel that most of these filmmakers fell into the trap of trying to employ an essentially male-oriented bourgeois notion of film—the notion of film as a window on the world, and have simply chosen to shoot out of other windows than did most filmmakers before the women's movement.[23]

It is not clear that "shooting out of other windows" could not be a very illuminating and subversive activity. For instance, Ann Kaplan has suggested that although the movement films do not demystify the system of representation, they can "reorder the signs within the convention, giving us unfamiliar images of women; we make unfamiliar identifications, sympathies and alliances and are given new perceptions."[24]

Before pursuing this argument further, I want to examine how film theory went beyond the notions of identification and recognition employed in Althusser's view of the subject, going back to their source in Lacanian psychoanalysis. Here was found a theory of subject formation which has been appropriated by feminists as an explanation of the non-representability of women in the cinema.

For Cook and Johnston, Barthes' concept of the naturalized connotation offered an explanation of how the photographic image of woman becomes a signifier in patriarchal discourse without any sense of violence being done to it. In their study of *The Revolt of Mamie Stover*, the image of woman is a sign emptied of its hypothetical denotation referring to the actual woman photographed (meaning "this is a woman," or "Mamie Stover") to become the dehistoricized signifier of the patriarchal connotation—"non-male."[25] In elaborating this argument they move from Barthes' notion of "myth" to Lacanian psychoanalysis. Thus reasons are found why the iconic image of woman must produce a patriarchal meaning, and why "women as women" are silent in our culture. In these terms, representation has less the force of a purposive cultural activity than of a compulsive psychoanalytic mechanism centering on the female figure. Mulvey gives an unequivocal statement of this: "The paradox of phallocentrism in all its manifestations is that it depends on the image of the castrated woman to give order and meaning to its world."[26] In Cook and Johnston's account, the cinematic image presents the body of woman as a spectacle for the erotic male gaze, at the same time rendering her as "non-male," so that her image may become the substitute phallus necessary to counter the castration threat to men posed by women's lack of a penis. Thus the very act of representation ipso facto involves the objectification of women and the repression of female sexuality.

The article in *Camera Obscura*, no. 1, by Jean-Louis Baudry, and later writings of Johnston[27] situate the reality effect not in techniques of verisimilitude, but in the construction of the spectator's relation to the film in a position of "plenitude" or "unity." There are several aspects to the notion of unity: the desire to be united with reality, with the others who confer on one a sense of identity, and with one's speech and its meanings. What terrifies is separation, difference, lack. An intimation of this desired state of being is first experienced by the baby at the breast, but this illusion of plenitude in unity with the mother is soon thrown into question by the experience of separation and loss when the mother leaves the baby to go about her own affairs. The pleasure of the cinema lies in its reconstruction in the spectator of an illusory sense of this imagined early experience of unity.

As the baby develops, however, it enters a second phase of illusory unity described as the "mirror phase," in which the baby's emerging subjectivity achieves an *imaginary* unity with its own idealized image reflected in a mirror—a fragmentation first indicated in the return look of the mother/ "other" that confirms for the baby the identity between itself and its reflection. This forms the basis of the fragmentation through which the ego is formed to become conscious of self. In "Towards a Feminist Film Practice: Some Theses," Johnston describes how the filmic text constructs a place for the spectator which reproduces this illusory identification.[28] This is achieved by an identification with the imaginary spectator implied in the presentation of a shot ("this scene is being looked at by someone") which in the reverse shot is then transferred to a fictional character, so denying the return look of the image and the separateness of the viewer in the auditorium, and stitching her or him into the fiction (suture) and into the subject place which the filmic text constructs.

If unity and identity are illusions, then the crucial reality is difference. The splitting of self which takes place when the ego separates out from the imaginary unity of image and self-image during the mirror phase is coincident with the beginnings of language. With the ego and language begins the differentiation in the world of objects and others from each other and from the self, and at the same time the gradual establishment of an individual subject in the place marked out for it through a series of prohibitions and approbations. The child gradually finds out who it is, who it has to become. Finally and most crucially for an analysis of patriarchy, the child acquires the sexed place indicated by the pronoun positions of "he" and "she" and everything that is socially and culturally predicated on them.

The crucial role of difference in this process arises from the structural linguistics of Ferdinand de Saussure. He argued that there are no positive terms in language—single words united and full with their single meanings and their referents in the real world—but only a system of related differences or oppositions. For instance, the meaning of the word "sheep" in English is not the meaning of "mouton" in French because English also has "mutton," which French does not. "Sheep" only has meaning in terms of its difference from "mutton" (and from a whole series of other interconnected differences, to pursue which would mean reading the dictionary of the English language). According to the logic of psychoanalysis, the starting place in this relay of differences is the first perception of sexual difference in the woman's lack of a penis.

In this instance the term difference becomes highly loaded. It is not a matter of functional opposition, as in the difference of "t" and "d" or "sheep" and "mutton." Sexual difference is said to be the key opposition in which presence (the phallus symbolized by the penis) is faced with absence (no penis).[29] Here for the emerging human subject a bitter paradox enters. Plenitude is only experienced in terms of the mother; for a short time, she "is the phallus" (symbol of plenitude) for the child—retrospectively, that is, for the mother offers that plenitude the possibility of which the phallus will later come to represent as a memory. But then the child is faced not only with the fact of the mother's necessary absences, but also with her betrayal of her exclusive relation to the child in that she is possessed also by the father. Thus the maternal identification is broken by the entry of "the father"—the third term representing the look of "the other" suppressed during the mirror phase—whose prohibition against incest turns the perception of sexual difference into the threat of castration. The traumatic experience of this oppositional difference sets in motion the acquisition of the organized relay of linguistic differences which constitute language and so the human subject.

The drive which will impel the child onward from the realization of castration into culture and the resolution of the Oedipus complex will be haunted by the memory of his original illusory experience of plenitude when baby and world were at one. As this subject is constructed through language, so desire is constituted as the attempt to recapture these illusions through language, which is the subject's only means of knowing the world and so of gaining control over it. But the language user has to submit to the rules of a language he or she has not made; moreover, there is an unbridgeable gap between the uttering ego, the moment of utterance, and reception of the utterance by the other. The desire of the subject is doomed to failure. Hence the double importance of the iconic media, which appear to promise an escape from the constraints of language and a return to the pleasure of an achieved unity between subject and reality.

At this point we can examine the differential entry of the male and female child into the patriarchal order, a difference that turns on the crucial role of the penis/no penis opposition in the institution of language. The mother originally represents the place of the phallus, but then with the entry of the third term betrays the child by her lack. For the boy, the father's penis demonstrates a comforting and recuperative presence. Thus the penis stands in for the phallus, the key signifier, the importance of which is that it is a kind of end-stop to the otherwise endless chain of signifiers. It represents the possibility of arriving back where one wants to be, a kind of finality which makes the production of meaning possible from the play of difference. The patriarchal fact that the penis can be the signifier of the phallus is paralleled by the boy's reassuring expectation that one day he will himself wield such a penis, taking the place of his father, and once more gain symbolic possession of his mother in the person of his wife. The terror of castration and lack can be evaded at the same time as the fact of difference facilitates entry into the symbolic order of human culture. Thus through the correspondence between his anatomy and the possibility of wielding language the boy can escape from the illusory unity of the imaginary and enter the symbolic, the sphere of articulation, of signification, and the expression of desire.

If the boy enters into a position of command within the patriarchal symbolic order, what is the girl's position in patriarchy? For our purposes there are two questions: What is the relation of women to language as speaking subject? What is the role of the representation of women in cultural artifacts? Put simply: *Can women speak, and can images of women speak for women?* The answers would seem to be negative. First, women anatomically play a key part in the production of the symbolic (language and culture), but by virtue of this role (castration) women can only have a negative relation to language; they cannot wield control over the symbolic; they do not carry in themselves the symbol of the signifier, the phallic authority for signification, only the absence which sets the signifier in place. Thus their entry into human discourse must be tentative, highly negotiated, and ambiguous. Second, though the threat of castration is necessary to the production of the speaking subject, the subject only speaks to obliterate that possibility. Thus female sexuality cannot be expressed; the symbolic activity of language and culture is set into motion in an attempt to liquidate the very lack that women are said to represent. For women themselves to attain mastery within this system, they would have to want to liquidate themselves. Hence the enigmatic silence of women.

So the answer to the first question (can women speak?) is no, or only in a highly negotiated fashion, because the subject position from which mastery of language is possible is a male construct—one which women help to form but which they cannot operate.

> Woman's desire is subjected to her image as bearer of the bleeding wound, she can exist only in relation to castration and cannot transcend it. She turns her child into the signifier of her own desire to possess a penis (the condition, she imagines, of entry into the symbolic). Either she must gracefully give way to the word, the Name of the Father and the Law, or else struggle to keep her child down with her in the half-light of the imaginary. Woman then stands in patriarchal culture as signifier for the male other, bound by a symbolic order in which man can live out his phantasies and obsessions through linguistic command by imposing them on the silent image of women still tied to her place as bearer of meaning, not maker of meaning.[30]

In these terms, then, the answer to the second question is similarly negative: images of women cannot speak for women. Because of the role played by the image of woman in the formation of the (masculine) subject, representations of women in cultural artifacts are bound to return to and play on the regressive desire to reestablish for the viewer the desired unity with the real—thrown into question by the possibility of castration—difference. So "woman as woman" can be presented in classic film representation only as a fetishized image constituting a denial of female sexuality and desire. Johnston describes how this fetishization is achieved cinematically, and at the same time reverses the claims usually made for Mae West.

> Many women have read into her parody of the star system and her verbal aggression an attempt at the subversion of male domination in the cinema. If we look more closely there are many traces of phallic replacement in her persona which suggest quite the opposite. The voice itself is strongly masculine, suggesting the absence of the male, and establishes the male/non-male dichotomy. The characteristic phallic dress possesses elements of the fetish. The female element which is introduced, the mother image, expresses male oedipal fantasy. In other words, at the unconscious level, the persona of Mae West is entirely consistent with sexist ideology; it in no way subverts existing myths, but reinforces them.[31]

The connotation "non-male" or "substitute phallus" required by patriarchal ideology is imposed through a system of iconic rather than fictional or narrative codes, so that women are realized filmically as "to-be-looked-at" images rather than in speech or action.

> Lighting, camera angles, the cutting between actors and use of close shot v. long shot—all the techniques of filming are used to differentiate radically the presentation of men and women on the screen...tech-

niques normally used...for women in films...essentially produce a specularity in relation to the character in a way which places her role in the film as iconic rather than diegetic; i.e., the classical sexual objectification of women in films.[32]

Mulvey in "Visual Pleasure and Narrative Cinema" uses the Lacanian interpretation of this visual objectification of women to argue that because the superabundant iconicity of the female image also threatens an eruption of extreme unpleasure—castration—classic Hollywood cinema has developed various devices and structures to give the male hero and, by proxy, the male spectator, control over this enchanting and threatening image.

This potential "unpleasure" provides for many theorists the key to a feminist counter-cinema, in which "difference," now equated with the "feminine," and, perhaps masochistically, associated with castration, is reintroduced to challenge and radically unsettle patriarchal consciousness. In her article on *Anne of the Indies*, Johnston sees the girl child's masquerade, her disguise as a pirate, as a destructive refusal of the feminine position within the symbolic order.[33] In so doing she asserts sexual difference in the face of the male fear of castration. Johnston defines this in terms of the Barthesian notion of "radical heterogeneity" developed in *The Pleasure of the Text* and *S/Z*. In these terms, the means of attack on patriarchy consist in the assertion of castration and the fundamental difference it opens up. In "Towards a Feminist Film Practice" she argues that the union of signifier and signified in patriarchal and classic filmic discourse ipso facto represses the feminine because it constitutes a denial of difference. Thus Woman is "the unnameable, the unsaid." Feminist practice must work toward dislocating and restructuring the symbolic order in order to change the function, in the moment of perception of sexual difference, of the entry of the third term in the production of the symbolic signifier; thus a new subject will be created together with a new order of language that will assert rather than repress sexual difference.

What is important for feminist analysis of patriarchal culture is how psychoanalysis affects our understanding of the nature of reality, for in changing this it changes our point of attack. The first question that arises is the problematic relation of the patriarchal symbolic order to the material existence of men and women and their social practices, which in orthodox Marxist terms constitute reality. The problem with orthodox Marxism, it is claimed, is that socioeconomic determinants are seen as operating within already constituted, and therefore potentially autonomous, subjects.[34] Thus the recourse to Lacan seeks a "materialist" theory of the subject in the discovery of the so-called primary processes that construct it. The problem here is that the theoretical juncture of Lacan and Althusser in the decentering of individuals from their consciousness seems to remove them from much else as well, for although the Lacanian subject accounts for different sexual locations in the symbolic order, it says little about class; the constitutive force of language, primary in both a chronological and formative sense, appears to displace the effectivity of the forces and relations of production in the social formation. The coincidence of ideology in general with bourgeois ideology suggests that language constructs not only individuals but bourgeois individuals. It is thus unclear what effectivity class or racial location has in this process, or in what sense individuals can be said to be differentiated class members. This suggests that a materialist theory of the subject has simply displaced the dialectical process of history and class struggle rather than interacting with it. Sexual difference has become the key structural contradiction in place of the social forces and relations of production.

For women this substitution has paradoxical consequences. On the one hand we are faced with almost total repression of femininity within patriarchal culture; on the other with the intensification in the twentieth century of struggles around the economic and political emancipation of women. The issue then, is the relation of the construction of the subject to the social structure; for feminists this could be posed as a question about the relation of the penis to the phallus. For if the trauma of castration is relieved by the phallus, what needs explaining is why the penis is able to escape the linguistic rule of negativity and signify it. *Unless patriarchy is a product of chance, the role of the penis as support for the symbolic signifier seems to be predicated on patriarchal dominance as an already constituted fact.* Burniston, Mort and Weedon argue against the claim made by Lacan that the "Law of the Father" represents a symbolic position, not necessarily involving the subordination of women:

> ... However, in the development of the human infant, its entry into a specific form of sexed subjectivity, in accordance with the laws of culture, is predicated on a specific resolution of the Oedipus complex, which functions through the recognition of *anatomical* difference. This difference, having or not having the penis, comes to mean, in cultural terms, having or not having the phallus. Although this position is based on misrecognition, in the sense that no one can actually possess the phallus, i.e., become the source of the laws which structure human sociality, it is nonetheless men, as possessors of actual penises, who are able to identify with this position of control.... The supposedly *pure symbolic* function of the phallus cannot be explained solely in terms of the internal logic of Lacanian theory whilst it relies on an anatomical difference. It is this which constitutes the *phallocentrism* (privileging of the phallus/penis) of Lacan's theory. Once we reject the notion of a necessary, ever pregiven patriarchal structure for the organization of desire (and it is here that a feminist critique of Lacan, as of Freud, must centre), the dominance of the phallus, in its equation with penis, can only be explained historically and materially, by an analysis of the structural relations between the sexes, which are manifest in material practices. It is only this materialist

analysis which can ground the phallus as a symbol of the social organization of sexuality at the level of the unconscious.[35]

The hiatus between the feminine position as constructed in language and women as produced by historical, social and economic forces is more marked if we question further the relation of patriarchy to capitalism and bourgeois ideology. In these terms patriarchy is coincident with ideology in general (and, by implication, bourgeois ideology) and would appear to be a condition of any other form of oppression. This raises two general problems. First, a feminist theory and cultural practice that seeks practical political effectivity must be able to take account of the intersection of gender with class and racial differences among others. In political terms, it would seem essential to have recourse to some form of recognition through which women can identify with themselves as women and as an oppressed group, yet at the same time relate this to their class experience. The second problem is the magnitude of the task facing feminists if patriarchy can be shifted only by an assault on the structure of the subject and ideology in general. Our understanding of this task has been given us in terms of psycholinguistic representational structures to which fictional and cinematic forms of representation are understood as being homologous. But we are in a very weak political position if rupturing the place of the subject in representation is our chief point of entry. There clearly is a danger in posing the question in chicken-and-egg terms. But the problem remains if we are to locate an effective point of feminist attack: How are the socioeconomic structures of power and subordination articulated with the repression of femininity in the psycholinguistic construction of the subject? and: How can one level effect changes in the other?

Confronted with such a massive critique of mainstream cultural production, the question is still what feminists *do now*: What films do we make and for whom? How do we function as critics? What do we teach? Traditionally, Marxist aesthetics has avoided a total identification of art and ideology, and a theory of the "subversive" potential of artistic practice has emerged, capable of providing progressive readings of "bourgeois" texts. For the antirealist position describes, in a sense, the *ideal* project of the dominant ideology in its attempt to turn artistic practice to its own ends by producing the transparent text. Art, however, deals in *material structures and forms*, which may be made more or less perceptible, more or less radically productive. For a while, before psychoanalysis claimed that all apparent play with difference was but a prelude to the reinstatement of the same, film theory supported the "rescue" of former Hollywood auteurs, and even discovered new ones (e.g., Sirk and Tashlin) under the rubric of "distanciation," "irony" and the progressive counter-readings these notions made possible. Feminism appropriated this critical method in order to support the films of women directors working in Hollywood or in forms that seemed to break with the received canons of what made a "good film"—e.g., the work of Dorothy Arzner, Ida Lupino, Nelly Kaplan or Stephanie Rothman.[36] At the same time it became necessary to expose those Hollywood genres or forms of European art cinema which claimed to produce independent or positive heroines, based often on the charisma of particular female stars, or on recognition of some aspect of the "women problem," e.g., *The Revolt of Mamie Stover, Klute,* and *Coma.* The point was to demonstrate the dominance of patriarchal narrative control over the apparent moments of "escape" or "excess" produced by the female star or character, and of the masculine fetishistic structure of representation over the figure of the woman. Inherent in the first strategy was the development of a notion of the "woman's discourse"; in the second, the refusal of the offered identification. The struggle to make these strategies work for feminism demonstrates in a productive and concrete way some of the problems raised above.

In "Dorothy Arzner: Critical Strategies," Johnston utilizes the notion of "making strange" in conjunction with the concept of "discourse" to argue the case for the progressive potential of Dorothy Arzner's films. The ideologically coherent text manages the potential heterogeneity posed by the variety of discourses that may intersect in it by gathering them under the dominance of that discourse which speaks for the ruling ideology, which is thereby empowered to judge or "speak" the truth of the others. In the patriarchal text these discourses are so organized along gender lines as to give priority to the male discourse. This priority is a further structural reason why the voice of woman—even as constituted in socially oppressed terms—is not heard.

In Johnston's analysis, the progressiveness of Arzner's work rests in the way it changes the terms under which male and female discourses are heard. By utilizing the notion of "making strange," Johnston seeks to locate in Arzner's films a different structuring principle—the woman's voice—which, if it cannot abolish the male discourse, at least de-centers it, subjects it to interrogation rather than the other way round:

> In Arzner's work the discourse of the woman, or rather the attempt to locate it and make it heard, is what gives the system of the text its structural coherence, while at the same time rendering the dominant discourse of the male fragmented and incoherent. The central female protagonists. . . do not sweep aside the existing order and found a new, female, order of language. Rather, they assert their own discourse in the face of the male one, by breaking it up, subverting it and in a sense, rewriting it.[37]

> In this way, the discourse of the male can no longer function as the dominant one, the one which speaks the truth of the secondary discourses in the films. . . . It is . . . for this reason that the narrative appears disjointed and fragmented; the conventions of plot and development are quite fully in evidence, but the work of the woman's discourse renders the narrative strange, subverting and dislocating it at the level of meaning.[38]

The notion of discourse is potentially valuable in that it cuts across the form/content division which would seek to judge form by its capacity to express content, and the text/society division which seeks to constitute the text outside any referential function.

What this seems implicitly to suggest is a space in the analysis of patriarchal culture for the forms—fictional, iconic, economic, social—through which actual women experience themselves. For instance, Johnston's analysis of a "subversive" moment in *Craig's Wife*:

> Here, the rituals of housework and the obsession with order acquire, as the film progresses, a definite validity, and it is evidence of people living and breathing in the house which is rendered strange. The marks of a trunk having been pulled along the floor or someone having sat on the bed acquire a sinister meaning within the text of the film.[39]

For this moment to be "rendered strange" there must first have been a recognition of and past identification with the rituals of housework.

In contrast, Cook and Johnston's earlier work on *The Revolt of Mamie Stover*, in which they use the concept of fetishism to analyze the film's so-called independent heroine, effectively denies the emergence of the woman's discourse and reduces the subversive possibilities of aesthetic play. Reading *The Revolt of Mamie Stover* is less a matter of activating subversive contradictions than it is tracing the preordained path by which the patriarchal subject is constructed in the text in spite of, or because of, its potentially subversive theme—the female speculator in sex and property. As Cowie has summarized their position, the film is not about the struggles of an independent heroine in the figure of Jane Russell/Mamie Stover, but about Richard Egan/Jimmy's rejection of her.[40] The film reproduces the fetishistic structure whereby Jane Russell cannot represent the woman (Mamie Stover) but rather must become a signifier of patriarchal desire; the attempt to produce an independent woman stereotype is ideologically recuperated. In order to evoke the independent heroine the narrative has to offer her access to those conjunctures in the plot where dominance is established: the power of the look (Jane Russell/Mamie Stover glowers back at the audience in the beginning of the film); entry to the circulation of money, the symbol of phallic potency (Mamie Stover ruthlessly profiteers real estate while the men are away at war); the rejection of the passive female roles of fiancée or wife (Mamie Stover secretly returns to her career at "The Bungalow" while the man she is engaged to is at war); and a symbolic attempt to take control of the discourse (Mamie asks the author, Jimmy, to write *her* story). Despite these narrative gestures toward independence, the patriarchal laws of representation and fictional construction ensure her entrapment and defeat.

> The central contradiction of her situation is that she can only attempt to assert herself as subject through the exploitation of a fetishized image of woman to be exchanged within the circulation of money; her independ-

ence and desire for social and economic status all hinge on this objectification.[41]

The issue raised by the contrast between this psychoanalytic reading of *The Revolt of Mamie Stover* and the subsequent subversive readings of Arzner is the relation of the patriarchal subject constructed by the text and the female reader/spectator. What function does the image of the fetishized woman have for the female audience, for whom castration is not a threat but an already accomplished "fact"? If the entry into language is the chief determinant in the construction of the human psyche in which the desire of women is repressed and femininity distorted, then, presumably, women acquiesce in the narrative exorcism of the threat of the feminine to the symbolic and civilized order.[42] Yet inevitably, women make other use of the female image offered to them. For example, they pick up codes in the construction of characters and of the female discourse which signal contradictory aspects in the determination of women—socioeconomic factors, psychological elements, cultural attributes—the notion of career, for instance (Judy in *Dance Girl Dance*); or self-expressive sexuality (Lucille Ball as Bubbles); or problems of female employment (the dancing troupe).

Once such extra-cinematic constructions of women are taken into account, however, a different problem confronts feminist analysis. A progressive reading of Arzner's work in terms of the woman's discourse alone can still be undermined by a discourse of class. This arguably is the case in *Dance Girl Dance*, where what Johnston construes as an effective, if momentary, break with patriarchal ideology—when Judy refuses her role as spectacle and turns on the vaudeville audience—is also the assertion of a ruling-class discourse in terms of Judy's high art ambitions over/against the crude vulgarity of the burlesque, which also includes judgment on another woman, Bubbles. Judy's momentary power to stun her audience into silence lies in her class tones, the class authority of her role as a "serious artist," as well as her high-toned moralism, behind which lurks the stereotype "prude" contrasted with Bubbles "good sport."

This problem is further compounded by the incapacity of the notion of the subject—constructed at such an early stage in the individual's life—to call into play all the socioeconomic and cultural variables arising out of class, race, education and so on. These variables differentiate one audience member from another and constitute the determining context in which he or she makes a reading.

Cook's approach to Arzner is in part an attempt to deal with this problem by proposing a subversive strategy which sets subject and spectator at odds in a process of distanciation:

> To approach films...is...to see them as texts (complex products demanding an *active reading in terms of the contradictions at work* in

them), which are produced within a system of representation which *tries* to fix the spectator in a system of closed relationship to the film.[43]

What prevents the crystalization of this "closed relationship" is the way Arzner's work foregrounds the dilemma of her heroines' attempts at self-realization through the only terms available to them, the patriarchal system of representation. Cook uses a notion of aesthetic play which impedes the completion of the patriarchal structure of representation through distancing devices that make the spectator aware of the contradictions between the needs and desires of women and the female image. For instance, her analysis of a moment in *Merrily We Go To Hell*:

> The party is well under way, except for the marked absence of Gerry. Joan's father comes to the top of the stairs, the camera behind him as he dominates the party below. Cut to Joan dancing with her friend Gregg. They are chatting and move towards a large mirror on the far side of the room from the stairs and dance before it for a moment before Joan suddenly becomes aware of the "image" of her father on the stairs, looking at her, reflected in the mirror. She stands for some seconds gazing at her own reflection in the mirror and the "image" of her father in the background before she moves across the room to talk to him. She seems fascinated, held in a fixed relation to the "image" in the mirror, and as *we* are faced with that image of fascination we are aware of a tension between desire and patriarchal law.[44]

The question remains how far such readings are not still made through identifications and recognitions, albeit with a self-conscious awareness of the heroine or of the woman's discourse as a textual production. The fact that we can locate these moments derives from the problems we as feminists encounter in negotiating the "roles as image" which society constructs for women.

The problem highlighted here becomes sharper if we look again at the Cook/Johnston analysis of *The Revolt of Mamie Stover*. For we are dealing here with the independent woman stereotype which was much in evidence in the Hollywood of the 1930s and 1940s, and which relates to the current search of the women's movement for positive heroines. Cook and Johnston's account of Jane Russell/Mamie Stover is of a woman's struggle to realize her desire, and of her defeat:

> Her drive is to. . . transgress the forms of representation governing the classic cinema itself, which imprison her forever within an image. As the credits of the film appear on the screen, Rosalind [sic] Russell looks into the camera with defiance. . . . Asserting herself as the subject rather than the object of desire, this look into the camera represents a reaching out beyond the diegetic space of the film and the myths of representation which entrap her. The central contradiction of her situation is that she can only attempt to assert herself as subject through the exploitation of a fetishized image of woman to be exchanged within the circulation of money; her independence and her desire for social and economic status

all hinge on this objectification. . . . The forms of representation generated by the classic cinema—the myths of woman as pin-up, vamp,
"Mississippi Cinderella"—are the only means by which she can achieve
the objective of becoming the subject rather than the object of desire.[45]

On one level the reading Cook and Johnston make of *The Revolt of
Mamie Stover* commands a lot of assent both in terms of the feminist
understanding it produces and the demonstration of the work that narrative
and thematic organization performs to accommodate and recuperate ideologically challenging developments like the independent woman stereotype. In
this sense the psychoanalytic framework can be taken metaphorically. But the
polemical intent of Cook and Johnston's piece is to expose the patriarchal
function of this stereotype as an object of male fascination. Consequently
their readings work reductively rather than metaphorically, as if to peel away
the accretion of fictional and generic elaboration and the heterogeneity of the
discourse, in order to drive back the pseudo-female image to the point where
it reveals its patriarchal origin and complicity. But even so, in Cook and
Johnston's account just quoted, the energy of the stereotype asserts itself; Jane
Russell/Mamie Stover appears an almost autonomous character struggling
against her role in patriarchal discourse, and her consequent location in the
world of fiction.

The real issue for feminism is the potential contradiction between
woman as characterization in terms of the independent woman stereotype
and woman as sign in a patriarchal discourse. Whatever the economic,
aesthetic or patriarchal reasons for the production of the stereotype—e.g., the
industry's attempt to exploit the female market for film, the aesthetic and
generic need for innovation, patriarchy's need to encounter and exploit the
psychic threat of women—the question remains of the use a female audience
may make of such a heroine. Molly Haskell observed of Hollywood's narrative recuperation of the independent woman stereotype that even though she
is rejected and humiliated by the end of the film, she has one and a half hours
of struggle and self-assertion before this defeat, and it seems possible that
aesthetic play with such an image might be very risky for patriarchal ideology.[46] Ultimately, I would suggest, the problem for feminists attempting to
utilize current developments in film theory and ideological analysis lies in the
need to conceptualize the triple relation subject/reader/audience. While the
work on Arzner implicitly allows some space within which particular
audience members might operate, given a feminist perspective and some
knowledge of film, the analysis of *The Revolt of Mamie Stover* discounts the
level at which the female audience might exploit the contradiction of a
patriarchal production of an independent woman stereotype. The general
lack in film theory of a means to conceptualize the social relations in which a
specific audience is constituted can lead to severe limitations on proposals for
subversive cultural activity.

Recent developments in feminist film theory rest on the meeting of three different strands in neo-Marxist analysis: the Althusserian designation of lived experience, empirical reality, as the materialization of ideology; the Lacanian theory of the primacy of language in the construction of the subject in which visual representation of woman plays a key role; and the designation of cinema as an iconic medium ideologically complicit with an epistemology of vision based on the self-evident character of phenomenal appearances, and devoted to replaying the process of the construction of the subject in order to reconfirm the ideological unity of the patriarchal subject outside contradiction.

A major problem, it seems to me, lies in the attempt to make language and the signifying process so exclusively central to the production of the social formation. Under the insistence on the semiotic production of meaning, the effectivity of social, economic and political practice threatens to disappear altogether. There is a danger of conflating the social structure of reality with its signification, by virtue of the fact that social processes and relations have to be mediated through language, and the evidence that the mediating power of language reflects back on the social process. But to say that language has a determining effect on society is a different matter from saying that society is nothing but its languages and signifying practices.

Once the social construction of reality and women is defined in terms of signifying practice alone, the process of realist representation can only be ideologically complicit, for it is itself based on an "imaginary" unity between signifier and signified, and the suppression of semiotic difference. From this originates our illusory sense of the real world in the first place. Thus in Barthes' *The Pleasure of the Text* and *S/Z*, part of his rejection of realism is that it demands that writers make a choice between meanings; for within the antirealist epistemology, the only way to avoid ideology is to put off the signified—the moment of closure, of ideological fixity—for as long as possible, to stay within process, the infinite play of meanings. From the point of view of the Women's Liberation Movement, or any other political grouping, this demand has serious implications; there are some meanings associated with the image of women that have to be forcibly rejected. That "realism" has been dominant as an epistemology and aesthetic goal since the Renaissance seems to be an inevitable part of materialist history, in so far as we are seeking to free ourselves from superstition, religion, idealism in order to gain control over our material, social and psychological world. Thus, in the days of the revolutionary bourgeoisie, visual and fictional techniques were developed, aimed at grasping the concrete world of human practice rather than the spiritual hierarchy of feudalism. If a radical ideology, such as feminism, is to be defined as a means of providing a framework for political action, one must finally put one's finger on the scales, enter some kind of realist epistemology.

Afterthoughts

It now seems that the "main problem," for feminists at least, is not only the exclusive centrality attributed to signifying processes in the production of the social formation. After all, some of the most interesting and energetic feminist film criticism has developed out of this theoretical trajectory. Nevertheless, the specter of "essentialism," especially problematic for feminism where the whole question of gender definition is so loaded, compounds the post-structuralist refusal of representation and identification. We reject given social definitions of women or femininity as mere indicators of social construction at work. Assertion of our social difference—maternity, feeling, irrationality—seems only to make patriarchal equations: woman as earthmother, woman as other. On the other hand, constructions of our culture-heroines as strong and powerful bring charges of male identification, or substitution. We seem trapped. However we try to cast our potential feminine identifications, all available positions are already constructed from the place of the patriarchal other so as to repress our "real" difference. Thus the unspoken remains unknown, and the speakable reproduces what we know, patriarchal reality. Hence the attractiveness of equating the feminine with difference itself, a motive force keeping everything in process, refusing the sedimentation into fixed positions of the masculine and feminine.

Location of femininity in difference, however, raises its own problems. First, within the Lacanian framework, difference is *sexual* difference founded in castration—either projected onto the female body, or introjected as a threat to the male body. Socially constructed gender differences are secondary to, a corollary of, the role of sexual difference in the construction of the patriarchal subject. They do not warrant the same attention from a film theorist as might be given them by sociologists, anthropologists or ethnographers. Second, the definition of femininity in terms of difference—the process of continually putting patriarchy to the challenge—has not yet evaded the problem of essentialism; only now the essence is posited in narrative structuration (what we oppose), or projected into a future practice that is very difficult to conceptualize except in typically avant-garde terms. How are women to be roused to this activity without a more concrete sense of how their day-to-day experience relates to it, or of what precisely it is we want to change? Finally, since the difference we invoke in the name of femininity is conceived as so repressed and "monstrous" in patriarchy, we are in danger of perpetuating the negative self-images with which women have always been confronted. It is not a question of closing our eyes to what is going on in the patriarchal camp, but of locating those spaces in which women, out of their socially constructed difference as women, can and do resist.

Women are constructed in a set of social relations and discourses which position them differently from men in the social formation. These relations also position women *and* men differently to each other in respect to class. Women experience work, parenthood, and personal, heterosexual and family relations differently from men. These are not merely given differences, but ones that arise out of the variant material conditions of women and men. These differences seem to me the ground on which we have to work in order to find the object of struggle and the material for constructing difference in a more egalitarian and productive way. Maternity/paternity, sexual display/ sexual action, feeling/rationality point not only to oppressive locations within unequally distributed and valued ideological categories constructed in patriarchy for the subordination of women, they also indicate differences *produced* by women in negotiating the contradictions entailed in the institutionalization of such categories, e.g., different rational/emotional/sexual modes of operation. Tessa Perkins' work on stereotypes offers valuable insights into material realities and differences which are transformed in patriarchal discourse:

> Part of the stereotype of women concerns their inability to concentrate on one issue at a time, their mental flightiness, scattiness and so on. In the middle of a conversation about one issue they skip to something completely different. This is all part of the "irrational, illogical, inconsistent" (female logic) stereotype. Now what this seems to me to relate to is a mode of thinking which is essential to the housewife's job. Most other jobs demand concentration on a single issue and the application of one skill at a time; the capacity to keep shifting attention back and forth, and changing skills, is characteristic of a housewife's job. What the stereotype does is to identify this feature of the women's job situation, place a negative evaluation on it, and then establish it as an innate female characteristic, thus inverting its status so that it becomes a cause rather than an effect. It is these features of stereotypes which explain why stereotypes appear to be false—indeed, *are* false. The point at the moment is to identify their validity, because the strength of stereotypes lies in this combination of validity and distortion.[47]

But how are we to regard these moments of "validity"? While they describe some of the contradictions within which "women" are produced, the "differences" they indicate potentially open up a challenge to patriarchal assumptions, making visible a whole regime of practices, modes of feeling and thought which generally go unrecognized even by women themselves. To work on this level will be to understand more of the construction and functioning of sexual and gender differentiation. It will also release the repressed differences produced in the experience of women from mere sex specification to become a general social potential.

This, as yet generalized, attempt to reconceptualize difference also implies a different conception of the relationship between "real material relations" and social discourses. Perkins maintains that stereotypes reference real social practices, while at the same time relocating them in the terms of particular patriarchal discourses. Such discourses have a material role in constructing how social reality is lived, but maintain their connection with the underlying social relations and differences they transform. Cultural analysis can work on such stereotypes and the discourses that put them into play by activating these contradictions—recognizing the boundaries and differences between distinct discourses and social practices, but never losing sight of their interrelations.

In the analysis of cultural products this model seems to me to offer a valuable alternative to that of a psychoanalytically conceived narrative discourse, predicated on difference as *sexual* difference. In the latter, classic narrative plays on the process of the subject in relation to desire. While desire is the desire to repeat a past, ultimately primary, pleasure, such repetition can only be perceived through the gap introduced by difference, with its threat of endless process and dissolution of the subject. Classic narrative, then, is committed to a compulsive play on the pleasure/terror opened up by difference and process, but predicated on the safety of an already known closure. So that while difference is continually evoked, and most pertinently the sexual difference implied in the figure of the woman, it is always brought back to the patriarchal same. I would argue that this represents an essentialist view of the power of narrative structure, abstracting it from the material conditions in which it functions for an audience. Behind this lies the insistence of "discourse theory" on the discrete effectivity of different discourses. While these discourses come into contradiction in a formal sense, they are not seen as productive of interaction or new positions when they meet in the lived experience of the subjects whom they help construct. In the analysis of fictional forms, then, there is little justification for thinking that the discourse of narrativity will not dominate. The material effectivity of other discourses in the subject's experience fades under pressure from the narrative, and the capacity of different discourses and social practices to reference each other is denied.[48] Narrative deconstructs and reforms to its own ends any extra-cinematic discourses it mobilizes as part of its material. The model Perkins offers, on the other hand, demands that cultural analysis hold the extra-discursive and discursive together as a complex and contradictory inter-relation. If we do this there seems to me no guarantee of the primacy of narrative closure in determining how we gain access to moments of difference, or of the ideological effectivity of the various positions the spectator may be asked to adopt as a side effect of some narrative or aesthetic strategy.

A wide range of discourses and practices arise from, speak to, the real and contradictory conditions of women's existence. There are the discourses of the dominant institutions—medicine, the law, education, welfare—which seek to locate and maintain difference as part of the natural order of things, rather than the consequences of a particular social structure. There are also those official discourses and practices, produced for and often by women, which speak to the fact that differences and contradictions do not disappear because ideology writes them out—agony columns, mother and toddler groups, women's magazine fiction, soap operas. These discourses negotiate the "problem" of a woman's existence and its contradictory demands, rearticulating them in terms of dominant, positive values, providing an outlet for frustration, catching up something of the "commonsense" wisdom in circulation among women. Finally, there are the unofficial discourses, hardly investigated, of women themselves, through which they negotiate dominant institutions and their contradictions for women.[49]

To reference this social effectivity when such discourses provide material for fiction—as in the woman's film, melodrama or soap opera for instance—is not a matter of playing off the fiction against some putative "objective reality," or "pure feminine discourse." Rather, it gives more weight to the "reality" of the production of discourses.

NOTES

1. Sharon Smith, "The Image of Women in Film: Some Suggestions for Future Research," *Women and Film*, no. 1 (1972), p. 13. See also Naome Gilbert, "To Be Our Own Muse: The Dialectics of a Culture Heroine," *Women and Film*, no. 2 (1972); and Claire Johnston, "Women's Cinema as Counter-Cinema," in *Notes on Women's Cinema*, Screen Pamphlet no. 2 (March 1973).

2. Julia Lesage comments on Joan Mellen's *Women and Their Sexuality in the New Film* (New York: Horizon Press, 1973) that Mellen rejects characters she finds "unpleasant." Thus Chloe in Eric Rohmer's *Chloe in the Afternoon* is "plain, with shaggy, unwashed hair falling in her eyes. Her complexion is sallow and unaided by makeup. Her sloppiness is intensified by a decrepit raincoat without style." (In "Whose Heroines?" *Jump Cut*, no. 1 [May/June 1974], pp. 22-24.)

3. Roman Jakobson, "On Artistic Realism," in *Readings in Russian Poetics*, ed. Ladislav Matejka and Krystyna Ponovska (Cambridge, MA: MIT Press, 1971).

4. Hans Magnus Enzensberger, "Constituents of a Theory of the Media," *New Left Review* 64 (November/December 1970).

5. Claire Johnston, "Nelly Kaplan: An Introduction," in *Notes on Women's Cinema*.

6. Richard Dyer's essay on the Musical, "Entertainment and Utopia," *Movie*, no. 24 (Spring 1977), and the concluding chapter of Terry Lovell's *Pictures of Reality: Aesthetics, Politics and Pleasure* (London: British Film Institute, 1981) begin this work.

7. Roland Barthes, "Myth Today," in *Mythologies* (New York: Hill and Wang, 1972).

8. _____ , "The Rhetoric of the Image," *Working Papers in Cultural Studies*, no. 1 (Spring 1971).

9. _____ , "Myth Today," pp. 116-117.

10. Eileen McGarry, "Documentary, Realism and Women's Cinema," *Women and Film*, no. 7 (Summer 1975).

11. *The Woman's Film* by the Newsreel Group, USA (1971); *Women of the Rhondda* by the London Women's Film Group (1973); *Women Against the Bill* by Esther Ronay and members of the Notting Hill Women's Liberation Group, London (1972).

12. Tessa Perkins, "Rethinking Stereotypes," in *Ideology and Cultural Production*, ed. Michèle Barrett et al. (London: Croom Helm, 1979), argues that stereotypes are produced out of social practices which they are then, in a reversal of cause and effect, taken to explain.

13. Elizabeth Cowie, "Women, Representation and the Image," *Screen Education*, no. 23 (Summer 1977).

14. Johnston, "Women's Cinema as Counter-Cinema," p. 28.

15. Louis Althusser, *Marxism and Humanism* (Harmondsworth, UK: Penguin Books, 1969), p. 233.

16. Ibid., pp. 161-162.

17. Louis Althusser, "A Letter on Art," in *Lenin and Philosophy and Other Essays*, trans. Ben Brewster (London: New Left Books, 1971).

18. The account of bourgeois ideology which I draw on in this article is that given by Stuart Hall: "Culture, the Media and the 'Ideological Effect,' " in *Mass Communication and Society*, ed. James Curran et al. (Beverly Hills, CA: Sage Publications, 1979).

19. "Yvonne Rainer: An Introduction," *Camera Obscura*, vol. 1, no. 1 (Fall 1976), p. 59.

20. Ibid.

21. Ibid., p. 68.

22. "Yvonne Rainer: Interview," *Camera Obscura*, vol. 1, no. 1 (Fall 1976), pp. 76-96.

23. "Yvonne Rainer: An Introduction," p. 60.

24. E. Ann Kaplan, "Aspects of British Feminist Film Theory," *Jump Cut*, no. 12/13 (December 1976), p. 52.

25. Pamela Cook and Claire Johnston, "The Place of Women in the Cinema of Raoul Walsh," in *Raoul Walsh*, ed. Philip Hardy (Edinburgh, UK: Edinburgh Film Festival, 1974).

26. Laura Mulvey, "Visual Pleasure and Narrative Cinema," *Screen*, vol. 16, no. 3 (Autumn 1975), p. 6.

27. Claire Johnston, "Towards a Feminist Film Practice: Some Theses," *Edinburgh '76 Magazine* (Fall 1976), pp. 50-59.

28. Ibid.

29. It is argued that penis and phallus should not be confused. While the penis refers to the anatomical organ, the phallus, which the penis is able to symbolize, represents the object of desire as it is structured under patriarchy. (However, see p. 34 of this paper.) The account of Lacanian psychoanalysis given here was largely drawn from Steve Burniston and Christine Weedon, "Ideology, Subjectivity and the Artistic Text," *Working Papers in Cultural Studies*, no. 10 (1977); Laura Mulvey, "Visual Pleasure and the Narrative Cinema"; Colin MacCabe, "Principles of Realism and Pleasure," *Screen*, vol. 17, no. 3 (Autumn 1976). More recently, Terry Lovell has mounted a cogent critique of this interpretation of sexual difference in *Pictures of Reality* (pp. 44-46).

30. Mulvey, p. 7.

31. Johnston, "Women's Cinema as Counter-Cinema," p. 26.

32. Elizabeth Cowie, "Feminist Film Criticism: A Reply," *Screen*, vol. 16, no. 1 (Spring 1975), p. 138.

33. Claire Johnston, "Femininity and the Masquerade: *Anne of the Indies*," in *Jacques Tourneur*, ed. Claire Johnston and Paul Willemen (Edinburgh, UK: Edinburgh Film Festival, 1975), pp. 36-44.

34. For a discussion of this problem, see the collective article "Psychology, Ideology and the Human Subject," by the editorial board of *Ideology and Consciousness*, no. 1 (May 1977).

35. Steve Burniston, Frank Mort and Christine Weedon, "Psychoanalysis and the Cultural Acquisition of Sexuality and Subjectivity," in *Women Take Issue: Aspects of Women's Subordination*, ed. Women's Studies Group, Centre for Contemporary Cultural Studies, University of Birmingham (London: Hutchinson, 1978), p. 117.

36. Claire Johnston, ed., *The Work of Dorothy Arzner: Towards a Feminist Cinema* (London: British Film Institute, 1975); Pamela Cook, "'Exploitation' Films and Feminism," *Screen*, vol. 17, no. 2 (Summer 1976).

37. Claire Johnston, "Dorothy Arzner: Critical Strategies," in *The Work of Dorothy Arzner*, p. 4.

38. Ibid., p. 6.

39. Ibid.

40. Cowie, "Feminist Film Criticism."

41. Cook and Johnston, p. 100.

42. Laura Mulvey, in "Afterthoughts on 'Visual Pleasure and Narrative Cinema' inspired by *Duel in the Sun*," *Framework* 15/16/17 (Summer 1981), has elaborated the notion of transsexual identification, based on the pre-oedipal and phallic "phantasy of omnipotence" shared by girls and boys, to account for how women negotiate the "masculinization" of the spectator position in classic Hollywood cinema: "However, for the female spectator this situation is more complicated, and goes beyond simple mourning for a lost phantasy of omnipotence. The masculine identification, in its phallic aspect, reactivates for her a phantasy of 'action' that correct femininity demands should be repressed. The phantasy 'action' can only find expression, its *only* signifier for a woman, through the metaphor of masculinity." (p. 15.)

43. Pamela Cook, "Approaching the Work of Dorothy Arzner," in *The Work of Dorothy Arzner*, p. 9.

44. Ibid., p. 15.

45. Cook and Johnston, p. 100.

46. Molly Haskell, *From Reverence to Rape* (New York: Holt, Rinehart and Winston, 1978), pp. 3-4.

47. Perkins, p. 154.

48. See much of the writing in the British feminist journal *m/f*; for example: Rosalind Coward, "Sexual Liberation and the Family," *m/f* 1 (1978); Elizabeth Cowie, "The Popular Film as a Progressive Text—a Discussion of *Coma*," *m/f* 3/4 (1979/80); Delia Dumaresq, "Rape-Sexuality in the Law," *m/f* 5/6 (1981).

49. Work has begun in these areas—for instance, Tania Modleski's work on television soap opera ("The Search for Tomorrow in Today's Soap Operas," *Film Quarterly*, vol. 33, no. 1 [Fall 1979]) and Harlequin Romances ("The Disappearing Act: A Study of Harlequin Romances," *Signs*, vol. 5, no. 3 [Spring 1980]); Dorothy Hobson's ethnographic studies of female television viewers at the Birmingham Centre for Contemporary Cultural Studies ("Housewives and the Mass Media," in *Culture, Media, Language*, ed. Stuart Hall et al. [London: Hutchinson, 1980], and *'Crossroads': The Drama of a Soap Opera* [London: Methuen, 1982)]; and Charlotte Brunsdon's work (" 'Crossroads': Notes on a Soap Opera," *Screen*, vol. 22, no. 4 [Winter 1981]). See also The American Film Institute Monograph No. 2, *Regarding Television: Critical Views—An Anthology*, ed. E. Ann Kaplan (Los Angeles, CA: The American Film Institute, 1983) which has a section on soap operas.

The Woman at the Keyhole:
Women's Cinema and Feminist Criticism

Judith Mayne

The term "women's cinema" seems, if not necessarily simple to define, then at least straightforward enough. But the term "women's cinema" has acquired two different meanings which, to some minds, are diametrically opposed. It is at the hypothetical intersection of these two meanings, rather than with the favoring of one over the other, that I begin.[1] First, women's cinema refers to films made by women. The filmmakers range from classical Hollywood directors like Dorothy Arzner and Ida Lupino to their more recent heirs, like Claudia Weill and Joan Micklin Silver; and from directors whom many feminists would just as soon forget, like Leni Riefenstahl or Lina Wertmüller, to other contemporary European directors concerned directly and consciously with female modes of expression, like Chantal Akerman and Helke Sander. They range as well from independent documentary film-makers like Julia Reichert (co-director of *Union Maids*) and Connie Fields (*The Life and Times of Rosie the Riveter*) to more experimental independents attempting to reconcile feminist politics and avant-garde form, like Michelle Citron (*Daughter Rite*) and Sally Potter (*Thriller*). To attempt to account for the wide diversity of films represented in even this simple definition of "women's cinema" is a gigantic task in and of itself.

The term "women's cinema" or more precisely, the "woman's film," has acquired another meaning, referring to a Hollywood product designed to appeal to a specifically female audience. Such films, popular throughout the 1930s, 40s, and 50s, were usually melodramatic in tone and full of high-pitched emotion, from which came the pejorative title "the weepies." Indeed, Molly Haskell characterizes the "woman's film" as the "most untouchable of film genres." Here is how Haskell defines the genre:

> At the lowest level, as soap opera, the "woman's film" fills a masturba-
> tory need, it is soft-core emotional porn for the frustrated housewife.

> The weepies are founded on a mock-Aristotelian and politically con-
> servative aesthetic whereby women spectators are moved, not by pity
> and fear but by self-pity and tears, to accept, rather than reject, their lot.
> That there should be a need and an audience for such an opiate suggests
> an unholy amount of real misery.[2]

A typical theme of the "woman's film" is obsessive sacrifice to one's children at the expense of self: at the conclusion of *Stella Dallas* (1937), Barbara Stanwyck is the female equivalent of a skid-row bum as she peeks longingly through the window of an elegant mansion where her daughter's wedding is taking place. Another typical theme concerns affliction: Jane Wyman is stricken blind in *Magnificent Obsession* (1954) and is nursed back to emotional and physical health by her doctor, Rock Hudson. The very notion of a "woman's film" evolved, of course, as a marketing strategy, one that has recently been revived. In films like *Julia* (1977) and *The Turning Point* (1977), the format of the woman's film has been refurbished and updated.

Perhaps ultimately films made by women have little or nothing to do with Hollywood women's films. The tendency, of course, is to establish a rigorous opposition between those Hollywood films, made by men for a female audience, and films by women, between the "inauthentic" and the "authentic" portrayals of female experience. But even while Molly Haskell condemns the facile pathos of the woman's films, she wonders why it is that emotional response should be so devalued as to be relegated to an "inferior" genre.[3] And in keeping with Haskell's love-hate relationship to the woman's film, I prefer to *affirm* the ambiguity of the term "women's cinema." For in order to understand how women make movies, there needs to be some consideration of what relationships women have had, traditionally and historically, as filmmakers and as film consumers, to the medium.

But even with this oscillation between production and consumption, the term "women's cinema" elides the context in which women have had the most visibility in the cinema, and that is on screen. Here again, Hollywood comes immediately to mind. We know that women function in the classical cinema as objects of spectacle, a function exemplified by the extreme: Marilyn Monroe. Remember *Gentlemen Prefer Blondes* (1953), for example—every time Monroe enters a room, be it a restaurant, a hotel room or a courtroom, the space immediately becomes a stage, and onlookers become spectators, consumers of this image of femininity. A feminist analysis of the phenomenon of Marilyn Monroe seems so *simple*. She is a passive object, nothing more than the projection of male fantasies. But this "ideology of the spectacle," so to speak, is more complex than even the cliché of Marilyn Monroe would suggest. By identifying women's presence in the Hollywood cinema through a spectator-spectacle relationship, we are asking the question: How are the relations of seeing, the relation of a person looking and a person looked at, power bound?[4] As film viewers, we have spent more time than we realize watching men and women look at each other, and, most emphatically, watching men watching women.

Again there is the temptation to establish a rigorous opposition. If women have been "falsely" represented in distorted images in the classical cinema, then women filmmakers will be more likely to present "accurate," "undistorted," not to mention "positive" images of women—which will then be eagerly consumed by the film viewer. But I am not only unconvinced that such clear-cut alternatives are possible, I am not convinced that they are even desirable. Once again, the work of women filmmakers always needs to be seen against a background shaped and defined by the ways in which women have been associated with the cinema.

It is through the conventions of the traditional cinema that most of us, critics and filmmakers included, have learned how to "watch" the movies. The conventions of the traditional cinema—these are, first and foremost, narrative conventions, the descendants, in some sense, of the narrative conventions of the novel. Or, put another way, cinema combines narrative and spectacle, story-telling and display. Some of the particular problems and issues of women's cinema are worth considering against that background of a narrative tradition which for two centuries before the development of moving pictures was dominated by the novel.

Women have been most visible in the cinema as performers, and somewhat less so as spectators. As filmmakers, women have been virtually invisible. One thinks of the traditional middle-class novel, and of how novels in the eighteenth century, that period of the "rise of the novel," tended to focus upon and problematize female experience.[5] It has become a commonplace that women were, especially in the eighteenth century, the most important audience for the novel. Women wrote novels too, of course, but the frequent adoption of male pen names necessitated by the increasing acceptability of the novel as a legitimate art form suggests a situation like that of the woman filmmaker many years later.

The affinities between the middle-class novel and the cinema, above and beyond the status of women, have been described in a variety of ways. Some say that the novel is to eighteenth-century British society what the cinema is to twentieth-century American society; others, that the novel is an emblematic art form of a developing industrial society, and the cinema equally emblematic of its later stage of consumerism; and still others, that the novel provides a model of the connection between art and industry later expanded by the cinema, an industrialized art form *par excellence*. Perhaps most obvious is the narrative connection: as cinema evolved as a story-telling medium, it was drawn closer and closer to the devices of the novel.

The social space within which the novel (and later the cinema) developed was increasingly divided along the lines of private and public existence.

Public and private: on the one hand, the world of business and trade, eventually of industrial production, and of the social institutions related to them, and on the other, the world of the home, of family and personal ties. The narratives of middle-class novels began to function as meditations on the splits between these two spheres of private and public life. That the separation between private and public spheres—sometimes real, sometimes imaginary—has particular ramifications for women has been suggested, for example, by recent feminist theory that examines how women have been bound by, and have transcended, the split between the private and the public.[6]

Hence narrative becomes a form of negotiation between the private and the public. In Samuel Richardson's *Clarissa*, for example, two distinctly opposed notions of the "private sphere" clash. Clarissa wants to marry for love, for a private sphere that functions as a refuge. But for her family, marriage functions only as a direct reflection of economic and financial necessity. This process of negotiation concerns, as well, the very process of reading which, for women isolated from the social sphere and with unlimited leisure time, created a form of imaginary participation.[7]

If the very substance of the traditional novel is so closely aligned to the changing dimensions of the social and individual lives of women, then the obvious question is: What defines the work of the female writer, and later, the female filmmaker? It has always been tempting to define women writers as a subculture, marginal to the dynamics and preoccupations of patriarchal society. While women writers have been marginal to the *business* of writing, there has been an aspect of female writing which is not so much *other* than the preoccupations of male novelists, as it is a foregrounding, an intensification of that process of negotiation between private and public spheres. Consider, for example, the famous and often commented-upon opening sentence of Jane Austen's *Pride and Prejudice*: "It is a truth universally acknowledged, that a single man in possession of a good fortune, must be in want of a wife."[8] The phrase seems firmly to situate the reader in the realm of popular wisdom, in a public sphere of "universal truths." The sentence is reminiscent of what Roland Barthes calls the cultural code: phrases which assume a kind of universal agreement, like "it is well-known that..." or, "everyone is aware that..." Barthes calls such utterances "implicit proverbs" which state the "law of society."[9] But we quickly discover, in Austen's novel, that the popular wisdom evoked, this "law of society," reflects not so much a universal opinion as the peculiarities of Mrs. Bennet's vision of the world as clearly divided between marriageable and unmarriageable men. This fine example of Austen's irony serves equally well as a fine example of a female narrative perspective. For *Pride and Prejudice* begins in a hypothetical space between the personal and the social, where the boundary lines are not clear. Indeed, the entire novel becomes an attempt to consolidate two opposing spheres. Thus the marriage of Elizabeth Bennet and Darcy is a fantasy of reconciliation, between private and public, middle class and aristocracy, female and male.

But an enormous distance separates Jane Austen from Hollywood. Women's relationships to the novel form provide a valuable perspective on women's cinema, and I will argue that women filmmakers explore, as well, those hypothetical spaces and bridges between private and public realms. If Jane Austen gives us a sense of the social and narrative background from which female writing emerges, then we might turn, for initial possibilities of cinematic analogues, to a more contemporary example of female writing in which the cinema emerges with metaphoric significance.

Doris Lessing's *The Golden Notebook* explores the relations between female identity and artistic production. One such relationship is represented for Lessing through the cinema, where the woman is the viewer, man the projectionist, and the whole viewing process a form of control and domination. Writer Anna Wulf describes her vision of events from the past: films shown to her by an invisible male projectionist. The films represent what Anna calls her "burden of recreating order out of the chaos that my life had become."[10] Yet Anna is horrified by this vision of cinematic order:

> They were all, so I saw now, conventionally well-made films, as if they had been done in a studio; then I saw the titles: these films, which were everything I hated most, had been directed by me. The projectionist kept running these films very fast, and then pausing on the credits, and I could hear his jeering laugh at *Directed by Anna Wulf*. Then he would run another few scenes, every scene glossy with untruth, false and stupid.[11]

Lessing's cinematic metaphor is informed by an insight into the patriarchal nature of the relation of projectionist to screen, viewer to image. Put another way, the conditions of film viewing suggest, for Lessing, patriarchal domination.

Cinema is evoked in *The Golden Notebook* within the context of a female narrator's relationship to language and experience. The cinema concretizes what Christa Wolf, in *The Quest for Christa T.*, calls "The difficulty of saying 'I.'"[12] Indeed, there are many obstacles in the cinema for saying "I." Lessing's designation of the cinema as bound by control and domination is not just a literary imagination denigrating the cinema. And just in case literature might appear to be utopian, at least relatively speaking, one might recall that Susan Gubar and Sandra Gilbert begin their analysis of women writers with a query into the equivalence between the writer's pen and his penis.[13] Yet the equivalence does seem somewhat minor compared to the cinema, where the metaphorical status of the camera as eye, gun (shooting a camera and shooting a gun) *and* penis has made for a long history of sometimes tiresome cinematic figures. By now, it may seem as though aspiring women filmmakers might do better to turn away from this seemingly monolithic institution. But if cinema does suggest this reified form of domination, then explorations into the possibilities of women's cinema have a kind of strategic importance.

Lessing's cinematic metaphor in *The Golden Notebook* emerges as part of the journey of a first-person female narrator attempting to distill and clarify experience. Two cinematic parallels which immediately come to mind are Michelle Citron's *Daughter Rite* (1978), in which a female narrator speaks, over home movies shown in slow motion, of dreams and fantasies; and Sally Potter's *Thriller* (1979), in which the Mimi of Puccini's *La Bohème* conducts an investigation, of sorts, to discover who was responsible for her death. But the place of the voice, in cinema, is complicated by one of the most basic features of film narrative: voyeurism.

Voyeurism has become so institutionalized a feature of the cinema that we tend to take it for granted. Early films are enormously instructive in this respect, for they often express directly and baldly those figures of fascination which, in the course of film history, would become naturalized in a variety of ways. *A Search for the Evidence* (1903) is one such film: it is a simple example of cinematic voyeurism, and it demonstrates, in highly condensed form, some of the crucial implications of voyeurism for women's relations to film.

A Search for the Evidence shows us a man and a woman, presumably an angry wife and a man of the law, as they proceed down a hotel corridor in search of the "evidence": an adulterous husband. The woman peers into one room after another. As she does so, the camera imitates her vision, and we look into a succession of hotel rooms. On the screen the space of the rooms is framed by a keyhole mask, the visualization of the look. Thus a simple alternation informs the structure of this brief film, between the person looking and the object of the look, between the corridor and the individual room. Now a hotel corridor may not exactly represent a public sphere, but the movie theater (or university classroom) certainly does. From this vantage point, we also peek into a whole series of "private spheres." Finally there is the payoff. The evidence, a guilty husband enjoying a romantic toast with his lover, is found. The man in the hall bursts triumphantly into the room, followed by the angry wife. The sense of closure is created by a change in angle: we finally see a room from within, unfettered by the keyhole mask. The inner space of the room has been—excuse the expression—penetrated.

This early film has something to tell us about the cinema's lingering fascination with the spheres of private and public life, mediated through the voyeuristic space proper to the cinema. *A Search for the Evidence* also provides an appropriate metaphor for women's relationship to the cinema. On one side of the corridor is a woman who peeks, on the other, the woman who is, as it were, on display. Now there are, of course, men on both sides of the threshold as well. But with a difference—before we actually enter the room where the evidence is to be found, the woman in the hall gestures to her companion, and he looks through the keyhole. Thus he authorizes the penetration of the room.

The history of women's relationship to the cinema, from this side of the keyhole, has been a series of tentative peeks; that threshold separating corridor and hotel room is crossed with difficulty. And then, we might recall as well that the roles of women in the early cinema were often portrayed by men, female impersonators. I am not absolutely certain whether the woman in the hallway in *A Search for the Evidence* is a man in drag. But there is something entirely appropriate about this ambiguous sexual identity, as if even a timid peek through the keyhole required a certain transvestism.

That the cinema is a voyeuristic medium has become a commonplace of film theory and criticism. That cinematic voyeurism should have, for women, a peculiarly ambiguous status comes as no surprise. Feminist critics, and Laura Mulvey in particular, have described "visual pleasure" in the cinema as rooted in a hierarchical system whereby the male is the "bearer of the look," the woman the "object of the look"—the ideology of spectacle referred to earlier.[14] Hence Mulvey calls for a film practice that will destroy, in sum, the traditional forms of visual pleasure.[15]

But the issue is complicated, it seems to me, when we see that voyeurism often entails, as it does in *A Search for the Evidence*, a look into a room—into a home, one could say, or into a private sphere; in other words, into that realm which traditionally and historically has been women's space. A gaze cast into a room, and a gaze cast at a female body: these are not necessarily contradictory activities, and often the one supposes the other. But they are clearly not voyeuristic in exactly the same way. Metaphoric license allows us to use terms like "voyeurism" in ways far more general than their clinical implications. But I wonder just how far such license leads us. If women cast a cinematic gaze inside rooms, does this necessarily entail an identification with the entire system of cinematic voyeurism?

Many women filmmakers have turned around the voyeuristic gaze in order to critique the convention from within, as it were. Thus one of the most important definitions of women's cinema that has emerged is the "critique of spectacle." An equally important and vital aspect of women's cinema, it seems to me, concerns the construction of a narrative space. What I mean here, quite literally, is an architecture of connecting or isolated rooms and passageways, interior and exterior space. I would define this narrative space not so much as a critique of voyeurism or of woman as spectacle, but as an attempt to disengage the voyeuristic look from the space that surrounds it.

Dorothy Arzner was one of the very few women directors to have been successful in Hollywood from the 1920s through the 1940s. *Dance Girl Dance* (1940) is often referred to in feminist film criticism as a kind of model of what the critique of spectacle entails in women's cinema. A famous scene in the film shows a woman performer (Maureen O'Hara) on stage, who turns to her predominantly male audience, and tells them how she sees *them*. The effect is stunning, and this "return of the look" does indeed turn the convention against itself.[16] In another film by Arzner, *Craig's Wife* (1936), "female" connotes not so much the female body in terms of performance, but rather a conception of space. *Craig's Wife*, based on a stage play by George Kelley, shows us a woman so obsessively concerned with her house that nothing else is of interest to her. Harriet Craig married as "... a way towards emancipation.... I married to be independent." If marriage is a business contract, then Harriet Craig's capital is her house. Indeed, Harriet's sense of economy is pursued with a vengeance, and the men in the film are the victims, explicit or not, of her obsession. It is Harriet's husband who married for love, not money; and in the subplot of the film, a friend of Walter Craig is so obsessed by his wife's unfaithfulness that he kills her and then himself.

As an adaptation, Arzner's film is quite faithful to the Kelley play, but with an important difference. At the conclusion of the film, virtually everyone has cleared out of Harriet's house: her niece has left with her fiancé, her servants have either quit or been fired, and Walter has finally packed up and left in disgust. Harriet, who has actively pursued the separation of private and public realms, now seems pathetically neurotic and alone. The widow next door brings Harriet some roses. In Kelley's play, Harriet has become a mirror image of her neighbor: both are women alone, to be pitied. But virtually the same scene is acted out quite differently in Arzner's film. The neighbor represents Harriet's one last chance for connection with another human being. Thus the figure who, in the original play, is a pale echo of Harriet, becomes in the film the suggestion of another identity. There is, then, an effect of commentary in Arzner's film, both on the original dramatic source and on the basic plot of the piece which, in the play, does reek of a certain misogyny.

Harriet's neurosis is, after all, simply an extension of consumerist ideals. Houses and rooms may suggest women's sphere, but they also function, particularly in the Hollywood film industry, as what film historian Charles Eckert has called "living display windows." Eckert suggests that Hollywood "... did as much or more than any other force in capitalist culture to smooth the operation of the production-consumption cycle by fetishizing products and putting the libido in libidinally invested advertising."[17] Numerous tie-ins between the film industry and other manufacturers assured that specific products and brand names—of clothing, of appliances, of virtually every thing imaginable—would be given maximum visibility on the screen.[18] Harriet Craig's living room is, indeed, a "living display window." But the products on display, from furniture to clothing to Harriet herself, are designated as the symptoms of a neurosis, rather than presented in a naturalized way as innocent objects in a happy, healthy, consumer society.

Women's relationship to domestic space is problematized in Arzner's film. If Harriet Craig is the woman on the other side of the keyhole, the woman looking through the keyhole resolutely refuses to differentiate the female body (the object of voyeurism) from the space that surrounds it. In Germaine Dulac's 1922 film *The Smiling Madame Beudet* (often cited as the "first feminist film"),[19] the situation is reversed. Here, woman is on the inside, looking through the keyhole to the world outside. *The Smiling Madame Beudet* recounts the fantasy life of a woman married to a boorish merchant in a small provincial French town, who dreams, through music and poetry, of another life. Much of the film is shot from Madame Beudet's point of view, with abstracted images of water and imaginary lovers functioning as concrete representations of her fantasy life.

Most of the film takes place inside the Beudet apartment. Occasionally, however, images of "outside" appear. The film begins with images of a church, a bridge, a park; these are establishing shots of provincial life. Images of the town appear again approximately halfway through the film, showing the town awakening at the same time as Monsieur and Madame Beudet. These images function, like Madame Beudet's fantasies, as indications of some kind of alternative to the claustrophobic world of the Beudet apartment.[20] If private and public spheres are relatively independent of each other, this world outside constantly beckons.

Madame Beudet's fantasy life only leads, however, to a failed attempt to catch her husband at his own "suicide game." He keeps an empty revolver in his desk, and occasionally fires it at his temple to taunt his wife and amuse himself. She loads the gun, an event that occurs "off-screen" and is thus just as imaginary as her fantasy life. But for once, he points the gun at her, and only just misses her. He then naively assumes that she wanted to kill herself. He clings to her, and in the final image of the film we see the couple in the street, nodding to a passing priest. For the first time, we see Madame Beudet outdoors. But this realm has lost all of the utopian potential suggested earlier in the film.[21] The public sphere has also become a confining, claustrophobic space, as the very composition of the image indicates: Madame Beudet is framed by her husband on the one side and by the priest on the other.

We perceive cinematic space through cinematic time. French critic Claudine Hermann has suggested that the female experience of space and time has particular contours:

> Masculine system has until now required women to assume material continuity—of daily life and the species—while men assume the function of discontinuity, discovery, change in all its forms, in essence, the superior, differentiating function.[22]

Hermann's delineations of space and time correspond, of course, to the separation of private and public spheres. The "material continuity" of which she speaks is comprised of the routines of domesticity. Some women film-makers have resolutely insisted upon the representation of real time on the screen, in a spirit that chimes with Herrmann's perceptions of female space and time. Chantal Akerman is perhaps the best-known of these filmmakers. Her film *Jeanne Dielman, 23 Quai de Commerce, 1080 Bruxelles* is con-structed around the use of real time, and gives detailed attention to the everyday gestures of a woman. Akerman has said:

> . . . I give space to things which were never, almost never, shown in that way, like the daily gestures of a woman. They are the lowest in the hierarchy of film images. . . . But more than the context, it's because of the style. If you choose to show a woman's features so precisely, it's because you love them. In some way you recognize those gestures that have always been denied and ignored.[23]

Put another way, Akerman enlarges the scope of the camera, displacing cinematic voyeurism by focusing on what has traditionally been marginal. One can imagine, perhaps, a Chantal Akerman version of *A Search for the Evidence*, in which the triumphant entry into the room where the adulterous husband and his lover share a toast is overshadowed, as it were, by a scene in the kitchen where the preparation of the tray is shown in great detail.

All of Marguerite Duras' films are informed by a principle of duration. In *Nathalie Granger* (1973), the space of a house inhabited by two women is explored and recorded. There is little condensation of time. Gestures, looks, aimless wanderings, household tasks—these are also those "marginal ges-tures" which form the body (I use the word in a literal sense) of the film. But then there is a climax, of sorts: a traveling salesman enters the house and tries to convince the two women to buy a washing machine. He finally discovers that they already have the washing machine that he is trying to sell. The traveling salesman is one of the few male presences in the film. At the beginning of the film, we hear a radio announcer's broadcast about two killers loose in the area, and a husband (or so we presume) leaves. In the traditional cinema, of course, the broadcast and the husband's departure would be the first clues that the women in the house are soon to be murdered. But that plot never thickens. When the salesman enters the house, he is functioning in a traditional sense as a voyeur. But voyeurism is completely suspended. It is not quite accurate to say that the look is returned; it is, rather, deflated. Duras strips the space of the house of any narrative intrigue. The female look has crossed the threshold and is inside. But, unlike *The Smiling Madame Beudet*, the look is not projected outside; rather, it explores the space and the rhythms of the interior.

What I have chosen to call duration might be understood as a euphe-mism for boredom. Boredom is not high on anyone's list of desirable aesthetic responses. But perhaps it has an important function, perhaps its unattractive reputation is somewhat unfair.[24] What is boring about *Nathalie Granger* stems from the lack of investment of the two women characters in the structures of voyeurism. But what of the film viewer? Perhaps duration, or boredom, can function in Duras' film as a way of disengaging, in the viewer, the experience of space from the experience of intrigue.

The three films by Arzner, Dulac and Duras that I have described explore, in different ways, the interface between a female perspective and narrative space. These are films which, to return to *A Search for the Evidence*, stand on the threshold between the hotel corridor and the room. They do so in a variety of ways, foregrounding the relationship between the woman in drag peeking through the keyhole and the woman in the room. And so, in describing these films by women directors, I am putting forth at least a tentative definition of what "women's cinema" is and might be. But there are pitfalls in such definitions. Chantal Akerman puts it well: "It's really a hard problem to try to say what differentiates a woman's rhythm in film because a man can use these same forms of expression. . . . We speak of 'women's rhythm,' but it isn't necessarily the same for all women."[25] The danger thus concerns hegemony. We risk characterizing women's cinema as a series of consumable products rather than as a process which adopts a multitude of forms. Hence, the different explorations of narrative space in *Craig's Wife*, *The Smiling Madame Beudet* and *Nathalie Granger* should not be understood as summary expressions of Woman and the Cinema. They are, rather, indications of how films by women can explore a terrain different from that of the traditional cinema.

But there is another pitfall, decidedly more problematic, and that is a definition of women's cinema that considers only the film director. Dorothy Arzner worked in the studio system of Hollywood, moving upwards from her early employment as a film editor. Germaine Dulac had relative independence as a filmmaker, and was actively involved in distribution and exhibition as an active promoter of the ciné-club movement in France. Marguerite Duras is a writer turned filmmaker, essentially defined within a French tradition of the avant-garde. To say that the category "woman filmmaker" somehow transcends the important differences between these directors is patently absurd.

The issue is one of authorship. The concept of authorship has had a curious history in the cinema. It was not until the 1950s that "auteurism" became a fixture of film theory and criticism—auteurism being the view that the film director is the single force responsible for the final film, and that throughout the films of a given auteur a body of themes and preoccupations will be discernable. Such assumptions must seem, particularly to one versed in literary criticism, so basic as to be unquestionable. But the object of inquiry for auteurist critics was first and foremost Hollywood, and to begin to speak of a "Hitchcock" or a "John Ford" or a "Nicholas Ray" film, rather than a "John Wayne" or an "MGM" film, constituted a genuinely radical enterprise.

Notions of authorship have come under attack in recent years. Authorship presumes, of course, a single presence which produces the text, and the metaphors for such production are usually paternalistic. Here is how Roland Barthes, for instance, describes the fiction of the author:

> As institution, the author is dead, his civil status, his biographical person have disappeared; dispossessed, they no longer exercise over his work the formidable paternity whose account literary history, teaching, and public opinion had the responsibility of establishing and renewing. . . . [26]

Barthes goes on to describe our desires, as readers (one could say viewers, as well), *vis-à-vis* this mythical presence: ". . . in the text, in a way, *I desire* the author: I need his figure (which is neither his representation nor his projection), as he needs mine. . . ."[27] I wonder if Barthes' "I" is all-inclusive. If the fictions of authorship are controlled by an image of paternity, then are we all fictional sons of the author, in search of an origin?

The tendency to fetishize authorship is, of course, overwhelming. In film there is the added factor that, more so than in perhaps any art form, it is collectively produced. In our society, this means produced according to the division of labor: rarely have women been able to become film directors, except as independents. For all the recent chatter about the "new woman" in Hollywood cinema, the proportion of women directors in Hollywood remains abysmally low. To insist upon authorship as a model for women's cinema, then, is to virtually ignore the major ways in which women *have* been involved in the cinema: as actresses, as screenplay writers, as editors and cutters. This does not mean that we should declare every film in which women have had a part a potential "woman's film." This would put us in the somewhat embarrassing position of laying claim to *Jaws*, for example, (edited by Verna Fields) as a "woman's film." But I am suggesting that we expand our definition of "production" so as to include other influences than that of the director.

Consider, for example, the role of the actress. Some actresses seem to transcend their roles as sex-objects, to comment on the very nature of spectacle and voyeurism. When Marlene Dietrich puts on a tuxedo and sings "Who'll buy my apples" to a cabaret crowd in von Sternberg's *Morocco* (1930), not to mention that she kisses a woman in the audience, sexual ambiguity reigns supreme. Silvia Bovenschen writes, apropos of Dietrich and others, that "amazingly, it seems that even those images of femininity constructed by men or by the male art industry, are turning against their creators in ever-increasing numbers."[28] When Katharine Hepburn, in George Cukor's *Sylvia Scarlett* (1935), disguises herself as a boy ("Sylvester") in order to travel with her father, the sum effect is to turn the tables, and make "femininity" look like the disguise. Indeed, once Sylvia has become a boy, she has a hard time remembering how to act like a woman.

I initially suggested that, given the nature of cinematic voyeurism, and given cinema's position with relation to private and public spheres, women's cinema, somewhat like women's writing, is concerned with the itinerary from public to private space. This context for a discussion of women's cinema also needs to be opened up, to include in particular what is perhaps the most important element in the whole process: the film viewer. It has taken many years for film criticism to address the ways in which spectators not only identify with the screen, but interact with it to produce effects of meaning. We know that in order for the looks exchanged by characters on screen to be meaningful, there has to be a vantage point for the spectator. One wonders if male and female spectators have different vantage points. If cinematic voyeurism does indeed rest upon a firm foundation of active versus passive, male versus female, "bearer of the look" versus "object of the look," then it would appear that women are always *alienated* spectators. B. Ruby Rich describes the situation of the woman viewer in terms that are not quite so monolithic:

> ...for a woman today, film is a dialectical experience in a way that it never was and never will be for a man under patriarchy. Brecht once described the exile as the ultimate dialectician in that the exile lives the tension of two different cultures. That's precisely the sense in which the woman spectator is an equally inevitable dialectician....As a woman going into the movie theater, you are faced with a context that is coded wholly for your invisibility, and yet, obviously, you are sitting there and bringing along a certain coding from life outside the theater....The cinematic codes have structured our absence to such an extent that the only choice allowed to us is to identify either with Marilyn Monroe or with the man behind me hitting the back of my seat with his knees.[29]

Central to any definition of women's cinema is recognition of the complex nature of film viewing, and of the woman viewer as, in Rich's words, the "ultimate dialectician." Such recognition is particularly imperative for feminist film criticism. Women's cinema and feminist criticism: the work of the filmmaker and the work of the critic are substantially different, and "women's" and "feminist" do not mean the same thing, even though feminism is the attempt to theorize female experience into modes of resistance and action. It is the work of criticism to make connections—between the different contexts that define film (production, exhibition, reception), and between cinema and the sociohistorical context in which it is produced and received. And, perhaps most important, the task of criticism is to examine the processes that determine how films evoke responses and how spectators produce them.

Consider, for example, the backlash mentality which seems to inform many contemporary American films. The new horror films are an extreme case in point, but I am thinking more of a film like *Kramer vs. Kramer*. I have no basic quarrel with the view that this film essentially asks the spectator to respond to Ted Kramer's success at fatherhood by denigrating Joanna Kramer's desires for independence. But striking up one more film for patriarchy doesn't tell us much about the itineraries required to arrive at such conclusions. I would like to see more critical attention devoted to the following: like most people at the movie theater, I was invested in *Kramer vs. Kramer,* that is, I was intrigued by the film, moved at the appropriate moments. But by the time the house lights had come on, I began to think that I had been had. What interests me is that precise moment when, my nose still runny from that emotional investment, I say: "This is appalling." I have just "embraced" a film, and then there comes the moment of disavowal. I suspect that the "embrace" and the "disavowal" are, for many women viewers—feminists included—more intimately connected than most of us realize.

The woman at the keyhole in *A Search for the Evidence* stands as an appropriate metaphor for the filmmaker and the viewer. The keyhole represents something of both the vision of the camera and the vision onto the screen. The critic is also somewhat like the woman at the keyhole. Extending the metaphor somewhat, one can imagine the filmmaker behind the camera, and the viewer before the screen. The most appropriate place for the critic would seem to be next to that machine which is intermediary of sorts between the camera and the screen: the projector. In Lessing's *The Golden Notebook,* we recall, Anna Wulf sees the films of her life shown to her by an invisible, male, jeering projectionist. Would that the work of feminist criticism and women's cinema were so simple, that the "male" could just be replaced by "female," the "invisible" by "visible."

Filmmaker Maya Deren suggests, perhaps, some of the same distance as Lessing from this machine when she describes, in her notebooks, looking at a film on a malfunctioning viewer, but rejecting her husband's suggestion that she would be "better off using a projector":

> The immediate physical contact with the film, the nearness of the image, the automatic muscular control of its speed—the fact that as I wound, my impulses and reactions towards the film translated themselves into muscular impulses and so to the film directly, with no machine—buttons, switches, etc.—between me and the film. . . . This physical contact creates a sense of intimacy. It is not an image independent of me, projected on a wall, of which I am spectator. It is immediately, directly, uniquely for my eyes. It comes to life out of the energy of my muscles. Later, of course, I shall use the projector to get proper speed, etc. But first this ultimate copulation between me and the film must take place, and out of it will be born the independent child which will be projected at the Provincetown Playhouse while I sit in a bar across the street.[30]

Sign of humiliation and control for Lessing, and a peculiar representation of separation from the mother for Deren, the projector suggests technology at its most instrumental. The projector marks the distance between

spectator and screen, the distance perhaps necessary to the voyeuristic pleasure of cinema. Another view, similar and yet different, comes from the poet
H.D.:

> This is his gift:
> light,
> light
> a wave
> that sweeps
> us
> from old fears
> and powers
> and disenchantments;
> this is his gift;
> light
> bearing us aloft,
> enthusiastic,
> into realms of magic;
> old forms dispersed
> take fresh
> shapes
> out of nothingness;
> light
> renders us spell-bound
> enchants us
> and astounds;[31]

H.D. mythologizes the projector by way of a curious ambivalence: at the same
time that the cinema is demystified, it is reinvested with patriarchal significance. The projector is not so totally representative of control as with Lessing,
nor such a sign of separation as with Deren. H.D. published her poem in
1927, during a decade when the cinema had certainly become well-established
as a story-telling medium, a cultural institution in its own right. Yet she
writes, nonetheless, at a moment closer to the origins of cinema than either
Lessing or Deren, closer to the period when films like *A Search for the
Evidence*—made in 1903—would create little primal scenes of the cinema.
H.D. writes at a moment when the autonomy and instrumentality of the
projector are, perhaps, not so self-evident. We recall that when the first films
were shown in Paris in 1895, their subjects were of decidedly less importance
than the simple fact of their projection, "life size, on a screen before an entire
audience," as the advertisement went.

All feminist inquiry is, in a sense, a reading against the grain of patriarchal institutions, an unearthing of contradictions and ambivalences at first
invisible to the naked eye. In the cinema, such a reading against the grain
requires a certain memory of how cinematic structures, like voyeurism,
evolved and became naturalized. The projector might well serve, in this light,

as an appropriate figure for the tasks of feminist criticism. Through projection, individual frames of celluloid are shot through with light and acquire the semblance of continuity. When the woman at the keyhole turns to cast a gaze at the machine, the projection of voyeuristic structures onto the screen is momentarily interrupted: the gesture is not so much one of destruction, but of a slowing-down of film into a series of celluloid fragments.

NOTES

1. This paper was first presented as a lecture in the Women's Studies Research Colloquia, Ohio State University, May 1981. This article was reprinted from *New German Critique* 23 (Spring/Summer 1981).

2. Molly Haskell, *From Reverence to Rape* (New York: Penguin Books, 1973), p. 155.

3. Ibid.

4. The issue is explored, in terms relevant to the cinema, in John Berger, *Ways of Seeing* (New York: Viking Press, 1972).

5. The classic study, of course, is Ian Watt, *The Rise of the Novel* (Berkeley, CA: University of California Press, 1957).

6. See, for example, Ann Foreman, *Femininity and Alienation* (London: Pluto Press, 1977); Joan Kelly, "The Doubled Vision of Feminist Theory," *Feminist Studies*, vol. 5, no. 1 (Spring 1979), pp. 216-227; and Sheila Rowbotham, *Woman's Consciousness, Man's World* (1973; rpt. Baltimore, MD: Penguin Books, 1974).

7. For a further discussion of the relationship of narrative to private and public existence, see my "Mediation, the Novelistic, and Film Narrative," in *Narrative Strategies*, ed. Syndy M. Conger and Janice R. Welsch (Macomb, IL: Western Illinois University Press, 1980).

8. Jane Austen, *Pride and Prejudice* (Boston, MA: Houghton Mifflin Co., 1956), p. 1.

9. Roland Barthes, *S/Z*, trans. Richard Miller (New York: Hill and Wang, 1976), p. 100.

10. Doris Lessing, *The Golden Notebook* (New York: Simon and Schuster, 1973), p. 619.

11. Ibid.

12. Christa Wolf, *The Quest for Christa T.*, trans. Christopher Middleton (New York: Delta Books, 1970), p. 170.

13. Susan Gubar and Sandra Gilbert, *The Madwoman in the Attic* (New Haven, CT: Yale University Press, 1979), p. 3.

14. Laura Mulvey, "Visual Pleasure and Narrative Cinema," *Screen*, vol. 16, no. 3 (Autumn 1975), p. 12.

15. Ibid., p. 18.

16. See Claire Johnston, "Dorothy Arzner: Critical Strategies," in *The Work of Dorothy Arzner*, ed. Claire Johnston (London: British Film Institute, 1975), pp. 1-8.

17. Charles Eckert, "The Carole Lombard in Macy's Window," *Quarterly Review of Film Studies*, vol. 3, no. 1 (Winter 1978), pp. 4, 21.

18. Ibid., p. 21.

19. See William Van Wert, "Germaine Dulac: First Feminist Filmmaker," in *Women and the Cinema*, ed. Karyn Kay and Gerald Peary (New York: E.P. Dutton, 1977), pp. 213-223.

20. Sandy Flitterman discusses these issues in "Montage/Discourse: Germaine Dulac's *The Smiling Madame Beudet*," *Wide Angle*, vol. 4, no. 3 (1981), pp. 54-59.

21. Flitterman says that "...the last shot of the film, which restricts this freedom of description by its focus on the diegetic couple, confirms its legibility as narrative space...." (Ibid., p. 59.)

22. Claudine Hermann, "Les Coordonnées féminines: espace et temps," in *Les Voleuses de langue* (Paris: Editions des femmes, 1976); trans. "Women in Space and Time," in *New French Feminisms*, ed. Elaine Marks and Isabelle de Courtivron (Amherst, MA: University of Massachusetts Press, 1980), p. 172.

23. Quoted in Stephen Heath, "Difference," *Screen*, vol. 19, no. 3 (Autumn 1978), p. 101.

24. For a discussion of boredom, see Ronald Rosbottom, "Boredom and Meaning: A Reading of Laclos' *Les Liaisons dangereuses*," *Forum*, vol. 16, no. 2 (1978), pp. 11-18.

25. Chantal Akerman, quoted in Heath, "Difference," p. 101.

26. Roland Barthes, *The Pleasure of the Text*, trans. Richard Miller (New York: Hill and Wang, 1975), p. 27.

27. Ibid.

28. Silvia Bovenschen, "Is There a Feminine Aesthetic?" *New German Critique* 10 (Winter 1977), p. 125.

29. B. Ruby Rich, in Michelle Citron et al., "Women and Film: A Discussion of Feminist Aesthetics," *New German Critique* 13 (1978), p. 87.

30. Maya Deren, "From the Notebook of 1947," *October* 14 (1980), p. 21.

31. H.D. (Hilda Doolittle), "Projector II Chang," *Close Up* 4 (October 1927), pp. 37-38. Anne Friedberg brought to my attention the writings of H.D. on the cinema, in a paper presented at the Ohio University Conference on Film History, April 1981.

The "Woman's Film": Possession and Address

Mary Ann Doane

Much of the effort of already classical feminist studies has been that of a certain recapture of the past, defined not as a rewriting of history but as its "filling out" or completion. The aim of such a project is the demonstration that, although women have been censored from the texts of history, they populate its reality and must be saved from obscurity. The underlying themes of such an approach are that women were "really there" or "did really do things," and that we can know in some direct and unmediated way what these things were. Feminist film theory and criticism have shown themselves to be particularly resistant to the empiricism of this methodology. Claire Johnston clearly delineates the difficulties in an attempt to situate the work of Dorothy Arzner:

> . . . do feminist critics simply want to introduce women into film history? To answer this question, it is necessary to examine the ideology which has dominated film history up to now. Film historians . . . have until very recently confined themselves to an accumulation of 'facts' and the construction of chronologies. From these, they have attempted by a process of induction to derive an interpretation of historical events closely linked to liberal notions of 'progress' and 'development'. The historicism and pseudo-objectivism of this approach leaves little room for theory of any kind. Indeed, it is commonly believed that the pursuit of theory must inevitably be at the expense of 'facts'. Merely to introduce women into the dominant notion of film history, as yet another series of 'facts' to be assimilated into the existing notions of chronology, would quite clearly be sterile and regressive. 'History' is not some abstract 'thing' which bestows significance on past events in retrospect. Only an attempt to situate Arzner's work in a theoretical way would allow us to comprehend her real contribution to film history. Women and film can only become

67

> meaningful in terms of a theory, in the attempt to create a structure in
> which films such as Arzner's can be examined in retrospect.[1]

The pseudo-objectivism Johnston refers to is especially apparent in the notions of the individual and agency which ground the "discoveries" of this woman's history. To retrieve and reestablish women as agents of history is to construct one's discourse upon a denial of the more problematic and complex aspects of subjectivity and sexuality.

On the other hand, the reaction against this crude historicism has often resulted in the virtual exclusion of the term "history" in its relations to the sexed subject which has become the focus of film theory's formulations. This is especially true of theories of spectatorship, of the consumption of the film object, its terms of address. What has been elided in the conceptualization of the spectator is not only historical but sexual specificity. The spectator purportedly anticipated and positioned by the text, defined by the psychical mechanisms of scopophilia or voyeurism, fetishism and a primary mirror identification, is inevitably male. In this context, Hollywood narratives are analyzed as compensatory structures designed to defend the male psyche against the threat offered by the image of the woman. Although this analysis has certainly been productive in understanding classical film narrative, it merely repeats the historical tendency of psychoanalysis to focus on the male psyche at the expense of that of the female. Furthermore, in a society which relies so heavily on a continual and pervasive inscription of sexual difference, it would seem problematic to assume that this sexual differentiation would not apply to spectatorship, to modes of looking and hearing, as well. The male spectator posited by film theory is a discursive construction; there is a female spectator who exists as a construction of the textual system and its discursive emplacement as well.[2] This is perhaps most apparent when one takes into account Hollywood's analysis of its own market, its own grouping of films along the lines of a sexual address. Thus, the nomenclature by means of which certain films of the 40s are situated as "woman's pictures"—a label which stipulates that the films are in some sense the "possession" of women and that their terms of address are dictated by the anticipated presence of the female spectator.[3]

The "woman's film" is not a "pure" genre—a fact which may partially determine the male critic's derogatory dismissal of such films. It is crossed and informed by a number of other genres or types—melodrama, film noir, the gothic or horror film—and finds its point of unification ultimately in the fact of its address. Because the woman's film of the 1940s was directed toward a female audience, a psychoanalytically informed analysis of the terms of its address is crucial in ascertaining the place the woman is assigned as spectator within patriarchies. The question then becomes: As a discourse addressed specifically to women, what kind of viewing process does the "woman's film" attempt to activate? A crucial unresolved issue here is the very possibility of constructing a "female spectator," given the cinema's dependence upon voyeurism and fetishism.

Given the apparent "masculinization" of the very process of looking in the cinema, these films often manifest a certain convolution and instability in their attempted construction of female fantasy. The narratives assume a compatibility between the idea of female fantasy and that of persecution—a persecution effected by husband, family, or lover. There is an almost obsessive association of the female protagonist with a deviation from some norm of mental stability or health, resulting in the recurrent investigation of psychical mechanisms frequently linked with the "feminine condition"— masochism, hysteria, neurosis, paranoia. It is as though the insistent attempt at an inscription of female subjectivity and desire, within a phallocentrically organized discourse such as the classical Hollywood text, produced gaps and incoherences which the films can barely contain. Because female identity in the cinema is constructed in relation to object-hood rather than subject-hood, an investigation of the contradictions resulting from an attempt to engage female subjectivity in a textual process such as the "woman's film" can be particularly productive. From this perspective, this essay has a quite limited aim—to trace certain obsessions which inhabit the texts across three different but related registers: the deployment of space and the activation of the uncanny; de-specularization and the medical discourse; and the economics of female subjectivity. All three registers are characterized by a certain violence which is coincident with the attribution of the gaze to the female.

The deployment of space in the "woman's film" is motivated rather directly by a fairly strict mapping of gender-differentiated societal spaces onto the films—the woman's place is in the home. Although this is quite clearly the case in the family melodrama (where the space of the house frequently dictates the weight of the *mise-en-scène*), I would like to shift attention to another subgroup of the genre in which the house is foregrounded in relation to mechanisms of suspense which organize the gaze. This cycle of films might be labelled the "paranoid woman's films," the paranoia evinced in the formulaic repetition of a scenario in which the wife invariably fears that her husband is planning to kill her—the institution of marriage is haunted by murder. Frequently, the violence is rationalized as the effect of an overly hasty marriage; the husband is unknown or only incompletely known by the woman. A scene in *Secret Beyond the Door* (1948) exemplifies this tendency: a long flashback which details the meeting of Joan Bennett and the man she is to marry culminates with the image of her future husband, emerging from the deep shadows of the church on their wedding day, accompanied by her surprised voice-over, "I'm marrying a stranger." The conjunction of sexuality and murder, the conflation of the two verbs, "to marry" and "to kill," is even more explicit in *Suspicion* (1941), in a scene on a windy hill in which Joan Fontaine's resistance to Cary Grant's attempts to kiss her is met with his question, "What did you think I was going to do—kill you?" As Thomas Elsaesser points out in reference to *Rebecca* (1940):

> Hitchcock infused his film, and several others, with an oblique intimation of female frigidity producing strange fantasies of persecution, rape, and death—masochistic reveries and nightmares, which cast the husband into the role of the sadistic murderer. This projection of sexual anxiety and its mechanisms of displacement and transfer is translated into a whole string of movies often involving hypnosis and playing on the ambiguity and suspense of whether the wife is merely imagining it or whether her husband really does have murderous designs on her...[4]

This "whole string of movies" includes, among others, *Suspicion, Rebecca, Secret Beyond the Door, Gaslight* (1944), *Undercurrent* (1946), *Dragonwyck* (1946), and *The Two Mrs. Carrolls* (1947).

In this cycle, dramas of seeing become invested with horror within the context of the home. The paradigmatic woman's space—the home—is yoked to dread, and a crisis of vision. For violence is precisely what is hidden from sight. While the mainstream Hollywood cinema organizes vision in relation to both spectacle and truth, and hence pleasure and fascination, the "woman's film" evinces a certain impoverishment of this mechanism. Laura Mulvey's very important analysis of "visual pleasure" focuses on films with a male protagonist.[5] Because the "woman's film" obsessively centers and re-centers a female protagonist, placing her in a position of agency, it offers some resistance to an analysis which stresses the "to-be-looked-at-ness" of the woman, her objectification as spectacle according to the masculine structure of the gaze. Thus, within the "woman's film," the process of specularization undergoes a number of vicissitudes which can be mapped. The textual assumption of a specifically female spectator also entails the assumption that she does not adopt a masculine position with respect to the cinematic image of the female body. In other words, because the female gaze is not associated with the psychical mechanisms of voyeurism and fetishism, it is no longer necessary to invest the look with desire in quite the same way. A certain de-specularization takes place in these films, a deflection of scopophiliac energy in other directions, away from the female body. The very process of seeing is now invested with fear, anxiety, horror, precisely because it is object-less, free-floating. As Jacqueline Rose has demonstrated, to the extent that the cinema does involve an imaginary structuration of vision, it also activates the aggressive component of imaginary processes.[6] In these films, the aggressivity which is contained in the cinematic structuration of the look is released or, more accurately, transformed into a narrativized paranoia. This subclass of the "woman's film" clearly activates the latent paranoia of the film system described by Rose. Its narrative structure produces an insistence upon situating the woman as agent of the gaze, as investigator in charge of the epistemological trajectory of the text, as the one for whom the "secret beyond the door" is really at stake.

Hence, one could formulate a veritable topography of spaces within the home along the axis of this perverted specularization. The home is not a homogeneous space—it asserts divisions, gaps and fields within its very structure. There are places which elude the eye; paranoia demands a split between the known and the unknown, the seen and the unseen. Thus, many of these films are marked by the existence of a room to which the woman is barred access. In *Gaslight* it is the attic where the husband searches for the dead aunt's jewels, in *Dragonwyck* it is the upstairs tower room where the husband exercises his drug addiction, in *Rebecca* it is both the boathouse-cottage detached from the house and Rebecca's bedroom, ultimately approached by the female protagonist with a characteristically Hitchcockian insistence on the moving point-of-view shot toward the closed door. *Secret Beyond the Door* bases itself upon the hyperbolization of this mechanism, a proliferation of rooms which the husband collects. In accordance with his architectural determinism (which, in a perverse reversal of German Expressionism, stipulates that a room does not reflect but determines what happens within it), the husband constructs exact replicas of rooms in which famous murders have taken place, concealing the final room—the wife's bedroom—from the eyes of both the public and his wife. The suspense generated by such strategies is no different in its dictation of subject positions from the more generalized cinematic suspense grounded by what Pascal Bonitzer refers to as the "rule of the look and nothing else":

> In this system, each shot engages the spectators as subjects (as potential victims) of another shot, and the 'image of the worst' governs the progression; each shot, in its difference of intensity, portends and defers 'the screen of the worst' for the spectators, subjects of the fiction: this is the principle of suspense. . . . Suspense is not just a genre. . . . It is, from the point of view I have just expounded, essential to cinema. . . . But only insofar as this system is one for ordering the depth of field, which constitutes the take not only as a passive recording of the scene, but as a productive force in its own right expressing, producing the *fading* of a point of view (and of a point of view that is. . . rather paranoiac).[7]

The cinematic generality of this system of suspense is specified by the "woman's film" in only two ways: through the localization of suspense in the familiarized female space of the home in relation to a close relative, almost always the husband; and in the violent attribution of the investigating gaze to the female protagonist (who is also its victim). This second specification effects a major disturbance in the cinematic relay of the look, resulting in so much narrative stress that the potential danger of a female look is often reduced or entirely avoided by means of the delegation of the detecting gaze to another male figure who is on the side of the law. (*Gaslight* is a particularly good example of this.) Nevertheless, in many of the films, and in the best tradition of the horror film, affect is condensed onto the fact of a woman investigating, penetrating space alone. And it is the staircase, a signifier which possesses a certain semantic privilege in relation to the woman as object of the gaze, which articulates the connection between the familiar and the unfamiliar, or neurosis and psychosis. An icon of crucial and repetitive insistence in the classical representations of the cinema, the staircase is traditionally the locus of specularization of the woman. It is *on the stairway* that she is displayed as spectacle for the male gaze (and often the icon is repeated, as though it were nonproblematic, within these same films—think of Joan Fontaine descending the stairs in *Rebecca* in the costume she mistakenly believes will please Laurence Olivier, or the woman in *Dragonwyck*, dressed in her best clothes, who poses on the staircase when her future husband comes to call). But the staircase in the paranoid woman's films also (and sometimes simultaneously) becomes the passageway to the "image of the worst" or "screen of the worst," in Bonitzer's terms. In *Dragonwyck*, film noir lighting intensifies the sense of foreboding attached to Gene Tierney's slow climb up the stairs in the attempt to ascertain what her suspicious husband does in the tower room prohibited to her. What Barbara Stanwyck finally discovers in the room at the top of the stairs in *The Two Mrs. Carrolls* is her own distorted and grotesque portrait, painted by her husband and evidence of his psychotic plan to kill her. The woman's exercise of an active investigating gaze can only be simultaneous with her own victimization. The place of her specularization is transformed into the locus of a process of seeing designed to unveil an aggression against itself.

The last site in this topography of spaces within the home with a pronounced semantic valence in relation to processes of specularization is the window. Within the "woman's films" as a whole, images of women looking through windows or waiting at windows abound. The window has special import in terms of the social and symbolic positioning of the woman—the window is the interface between inside and outside, the feminine space of the family and reproduction and the masculine space of production. It facilitates a communication by means of the look between the two sexually differentiated spaces. That interface becomes a potential point of violence, intrusion and aggression in the paranoid woman's films. In *The Two Mrs. Carrolls* the traces of the poisoned milk which Barbara Stanwyck throws out the window are discovered on the sill by her psychotic artist-husband Humphrey Bogart, who later penetrates her locked bedroom in a vampire-like entrance through the window. In *Rebecca*, Mrs. Danvers attempts to seduce Joan Fontaine into committing suicide at the window. In these films the house becomes the analogue of the human body, its parts fetishized by textual operations, its erotogeneous zones metamorphosized by a morbid anxiety attached to sexuality. It is the male character who fetishizes the house as a whole, attempting to unify and homogenize it through an insistent process of naming—Manderley, Dragonwyck, #9 Thornton Street.

Within the cinema, it is hardly surprising that the uncanny should be activated by means of dramas of seeing, of concealing and revealing. Freud himself in his article on "The Uncanny," repetitively and obsessively returns to the relations of vision to the uncanny effect—the "evil eye," the sight of himself in a mirror misrecognized, the fear of losing one's eyes embodied in "The Sandman." Even his etymological investigation of the word *"unheimlich"* (uncanny) revolves around the possibilities of seeing and hiding. Freud's rather long tracing of the linguistic deviations of the word serve finally to demonstrate that *heimlich* (belonging or pertaining to the home, familiar) is eventually equated with its opposite *unheimlich* (strange, unfamiliar, uncanny)—"Thus *heimlich* is a word the meaning of which develops towards an ambivalence, until it finally coincides with its opposite, *unheimlich*."[8] This sliding of signification is possible only because the word for "home" is semantically overdetermined and can be situated in relation to the gaze. For the home or house connotes not only the familiar but also what is secret, concealed, hidden from sight. The paradigmatic process by means of which what is familiar becomes strange is situated as the male's relation to the female body:

> It often happens that male patients declare that they feel there is something uncanny about the female genital organs. This *unheimlich* place, however, is the entrance to the former *heim* (home) of all human beings, to the place where everyone dwelt once upon a time and in the beginning...the prefix *"un"* is the token of repression.[9]

The female genitals are uncanny because they represent, for the male, the possibility of castration. In Samuel Weber's interpretation of Freud, the uncanny constitutes a defense against the negative perception of feminine castration, a vision which connotes nothing less than a "*crisis* of perception and of phenomenality."

> The uncanny is a defense which is ambivalent and which expresses itself in the compulsive curiosity...the craving to penetrate the flimsy appearances to the essence beneath....This desire to penetrate, discover and ultimately to conserve the integrity of perception: perceiver and perceived, the wholeness of the body, the power of vision—all this implies a *denial* of that almost-nothing which can hardly be seen, a denial that in turn involves a certain structure of narration, in which this denial repeats and articulates itself.[10]

Thus for both Freud and Weber, the uncanny is the return of the repressed, and what is repressed is a certain vision of the female body as the signifier of castration, and hence disunity. Suspense in the cinema—for Bonitzer the "rule of the look and nothing else"—therefore involves a kind of fetishization of vision itself, a reassertion of the integrity of perception along the lines of sexual difference.

But what does *this* have to do with the female spectator, for whom castration cannot pose a threat since she has nothing to lose? The different relation of the woman to the look must necessarily pose problems for a class of films which depends so heavily upon the mechanisms of suspense and the very possibility of attributing the gaze and subjectivity to the woman. In fact, the difficulty is not confined to the paranoid woman's films but pervades the genre, evinced in the continual inability to sustain a coherent representation of female subjectivity in the context of phallocentric discursive mechanisms. This is particularly explicit in the instability of certain privileged signifiers of enunciation—the voice-over and the point-of-view shot. The voice-over, introduced in the beginning of a film as the possession of the female protagonist who purportedly controls the narration of her own past, is rarely sustained (*Rebecca, Secret Beyond the Door*). Voice-overs are more frequently mobilized as moments of aggression or attack exercised against the female protagonist (*Gaslight, Undercurrent, Rebecca*). In *Suspicion*, the ending belies an inability to localize subjectivity in the point-of-view shot and the consequent collapse of the opposition between subjectivity and objectivity. In *Possessed* (1947), a scene in which Joan Crawford kills her stepdaughter is situated only retrospectively and traumatically as a subjectivized scenario—the image, in effect, lies.

Such an instability in the representation of female subjectivity, however, does not remain unrecognized by the texts, and is, instead, recuperated as the sign of illness or psychosis.[11] This is the operation of the second register—despecularization and the medical discourse. In the "woman's film," the erotic gaze becomes the medical gaze. The female body is located not so much as spectacle but as an element in the discourse of medicine, a manuscript to be read for the symptoms which betray her story, her identity.[12] Hence the need, in these films, for the figure of the doctor as reader or interpreter, as the site of a knowledge which dominates and controls female subjectivity—examples include *Now Voyager* (1942), *A Woman's Face* (1941), *Dark Victory* (1939), *Possessed* (1947), *Caught* (1949), *The Dark Mirror* (1946), *Shock* (1946), *Johnny Belinda* (1948), and *The Snake Pit* (1948).

In *Possessed*, Joan Crawford's illness is indicated immediately by her fixed stare and the fact that she can only repeat compulsively one word—the name of the man with whom she is in love. This situation causes certain difficulties of narration since she is the only one in the hospital room who knows and can therefore tell her own story. The dilemma receives a rather remarkable narrative solution which is, in a sense, exemplary for the "woman's film." The mute Joan Crawford is given an injection by the doctor which induces cinematic narrative. The thrill of her story, the pleasure of the cinema, is encapsulated in the doctor's words, "Every time I see the reaction to this treatment I get the same thrill I did the first time." The woman's narrative, as a repetition of that first time, is nevertheless held in check by recurrent withdrawals from her flashback account to the present tense of the doctor's diagnosis. For instance, the first part of her story illustrates, according to one of the doctors, "the beginning of a persecution complex," indicated by the fact that there is "no attempt to see the man's point of view." Within the encompassing masculine medical discourse, the woman's language is granted a limited validity—it is, precisely, *a* point of view, and often a distorted and unbalanced one.

In terms of both spatial configurations and language the female figure is trapped within the medical discourse of these narratives. In films like Ophuls' *Caught*, these framing procedures in the medical construction of the woman are quite apparent. Toward the end of the film there is a scene in which Barbara Bel Geddes' empty desk is used as a pivot as the camera pans back and forth between two doctors (James Mason and Frank Ferguson) discussing her fate. Obsessively moving across Bel Geddes' desk from doctor to doctor, the camera constructs a perfect symmetry by framing both of the men in their office doorways, ultimately returning to the woman's empty desk and closing the sequence with a kind of formal tautology. The sequence is a performance of one of the over-determined meanings of the film's title—Barbara Bel Geddes is "caught" spatially, between an obstetrician and a pediatrician. Furthermore, the obstetrician's final diagnosis of Bel Geddes consists of a rejection of the object which at the beginning of the film epitomized the woman's desire—a mink coat ("If my diagnosis is correct, she won't want that anyway."). Because the mink coat is associated with femininity as spectacle and image (its first inscription in the film is within the pages of a fashion magazine), the doctor's diagnosis has the effect of a certain de-specularization of the female body.[13] That body is, instead, symptomatic, and demands a reading.

It is therefore important, within this group of films, to *know* the woman as thoroughly as possible. Unlike the film noir, the "woman's film" does not situate its female protagonist as mysterious, unknowable, enigmatic. The site of potential knowledge about the woman is transferred from the Law to Medicine. This displacement is narrativized in *The Dark Mirror*, where the agent of the Law, the police detective, must appeal to a psychiatrist for a solution to the crime committed by one of two identical twins. Because the two women *look* exactly alike, a psychiatrist is needed to *see through* the surface exterior to the interior truths of the two sisters—in other words, to perform a symptomatic reading. And when the doctor falls in love with one of the twins, the discourse of desire merges imperceptibly with the discourse of psychiatry: "The more I know about you, the more I want to know, I want to know everything about you." Although the medical discourse is central to films like *Possessed*, *The Snake Pit*, and *Johnny Belinda*, it also informs and inflects the subgroup of "paranoid woman's films" discussed earlier. In both *The Spiral Staircase* and *Dragonwyck* the heroic male figure, a site of wisdom and safety, is a doctor. Many of the films depend rather heavily upon the tableau of the sick woman in bed, effecting the transformation of a site of sexuality into a site of illness and pain. In *Rebecca*, it is the doctor's discourse which provides closure for the story of the absent Rebecca, an answer to the hermeneutic question concerning her disappearance. Of particular interest in this respect is *Shock*, which merges conventions of the medical discourse with those of the paranoid films. Like Jimmy Stewart in *Rear Window*, the female protagonist in *Shock* looks out the window when she shouldn't, and sees what she shouldn't have seen—a husband murdering his wife. But unlike *Rear Window*, the woman goes into shock as a result of this sight, of this image which suggests itself as a microcosm of the cinema-spectator relation. The murderer turns out to be a psychiatrist who is called in to treat the catatonic woman suffering from what she has seen. All of his efforts are directed toward making her forget the image and maintaining her in a state in which she is unable to articulate her story.

The attribution of muteness to the woman is by no means rare in these films. In *Shock*, *Possessed*, and *The Spiral Staircase* the female character loses the power of speech as the result of a psychical trauma, while in *Johnny Belinda* she is mute from birth. But in all cases language is the gift of the male character, a somewhat violent "gift" in the case of *Shock* and *Possessed*, where the woman is induced to talk through an injection, and more benign, paternalistic in *Johnny Belinda*, where the doctor provides Belinda with sign language. This muteness is in some ways paradigmatic for the genre. For it is ultimately the symptoms of the female body which "speak" while the woman as subject of discourse is inevitably absent. In his case history of Dora (another "woman's narrative"), Freud posits a privileged relation between hysteria (often theorized as a specifically feminine illness, associated with the womb) and the somatic. "Somatic compliance" is the concept Freud elaborated to designate the process whereby the body complies with the psychical demands of the illness by providing a space and a material for the inscription for its signs. The female body thus acts in this context as a vehicle for hysterical speech. The marked ease of the metonymic slippage in these films between the woman, illness, the bed, muteness, blindness, and a medical discourse indicates yet another contradiction in the construction of a discourse which purportedly represents a female subjectivity.[14] If the woman must be given a genre and hence a voice, the addition of a medical discourse makes it possible once again to confine female discourse to the body, to disperse her access to language across a body which now no longer finds its major function in spectacle. Yet, de-specularized in its illness, that body is nevertheless interpretable, knowable, subject to a control which is no longer entirely subsumed by the erotic gaze. What that body no longer supports, without the doctor's active reading, is an identity.

The medical gaze, de-eroticized, constitutes the woman in these films not only as the object of the trained gaze, but as the object of speech and of knowledge as well, much in the manner of Foucault's speaking eye.

> Over all these endeavors on the part of clinical thought to define its methods and scientific norms hovers the great myth of a pure Gaze that would be pure Language: a speaking eye. It would scan the entire hospital field taking in and gathering together each of the singular events that occurred within it; and as it saw, as it saw ever more and more clearly, it would be turned into speech that states and teaches. . . . A hearing gaze and a speaking gaze: clinical experience represents a moment of balance between speech and spectacle.[15]

As the field of the masculine medical gaze is expanded, the woman's vision is reduced. Although in the beginning of *Possessed*, point-of-view shots are attributed to Crawford as she is wheeled into the hospital, she is *represented* as having an empty gaze, seeing nothing, blinded by the huge lamps aimed at her by the doctors. The ending of *Dark Victory* is crucial in this respect. The first sign of Bette Davis' impending death from a brain tumor is blindness. But because her husband is planning to attend a conference to present his medical discoveries—a conference which meets only twice a year—she must pretend to be able to see so that he won't remain with her and retard medical science by six months. Davis' heroism, then, is delineated as her ability to mime sight, to represent herself as the subject of vision.

The third register of the texts—the economics of female subjectivity—must be defined in relation to this process of miming—miming a position which can only be described as masochistic, as the perpetual staging of suffering. Addressing itself to a female audience, the "woman's film" raises the crucial question: How can the notion of female fantasy be compatible with that of persecution, illness, and death? In what way do these texts engage their spectator? Freud's explanation of paranoia and masochism relates them both to the assumption by the subject—whether male or female—of a feminine position. In Dr. Schreber's paranoid delusions, his body is transformed, painfully, into the body of a woman. The masochism which Freud assigns to the classical sexual pervert (usually male) is labelled "feminine" precisely because the fantasies associated with this type of masochism situate the subject in positions "characteristic of womanhood, i.e., they mean that he is being castrated, is playing the passive part in coitus, or is giving birth."[16] The economic problem of masochism, for Freud, lies in the apparent paradox of pleasure-in-pain. But this paradox is not unique to "feminine" masochism in Freud's typology, for there is a sense in which masochism is primary for the subject, ultimately, for Freud, a manifestation of the fundamental and inexorable death drive.

Nevertheless, when confronted with concrete clinical cases where masochism is embodied in a particularly insistent fantasy—"A Child is Being Beaten"—Freud is forced to make crucial distinctions along the lines of sexual difference. For it does, indeed, matter whether the subject of the fantasy is male or female. And it is not accidental that a certain ease of interpretation characterizes the psychoanalysis of the female masochistic fantasy which takes the form of a three part transformation of a basic sentence: (1) My father is beating the child whom I hate; (2) I am being beaten (loved) by my father; (3) A child is being beaten. In the construction of the male fantasy, Freud can isolate only two sentences: (1) I am being beaten (loved) by my father; (2) I am being beaten by my mother. Although both the female and the male instanciations stem from the same origin—an incestuous attachment to the father—their psychical meaning-effects are necessarily quite different. The woman's masochism can be located unproblematically within the terms of the "normal" female oedipal configuration, while the attribution of masochism to the man depends upon the possibility of an inverted oedipal attitude in which the father is taken as the object of desire. The man can, however, avoid the homosexual implications by remodeling his fantasy so that the mother takes the place of the father as the agent of the beating.

For my purposes here, there are two aspects of this sexual differentiation of the masochistic fantasy which assume paramount importance: the relationship established between fantasy and sexuality, and the presence or absence of spectatorship as a possible role in the scenario. On the first point, Freud is quite explicit. The erotic implications of the fantasy are acknowledged no matter what the vicissitudes of its transformation in the case of the male—sexuality remains on the surface. Furthermore, he retains his own role and his own gratification in the context of the scenario. The "I" of identity remains. On the other hand, the feminine masochistic fantasy, in the course of its vicissitudes, is desexualized: by means of the fantasy, "the girl escapes from the demands of the erotic side of her life altogether."[17] The fantasy, whose primary function in Freud's description is the facilitation of masturbation, becomes an end in itself. The women are prone to construct an "artistic super-structure of daydreams," fantasies which in some instances approach the level of a "great work of art" and eliminate entirely the need for masturbation. It is the fantasmatic gone awry, dissociated completely from the body as site of the erotic. But most crucially, the third sentence—"A child is being beaten"—which is significantly absent in male masochism, necessitates the woman's assumption of the position of spectator, outside of the event. The

"I" of the fantasy is no longer operative within its diegesis and, instead, the child who is being beaten is transformed into an anonymous boy or even a group of boys who act as the representatives of the female in the scenario.[18] Confronted with Freud's insistent question, "Where are *you* in this fantasy?," the female patients can only reply, "I am probably looking on."[19] Or, in Freud's eloquent summation of the sexual differentiation of the masochistic fantasy:

> ...the girl escapes from the demands of the erotic side of her life altogether. She turns herself in fantasy into a man, without herself becoming active in a masculine way, and is no longer anything but a spectator of the event which takes the place of a sexual act.[20]

Thus, simultaneous with her assumption of the position of spectator, the woman loses not only her sexual identity in the context of the scenario but her very access to sexuality.

Masochistic fantasy *instead* of sexuality. The phrase would seem to exactly describe the processes in the "woman's film" whereby the look is de-eroticized. In the paranoid subgroup, the space which the woman is culturally assigned, the home, through its fragmentation into places that are seen and unseen, becomes the site of terror and victimization—the look turned violently against itself. In the films which mobilize a medical discourse, where blindness and muteness are habitually attributed to the woman, she can only passively give witness as the signs of her own body are transformed by the purportedly desexualized medical gaze, the "speaking eye," into elements of discourse. The dominance of the bed in the *mise-en-scène* of these films is the explicit mark of the displacement/replacement of sexuality by illness.

There is a sense, then, in which these films attempt to reverse the relation between the female body and sexuality which is established and reestablished by the classical cinema's localization of the woman as spectacle. As spectacle, the female body *is* sexuality, the erotic and the specular are welded. By de-eroticizing the gaze, these films in effect disembody their spectator—the cinema, a mirror of control to the man, reflects nothing for the woman, or rather, it denies the imaginary identification which, uniting body and identity, supports discursive mastery. Confronted with the classical Hollywood text with a male address, the female spectator has basically two modes of entry: a narcissistic identification with the female figure as spectacle, and a "transvestite" identification with the active male hero in his mastery.[21] This female spectator is thus imaged by its text as having a mixed sexual body—she is, ultimately, a hermaphrodite. It is precisely this oscillation which demonstrates the instability of the woman's position as spectator. Because the "woman's film" purportedly directs itself to a female audience, because it pretends to offer the female spectator an identity other than that of the active male hero, it deflects energy away from the second "transvestite" option described above and towards the more "properly" female identification. But since the "woman's film" reduces the specularizable nature of the female body, this first option of a narcissistic identification is problematized as well. In a patriarchal society, to desexualize the female body is ultimately to deny its very existence. The "woman's film" thus functions in a rather complex way to deny the woman the space of a reading.

All of this is certainly not to say that the "woman's film" is in any way radical or revolutionary. It functions quite precisely to immobilize—its obsession with the repetition of scenarios of masochism is a symptom of the ideological crisis provoked by the need to shift the sexual terms of address of a cinema which, as Laura Mulvey has shown, is so heavily dependent upon masculine structures of seeing. The very lack of epistemological validity ascribed to these films—manifested in the derogatory label, the "weepies"— is an active recuperation of the contradictions which necessarily arise in attributing the epistemological gaze to the woman. For a body-less woman cannot see. The impossibility of the contract which these films attempt to actualize is most succinctly articulated in a line from *Rebecca*—"Most girls would give their eyes for a chance to see Monte."

NOTES

1. Claire Johnston, "Dorothy Arzner, Critical Strategies," in *The Work of Dorothy Arzner*, ed. Claire Johnston (London: British Film Institute, 1975), p. 2.

2. The phrase "discursive construction" is used here to indicate the operation whereby filmic texts anticipate a position for the spectator and outline the terms of their own understanding. This process pertains to both conscious and unconscious levels of understanding. Individual, empirical spectators may fail to assume such a position in relation to the text, but in this event a certain textual meaning-effect is lost. That meaning-effect may not be entirely dependent upon the filmic text's own mechanisms but may also be influenced by other discourses surrounding the film.

3. This article is a condensation of various motifs which will be elaborated more systematically in a book in progress—*The "Woman's Film": Possession and Address*. It is therefore very much a working paper. The book focuses on "women's films" of the 1940s. The notion of a "woman's picture," or a genre of films addressed specifically to women, is clearly not limited to the 1940s. However, the ideological upheaval signalled by a redefinition of sexual roles and the reorganization of the family makes the 1940s a particularly intense and interesting period for feminist analysis.

4. Thomas Elsaesser, "Tales of Sound and Fury," *Monogram*, no. 4 (1972), p. 11.

5. Laura Mulvey, "Visual Pleasure and Narrative Cinema," *Screen*, vol. 16, no. 3 (Autumn 1975), pp. 6-18.

6. Jaqueline Rose, "Paranoia and the Film System," *Screen*, vol. 17, no. 4 (Winter 1976/77), pp. 85-104.

7. Pascal Bonitzer, "Here: The Notion of the Shot and the Subject of the Cinema," *Film Reader*, no. 4 (1979), p. 113.

8. Sigmund Freud, "The Uncanny," in *On Creativity and the Unconscious*, ed. Benjamin Nelson (New York: Harper and Row, 1958), p. 131.

9. Ibid., pp. 152-153.

10. Samuel Weber, "The Sideshow, or: Remarks on a Canny Moment," *MLN*, vol. 88, no. 6 (December 1973), p. 1133.

11. The obsessive association of women with madness is clearly not limited to the film medium and is a phenomenon which can already claim a tradition of feminist study. See, for instance, Phyllis Chesler, *Women and Madness* (New York: Avon Books, 1972) and Shoshana Felman, "Women and Madness: The Critical Phallacy," *Diacritics*, vol. 5, no. 4 (Winter 1975), pp. 2-10.

12. As Lea Jacobs has pointed out to me, this statement should be qualified. In films like *Now, Voyager* and *A Woman's Face*, the woman's "cure" consists in a beautification of body/face. The doctor's work is the transformation of the woman into a specular object. (See Lea Jacobs, "*Now, Voyager*: Some Problems of Enunciation and Sexual Difference," *Camera Obscura*, no. 7 [Spring 1981], pp. 89-109.) Nevertheless, in both films the woman's status as specular object of desire is

synonymous with her "health"—her illness is characterized as the very lack of that status. The narratives thus trace a movement from the medical gaze to the erotic gaze in relation to the central female figure. In *Possessed*, on the other hand, Joan Crawford is still the victim of a psychosis at the end of the film and never quite regains her "looks."

13. For a more complete analysis of the medical discourse in *Caught* see my "*Caught* and *Rebecca*: The Inscription of Femininity as Absence," *Enclitic*, vol. 5, no. 2/vol. 6, no. 1 (Fall 1981/Spring 1982), pp. 75-89.

14. I make no distinction, in this section, between physical illness and mental illness because the films themselves elaborate strong connections between the two. They assume without question at the level of their manifest discourse a rather popularized Freudian notion of the psychosomatic.

15. Michel Foucault, *The Birth of the Clinic: An Archaeology of Medical Perception*, trans. A.M. Sheridan-Smith (New York: Vintage Books, 1975), pp. 114-115.

16. Sigmund Freud, "The Economic Problem in Masochism," in *General Psychological Theory*, ed. Philip Rieff (New York: Collier Books, 1963), p. 193.

17. Sigmund Freud, "A Child is Being Beaten," in *Sexuality and the Psychology of Love*, ed. Philip Rieff (New York: Collier Books, 1963), p. 128.

18. Freud's explanation for this sexual transformation is quite interesting and worth quoting in full: "When they [girls] turn away from their incestuous love for their father, with its genital significance, they easily abandon their feminine role. They spur their 'masculinity complex' (v. Ophuijsen) into activity, and from that time forward only want to be boys. For that reason, the whipping-boys who represent them are boys also. In both the cases of day-dreaming—one of which almost rose to the level of a work of art—the heroes were always young men; indeed women used not to come into these creations at all, and only made their first appearance after many years, and then in minor parts." (Ibid., pp. 119-120.) The positioning of the male as protagonist of the fantasy clearly makes a strict parallel between the "Child is Being Beaten" fantasy and the "woman's film" impossible. Nevertheless, the sexual transformation of female into male in the fantasy does parallel the de-eroticization of the female body in the masochistic women's films and the consequent loss of the "feminine" category of spectacle.

19. Ibid., p. 114.

20. Ibid., p. 128.

21. For a more thorough and detailed discussion of the female spectator's relation to the classical text see my "Film and the Masquerade: Theorising the Female Spectator," *Screen*, vol. 23, no. 3/4 (September/October 1982), pp. 74-88. For more on "transvestite" identification, see Laura Mulvey, "Afterthoughts on 'Visual Pleasure and Narrative Cinema' inspired by *Duel in the Sun*," *Framework* 15/16/17 (Summer 1981), pp. 12-15.

When the Woman Looks

Linda Williams

Whenever the movie screen holds a particularly effective image of terror, little boys and grown men make it a point of honor to look, while little girls and grown women cover their eyes or hide behind the shoulders of their dates. There are excellent reasons for this refusal of the woman to look, not the least of which is that she is often asked to bear witness to her own powerlessness in the face of rape, mutilation and murder. Another excellent reason for the refusal to look is the fact that women are given so little to identify with on the screen. Laura Mulvey's extremely influential article on visual pleasure in narrative cinema has best defined this problem in terms of a dominant male look at the woman that leaves no place for the woman's own pleasure in seeing: she exists only to be looked at.[1]

Like the female spectator, the female protagonist often fails to look, to return the gaze of the male who desires her. In the classical narrative cinema, to see is to desire. It comes as no surprise, then, that many of the "good girl" heroines of the silent screen were often figuratively, or even literally, blind.[2] Blindness in this context signifies a perfect absence of desire, allowing the look of the male protagonist to regard the woman at the requisite safe distance necessary to the voyeur's pleasure, with no danger that she will return that look and in so doing express desires of her own. The relay of looks within the film thus duplicates the voyeuristic pleasure of the cinematic apparatus itself—a pleasure that Christian Metz and Laura Mulvey have suggested to be one of the primary pleasures of film viewing: the impression of looking in on a private world unaware of the spectator's own existence.[3]

But even when the heroine is not literally blind, the failure and frustration of her vision can be the most important mark of her sexual purity. An illuminating example of this failed vision occurs in D.W. Griffith's 1911 two-reeler, *Enoch Arden*.[4] A remarkable illustration of the pleasures of voyeurism the cinema could offer audiences of that time, the film is entirely structured as a series of romantic or domestic scenes which are spied upon by two successive male voyeurs.

In a small fishing village Enoch Arden and Phillip Ray are rivals for Annie Lee's affections. After separate shots which introduce each of them, Enoch in the background spies upon what he presumes to be the happy love of Phillip and Annie Lee. Soon after the shot is repeated, but this time with Phillip as the outsider spying on Annie Lee and Enoch. A title provides Tennyson's lines, "Phillip looked, and in their eyes and faces read his doom."[5] The decision as to which of these rivals "gets" the girl is based on the abdication of an unseen onlooker who believes he "reads" the true desires of the couple. But since Enoch and Phillip have each read the same desire in the couple which excludes them, it becomes apparent that what matters is not so much the desire of the couple but the sad and jealous look of the outsider-voyeur who imagines—and thus constitutes—a happiness that must exclude him. Through this process Enoch wins Annie.

After some years of marriage, Enoch is forced to leave his happy home and family to go to sea. Annie Lee stands on the beach waving to Enoch's ship as it disappears in the distance, watching "to the last dip of the vanishing sail." The frustration of her look is emphasized by the spyglass she brings with her and through which she vainly peers for the next 20 years as she awaits Enoch's return.[6]

What Annie strains to see but cannot, Griffith's parallel editing permits us to see clearly: Enoch's shipwreck and long vigil on a desert island, scanning the horizon for the ship that will bring him home. Throughout their long separation Griffith is careful to maintain consistent screen direction in both Enoch and Annie Lee's looks "off." Annie always looks screen left, Enoch on his island looks screen right, thus preserving the spectator's hope that their gazes, and their paths, might one day meet. This is especially acute when Enoch is on the ship transporting him home. Throughout his long absence Annie has steadfastly resisted Phillip's renewed advances. Although she finally gives in to his offer of marriage "for the children's sake," she still refuses his embrace and remains loyal to Enoch by continuing to look out her window in the "correct" direction—away from Phillip and towards the absent Enoch.

But just as parallel editing informs us that Enoch is about to arrive home, an intertitle, for which we have had no visual preparation, informs us that "when her new baby came, then Phillip was her all and all." Given the visual evidence of Annie's rejection of Phillip's advances and her persistent watch out the window for Enoch, this baby comes as rather a surprise. It does not seem possible for it to have arisen out of any sexual desire for Phillip on Annie Lee's part. Griffith uses this baby, which will soon become the visual proof of Annie's happiness with Phillip *in Enoch's eyes*, as the proper maternal justification of Annie finally turning *her* eyes from the window and towards her new family now headed by Phillip. The baby thus functions as cause, rather than effect, of Annie's desire for Phillip. This remarkable reversal of the usual logic of cause and effect allows the narrative to deny Annie a look of desire in *both* directions—at both Enoch and Phillip. The film ends as it began, with the look of the male voyeur (this time a literal voyeur) as the long-lost Enoch creeps up to the window to spy on the happy family scene from which he is now excluded. Once again he "reads" their happiness and his own "doom."

Let us take *Enoch Arden* as one paradigm for the frustration of the woman's "look" in the silent melodrama. It is a frustration necessary for the male regime of voyeuristic desire already clearly articulated by 1911. Given this paradigm we can go on to examine the exceptions to it: those moments (still in the silent film) when the woman in the text not only tries to look, but actually sees.

The bold, smouldering dark eyes of the silent screen vamp offer an obvious example of a powerful female look.[7] But the dubious moral status of such heroines, and the fact that they must be punished in the end, undermine the legitimacy and authentic subjectivity of this look, frequently turning it into a mere parody of the male look.[8] More instructive are those moments when the "good girl" heroines are granted the power of the look, whether in the woman's film, as discussed by Mary Ann Doane in this volume,[9] or in the horror film as discussed below. In both cases, as Doane suggests, "the woman's exercise of an active investigating gaze can only be simultaneous with her own victimization."[10] The woman's gaze is punished, in other words, by narrative processes that transform curiosity and desire into masochistic fantasy.

The horror film offers a particularly interesting example of this punishment in the woman's terrified look at the horrible body of the monster. In what follows I will examine the various ways the woman is punished for looking in both the classic horror film and in the more recent "psychopathic" forms of the genre. I hope to reveal not only the process of punishment but a surprising (and at times subversive) affinity between monster and woman, the sense in which her look at the monster recognizes their similar status within patriarchal structures of seeing.

In F.W. Murnau's *Nosferatu* (1922), for example, Nina's ambiguous vigil by the sea is finally rewarded, not by the sight of her returning husband who arrives by land in a carriage, but by the vampire's ship towards which a wide-eyed Nina in a trance-like state reaches out her arms.[11] Later, from the windows of facing houses, Nina and the vampire stare at one another until she finally opens the window. When the vampire's shadow approaches, she again stares at him in wide-eyed terror until he attacks.

There are several initial distinctions to be made between what I have characterized above as the desiring look of the male-voyeur-subject and the woman's look of horror typified by Nina's trance-like fascination. First, Nina's look at the vampire fails to maintain the distance between observer and observed so essential to the "pleasure" of the voyeur. For where the (male) voyeur's properly distanced look safely masters the potential threat of the (female) body it views, the woman's look of horror paralyzes her in such a way that distance is overcome; the monster or the freak's own spectacular appearance holds her originally active, curious look in a trance-like passivity that allows him to master her through *her* look. At the same time, this look momentarily shifts the iconic center of the spectacle away from the woman to the monster.

Rupert Julian's 1925 version of *The Phantom of the Opera*, starring Lon Chaney and Mary Philbin, offers another classic example of the woman's look in the horror film. Christine, an aspiring young opera singer, is seduced by the voice of the Phantom speaking to her through the walls of her dressing room at the Paris Opera. She follows "her master's voice" by stepping through the mirror of her dressing room. Her first glimpse of the masked Phantom occurs as she turns to respond to the touch of his hand on her shoulder. Thus her look occurs *after* the film audience has had its own chance to see him—they are framed in a two-shot that has him standing slightly behind her; only when she turns does she see his masked face.

Similarly, in the famous unmasking scene, Christine first thrills to the sound of the organ music the Phantom plays ("Don Juan Triumphant"), then sneaks up behind him and hesitates several times before finally pulling the string that will drop his mask. Since both he and Christine face the camera in a two-shot (with Christine situated behind him) we again see the Phantom's face, this time unmasked, before Christine does. The audience thus receives the first shock of the horror even while it can still see the curiosity and desire *to see* on Christine's face.[12]

Everything conspires here to condemn the desire and curiosity of the woman's look. Our prior knowledge of what she will see encourages us to judge her look as a violation of the Phantom's privacy. Her unmasking of his face reveals the very wounds, the very lack, that the Phantom had hoped her blind love would heal. It is as if she has become responsible for the horror that her look reveals, and is punished by not being allowed the safe distance that ensures the voyeur's pleasure of looking. "Feast your eyes, glut your soul, on my accursed ugliness!" cries the Phantom as he holds her face up close to his.

When the men in this film look at the Phantom, the audience first sees the man looking, then adopts his point of view to see what he sees. The audience's belated adoption of the woman's point of view undermines the usual audience identification and sympathy with the look of the cinematic character. But it may also permit a different form of identification and sympathy to take place, not between the audience and the character who looks, but between the two objects of the cinematic spectacle who encounter one another in this look—the woman and the monster.

In *The Phantom of the Opera* Christine walks through her mirror to encounter a monster whose face lacks the flesh to cover its features. Lon Chaney's incarnation of the Phantom's nose, for example, gives the effect of two large holes; the lips fail to cover a gaping mouth. Early in the film women dancers from the corps de ballet argue excitedly about his nose: "He had no nose!" "Yes he did, it was enormous!" The terms of the argument suggest that the monster's body is perceived as freakish in its possession of too much or too little. Either the monster is symbolically castrated, pathetically lacking what Christine's handsome lover Raoul possesses ("He had no nose!"), or he is overly endowed and potent ("Yes he did, it was enormous!"). Yet it is a truism of the horror genre that sexual interest resides most often in the monster and not the bland ostensible heroes like Raoul who often prove powerless at the crucial moment. (*The Phantom of the Opera* is no exception. Raoul passes out when most needed and Christine's rescue is accomplished by her accidental fall from the Phantom's racing carriage.)

Clearly the monster's power is one of sexual difference from the normal male. In this difference he is remarkably like the woman in the eyes of the traumatized male: a biological freak with impossible and threatening appetites that suggest a frightening potency precisely where the normal male would perceive a lack. In fact, the Phantom's last act of the film is to restage the drama of the lack he represents to others. Cornered by a crowd more bestial than he has ever been, a crowd that wants to tear him apart, the Phantom pulls back his hand as if threatening to detonate an explosive device. The crowd freezes, the Phantom laughs and opens his hand to reveal that it contains...nothing at all.

It is this absence, this nothing at all so dramatically brandished by the Phantom, that haunts a great many horror films and often seems the most effective element of their horror. It may very well be, then, that the power and potency of the monster body in many classic horror films—*Nosferatu, The Phantom of the Opera, Vampyr, Dracula, Freaks, Dr. Jekyll and Mr. Hyde, King Kong, Beauty and the Beast*—should not be interpreted as an eruption of the normally repressed animal sexuality of the civilized male (the monster as double for the male viewer and characters in the film), but as the feared power and potency of a different kind of sexuality (the monster as double for the women).

As we have seen, one result of this equation seems to be the difference between the look of horror of the man and of the woman. The male look expresses conventional fear at that which differs from itself. The female look—a look given preeminent position in the horror film—shares the male fear of the monster's freakishness, but also recognizes the sense in which this freakishness is similar to her own difference. For she too has been constituted as an exhibitionist-object by the desiring look of the male. There is not that much difference between an object of desire and an object of horror as far as the male look is concerned. (In one brand of horror film this difference may simply lie in the age of its female stars. The Bette Davises and the Joan Crawfords considered too old to continue as spectacle-objects nevertheless persevere as horror objects in films like *Whatever Happened to Baby Jane?* and *Hush Hush Sweet Charlotte*.) The strange sympathy and affinity that often develops between the monster and the girl may thus be less an expression of sexual desire (as in *King Kong, Beauty and the Beast*) and more a flash of sympathetic identification.

In Carson McCullers' *The Member of the Wedding*, Frankie fears that the carnival freaks look at her differently, secretly connecting their eyes with hers, saying with their look "We know you. We are you!"[13] Similarly, in *The Phantom of the Opera*, when Christine walks through a mirror that ceases to reflect her, it could very well be that she does so because she knows she will encounter a truer mirror in the freak of the Phantom on the other side. In other words, in the rare instance when the cinema permits the woman's look, she not only sees a monster, she sees a monster that offers a distorted reflection of her own image. The monster is thus a particularly insidious form of the many mirrors patriarchal structures of seeing hold up to the woman. But there are many kinds of mirrors; and in this case it may be useful to make a distinction between beauty and the beast in the horror film.

Laura Mulvey has shown that the male look at the woman in the cinema involves two forms of mastery over the threat of castration posed by her "lack" of a penis: a sadistic voyeurism which punishes or endangers the woman through the agency of an active and powerful male character; and fetishistic over-valuation, which masters the threat of castration by investing the woman's body with an excess of aesthetic perfection.[14]

Stephen Heath, summarizing the unspoken other side of Mulvey's formulation, suggests that the woman's look can only function to entrap her further within these patriarchal structures of seeing:

> If the woman looks, the spectacle provokes, castration is in the air, the Medusa's head is not far off; thus, she must not look, is absorbed herself on the side of the seen, seeing herself seeing herself, Lacan's femininity.[15]

In other words, her look even here becomes a form of not seeing anything more than the castration she so exclusively represents for the male.

If this were so, then what the woman "sees" would only be the mutilation of her own body displaced onto that of the monster. The destruction of the monster that concludes so many horror films could therefore be interpreted as yet another way of disavowing and mastering the castration her body represents. But here I think it may be helpful to introduce a distinction into Mulvey's, Heath's, and ultimately Freud's, notion of the supposed "mutilation" of the "castrated" woman that may clarify the precise meaning of the woman's encounter with a horror version of her own body.

A key moment in many horror films occurs when the monster displaces the woman as site of the spectacle. In *King Kong*, Kong is literally placed on stage to "perform" before awed and fearful audiences. In *The Phantom of the Opera*, the Phantom makes a dramatic, show-stopping entrance at the Masked Ball as the Masque of the Red Death, wearing a mask modeled on the absences of his own face beneath. Count Dracula, in both the Murnau and the Browning versions, makes similarly show-stopping performances. Tod Browning's *Freaks* begins and ends with the side-show display of the woman who has been transformed by the freaks into part bird, part woman. These spectacular moments displaying the freakish difference of the monster's body elicit reactions of fear and awe in audiences that can be compared to the Freudian hypothesis of the reaction of the male child in his first encounter with the "mutilated" body of his mother.

In her essay, "Pornography and the Dread of Women," Susan Lurie offers a significant challenge to the traditional Freudian notion that the sight of the mother's body suggests to the male child that she has herself undergone castration. According to Lurie, the real trauma for the young boy is not that the mother is castrated but that she *isn't*: she is obviously *not* mutilated the way he would be if his penis were taken from him. The notion of the woman as a castrated version of a man is, according to Lurie, a comforting, wishful fantasy intended to combat the child's imagined dread of what his mother's very real power could do to him. This protective fantasy is aimed at convincing himself that "women are what men would be if they had no penises— bereft of sexuality, helpless, incapable."[16]

I suggest that the monster in the horror film is feared by the "normal" males of such films in ways very similar to Lurie's notion of the male child's fear of this mother's power-in-difference. For, looked at from the woman's perspective, the monster is not so much lacking as he is powerful in a different way. The vampire film offers a clear example of the threat this different form of sexuality represents to the male. The vampiric act of sucking blood, sapping the life fluid of a victim so that the victim in turn becomes a vampire, is similar to the female role of milking the sperm of the male during intercourse.[17] What the vampire seems to represent then is a sexual power whose threat lies in its difference from a phallic "norm." The vampire's power to make its victim resemble itself is a very real mutilation of the once human victim (teeth marks, blood loss), but the vampire itself, like the mother in Lurie's formulation, is not perceived as mutilated, just different.

Thus what is feared in the monster (whether vampire or simply a creature whose difference gives him power over others) is similar to what Lurie says is feared in the mother: not her own mutilation, but the power to mutilate and transform the vulnerable male. The vampire's insatiable need for blood seems a particularly apt analogue for what must seem to the man to be an insatiable sexual appetite—yet another threat to his potency. So there is a sense in which the woman's look at the monster is more than simply a punishment for looking, or a narcissistic fascination with the distortion of her own image in the mirror that patriarchy holds up to her; it is also a recognition of their similar status as potent threats to a vulnerable male power. This would help explain the often vindictive destruction of the monster in the horror film and the fact that this destruction generates the frequent sympathy of the women characters, who seem to sense the extent to which the monster's death is an exorcism of the power of their own sexuality. It also helps to explain the conventional weakness of the male heroes of so many horror films (e.g., David Manners in *Dracula*, Colin Clive in *Frankenstein*) and the extreme excitement and surplus danger when the monster and the woman get together.

Thus I suggest that, in the classic horror film, the woman's look at the monster offers at least a potentially subversive recognition of the power and potency of a non-phallic sexuality. Precisely because this look is so threatening to male power, it is violently punished. In what follows I would like to look closely at a different kind of horror film that offers a particularly self-conscious and illuminating version of the significance of the woman's look in the horror genre. And then, lest we get carried away with enthusiasm, I shall look at two other, more typically exploitative, examples of the recent evolution of the genre.

Michael Powell's *Peeping Tom* (1960) is a self-conscious meditation on the relations between a sadistic voyeur-subject and the exhibitionist objects he murders. Along with *Psycho* (also 1960), it marked a significant break in the structure of the classic horror film, inaugurating a new form of psychological horror. In these two films, a physically normal but psychologically deranged monster becomes the central figure of the narrative. For better or for worse (we will see later just how bad it can be) the audience is now asked to identify with the monster's point of view, and even to sympathize with the childhood traumas that produced his deranged behavior. In *Peeping Tom*, the first images we see are through the lens of Mark's 16mm camera as he murders a prostitute with a knife concealed in a leg of his tripod. We learn in the opening credits that Mark is a killer whose only apparent sexual gratification comes while watching from the womblike safety of his dark projection room the murders he commits in his own movies.

Peeping Tom suggests that Mark's obsession evolved as a protection against his father's voyeuristic experimentation upon him as young child. We see home movies showing the young Mark terrified by lizards placed in his bed, probed with lights and coldly spied upon by his father's camera. It becomes clear that Mark's only defense was to master the very system that had turned him into an exhibitionist object of scientific spectacle. In one of the home movies we see Mark receive a camera from his father and turn it, weapon-like, back upon the world, mastering his own victimization by gaining the means to victimize others.

Where Mark's father represents the sadistic power of the voyeur-scientist to scrutinize his subjects safe from any involvement with them, Mark's own manipulation is on a different level: he is the voyeur as romantic artist. His home movies are a desperate attempt to capture on film the perfect expression of the terror of his victims—a terror that might match his own. A classic voyeur, any actual contact with his victims disrupts the distance so necessary to his sadistic pleasure. It is precisely this distance that Helen, an artist herself (she has a book of stories about a "magic camera" that she wants Mark to illustrate) disrupts. Helen intrudes upon the inner sanctum of his screening room, looks herself at the home movies of Mark as a child, demands an explanation ("I like to understand what I'm shown!") and eventually switches on the projector to view his latest murder. Her own autonomous looking, her ambitious sense of herself as a creator of images in her own right, and her instinctive distrust of Mark's dependence on his camera to avoid contact with the world, force him to see her not as another victim, but as a subject with her own power of vision. All of his other victims, a prostitute, a movie stand-in, and a pornographer's model, have willingly accepted their positions as exhibitionist spectacles for his camera.

Helen's power of vision becomes dramatically evident in her ability to refuse the mirror-snare that ultimately gives this film its greatest horror. For Mark not only films his victims as he stabs them, the artist in him wants to perfect this image of their terror. To do this, he holds up before them, while filming and stabbing, a concave mirror that reflects the hideous distortion of their faces. Thus what Mark films is his victim at the moment of death looking at her own distorted reflection and not, as in the conventional look of horror, back at the monster. Our own awareness of this mirror is withheld until near the end when Mark finally turns the apparatus on himself, running on the knife as he looks into the distorting mirror, uniting voyeur and exhibitionist in a one-man movie of which he is both director and star.

In the classic horror film, the woman encountered a monster whose deformed features suggested a distorted mirror-reflection of her own putative lack in the eyes of patriarchy, although this supposed lack could also be construed as a recognition of the threat both beauty and the beast presented to this patriarchy. In *Peeping Tom*, however, the woman's look is literally caught up in a mirror reflection that does not simply suggest an affinity with the monster in the eyes of patriarchy, but attempts to lure her into the false belief that she *is* the monster. Mark's self-reflective cinematic apparatus uses its mirror-effect to haunt the woman with her own image, to trap her in an attitude of exhibitionism and narcissism that has traditionally been offered as the "natural" complement to the voyeur's sadistic pleasure.

The point of the film, of course, is to show that the woman is *not* the monster. Mark's attempt to convince her that she is, is simply a way of alienating her from her own look, of forcing her into a perverse reenactment of his own traumatic experience of being looked at. In making his films (the *mise-en-scène* of which is murder) Mark assumes the role of his sadistic father, mastering his own terror by becoming the victimizer himself. Then in watching his films he can relive his original experience of terror at a safe distance, identify with his own victims and repossess his own look of terror from a safer aesthetic distance.

Throughout the film we are invited to equate the art and technology of movie making with the sadist-voyeur's misuse of the female body. Mark lures the women he kills into exhibitionistic performances—the prostitute's come-on, the stand-in's frenetic jazz dance, the pornographic model's pose—which he captures with his camera-mirror-weapon and then punishes. Yet this punishment is clearly only a substitute for the revenge on his dead father that he can never accomplish. Ultimately he will turn the weapon back on himself and exult in his own terror as he dies before the distorting mirror.

Mark's regression to his original position of victim occurs when Helen refuses to occupy that same position herself. Helen is not transfixed by the mirror Mark holds up to her; she sees it for the distortion it is and has the power to turn away, to reject the image of woman as terrified victim and monster preferred by the male artist.

Helen's refusal of the mirror marks an important moment in the history of the woman's look in the horror film: in a rare instance her look both sees and understands the structure of seeing that would entrap her; her look is not paralyzed by the recognition of the horror she represents, and she therefore refuses the oppressive lie of the narcissistic mirror that the cinematic apparatus holds up to her.

Peeping Tom thus lays bare the voyeuristic structure of cinema and that structure's dependence on the woman's acceptance of her role as narcissist. Both Mark and his victims are trapped in a perverse structure of seeing that is equated throughout the film with the art of making "true-to-life" movies. Yet it is also true that Helen's ability to refuse the mirror is simply a result of her status as a non-sexual "good girl." As played by Anna Massey, Helen is the stereotypical "girl next door." She mothers Mark, feeds him, tells him not to work so hard and gives him a chaste goodnight kiss which he later, and much more erotically, transfers to the lens of his camera.

Helen's refusal of narcissism also turns out to be a refusal of the only way patriarchal cinema has of representing woman's desire. If she has the power to recognize and refuse the mirror-trap, it is because she is portrayed as ignorant of sexual desire altogether. She is like the one virginal babysitter who survives the attacks of the monster in the more recent *Halloween* (John Carpenter, 1978), or like Lila, Marion Crane's "good girl" sister in *Psycho*, who survives Norman Bates's final attack, or even like Helen's blind mother in *Peeping Tom* who immediately "sees"—in the tradition of the blind seer—the turbulence in Mark's soul. In other words, in most horror films, the tradition of the power of the woman "pure of heart" is still going strong; the woman's power to resist the monster is directly proportional to her absence of sexual desire.[18] Clarity of vision, it would seem, can only exist in this absence.

If *Peeping Tom* can be privileged as a progressive horror film, not so much for sparing the life of its "good girl" heroine as for exposing the perverse structures of seeing that operate in the genre, then we might compare two much more popular horror films in the same mode: Alfred Hitchcock's *Psycho* (made in the same year as *Peeping Tom*) and Brian De Palma's *Psycho*-inspired *Dressed to Kill* (1980). Both films offer insidious and much more typical forms of the narcissistic trap that frustrates the woman's look of desire.

Psycho has been the model for the new form of the "psycho at large" horror films that began to emerge in the early 1960s and which now dominate the market. There is no more convincing proof of the influence of this model than De Palma's flagrant imitation of it in *Dressed to Kill*. In both *Psycho* and *Dressed to Kill*, the primary female stars are killed off early by knife-wielding murderers who appear, to both their victims and the audience, to be female. In both films the snooping of a second heroine, who is similarly endangered but not killed, corrects the original vision: the attacking she is a he. But also in both films, the psychoanalytic voice of reason revises this vision as well: although the body of the attacker might appear to be male, it is really the woman in this man who kills.

In other words, both films offer yet another form of the look of recognition between the woman and the monster. The monster who attacks both looks like and, in some sense, *is* a woman. But unlike *Peeping Tom*, which exposes the lie of the female victim's encounter with her own horror in the mirror image that Mark holds up to her, *Psycho* and *Dressed to Kill* perpetuate this lie, asking us to believe that the woman is both victim and monster.[19]

In *Psycho* we learn that the mother did it. As the psychiatrist explains at the end of the film, Norman Bates had been dominated by his demanding and clinging mother whom he eventually killed. Not able to bear the crime of matricide, he maintains the fiction that she lives by dressing in her clothes and speaking in her voice. Each time he feels sexual desire for a woman, the mother he has killed rises up in him to murder the cause of this betrayal of her son's affections. Thus Norman, the matricide and killer of several other women, is judged the victim of the very mother he has killed.

Marion Crane is punished for sexual desires which put her in the wrong place at the wrong time. Yet her decision to return the money and go back to face the consequences of her theft makes her subsequent murder seem all the more gratuitous. One of the more insidious changes in Brian De Palma's reworking of the *Psycho* plot in *Dressed to Kill* is that Kate, the Angie Dickinson character who replaces Janet Leigh's Marion, is a sexually frustrated middle-aged woman whose desperate search for satisfaction leads directly to her death. Not only does a "woman" commit the crime but the female victim asks for it.[20]

In this and other ways De Palma's film *Dressed to Kill* extends *Psycho*'s premise by holding the woman responsible for the horror that destroys her. Here too the psychiatrist explains at the end that it was the woman in the man who killed—in this case the female, "Bobbie," half of Kate's schizophrenic therapist, Dr. Elliot. Bobbie wants the doctor to undergo a sex change operation so that "she" will become dominant. Bobbie kills Kate when she discovers that Kate's sexual desires have aroused the very penis that Bobbie would like to eradicate. But this time the murder is clearly meant to be seen as the fault of the sex-hungry victim who, in the words of the detective who solves the case, was "*looking* to get killed."

The film begins with a form of interior "looking" with Kate's violent sexual fantasy of being attacked in the shower. This fantasy, which begins with the blurring of Kate's vision by the steam of the shower, condenses Hitchcock's illicit love-in-a-motel-room scene with the famous shower sequence, encouraging us to believe that Kate's desire is to be the victim of the male aggression. The rest of the film will give her what she "wants."

A second instance of Kate's desiring look occurs during a therapy session with Dr. Elliot. She discusses her sexual frustrations with her husband and her unwillingness to confess her lack of satisfaction: "I moaned with pleasure at his touch, isn't that what every man wants?" The doctor assures her that the problem must lie in her husband's technique; she is perfectly attractive so there could be nothing wrong with *her*. The film thus assumes that sexual satisfaction must be given by the aggressive man to the passive and sufficiently attractive woman; there is no route to achieving it herself. This lesson is borne out by Kate's very next act; her aggressive proposition to Dr. Elliot leads not to sexual satisfaction but to humiliation and death.

Proof follows in an elaborate cat-and-mouse chase in the labyrinthine art museum where Kate tentatively pursues a strange man.[21] Throughout the sequence Kate's look and pursuit of the man is continually frustrated and outmaneuvered by his look and pursuit of her. It is as if the game for him consists in hiding from her look in order to surprise her with his.

Once again the camera adopts Kate's subjective point of view only to demonstrate her failure to see, while the objective shots reveal the many times she fails to look in the right direction to see the lurking figure of the man she seeks and whom we so easily see. Repeatedly, her look of expectation encounters thin air. She only encounters him when vision can give her no warning, as when she turns at the sudden touch of his hand, wearing her dropped glove; or outside the museum when he waves her lost glove, symbol of his triumph, at her from a cab.

When she thanks him for the glove he pulls her into the cab, aggressively undresses her and performs cunnilingus. Her ecstasy is mixed with the humiliation of watching the cab driver adjust his rear-view mirror to get a better view. Later, in the stranger's apartment, she encounters a second humiliating punishment for the dubious pleasure she has just received: a public health record attesting to the fact that the stranger has venereal disease. But these humiliations are only teases for the real punishment to come: the revenge of Bobbie, the tall blond in sunglasses, who slashes her to pieces in the elevator, spoiling her pretty white suit.

Bobbie wreaks her revenge on Kate as a substitute for the castration she has not yet been able to have performed on her male half. The film stresses the gory details of the transexual operation in no uncertain terms when Liz the hooker explains to Peter, Kate's son, just how a "penectomy" is performed. In *Psycho* the dead mother-villain was guilty of an excessive domination that figuratively castrated her son, eventually turning him into her entirely. In *Dressed to Kill* this figurative castration by the woman in the man becomes a literal possibility, and the desiring look of the female victim becomes a direct cause of the sexual crisis that precipitates her own death.

"If the woman looks, the spectacle provokes, castration is in the air."[22] Kate's crime is having tried to look, having actively sought the satisfaction of her desires. The film teaches that such satisfaction cannot be actively sought; it must be received, like rape, as a gift from the gods. And if Kate dies while Liz the hooker and ostensibly promiscuous woman, survives (much as Marion Crane's "good girl" sister survives in *Psycho*) it is because Kate's desires have made disturbing demands on the male that Liz does not make.

Thus, although the film gives the impression of reversing the conventions by which the "good girls" are saved and the promiscuous ones punished, it actually reinforces the convention by redefining the "good girl" as the professional sex machine who knows how to satisfy but makes no demands of her own.

The film leaves us with one last, nagging "insight" as to the nature of woman's desire: Liz's dream of the return of Bobbie to murder her as she steps out of the shower that was the scene of Kate's original fantasy. She awakens from the dream and is comforted by Peter as the film ends. But there can be no comfort for the female spectator, who has been asked to accept the truth of a masochistic female imagination that envisions its own punishment at the hands of the sick man whose very illness lies in the fact that he wants to become a woman.

In the 22 years since *Psycho* and *Peeping Tom* began the new horror tradition of the psychopathic hero, one of the most significant changes in the genre has been the deepening of the woman's responsibility for the horror that endangers her. We have seen that in the classic horror film the woman's sexually-charged look at the monster encounters a horror version of her own body. The monster is thus one of many mirrors held up to her by patriarchy. But, as I have tried to suggest, she also encounters in this mirror at least the possibility of a power located in her very difference from the male.

In the more recent psychopathic horror films, however, the identification between woman and monster becomes greater, the nature of the identification is more negatively charged, and women are increasingly punished for the threatening nature of their sexuality. *Peeping Tom* is both exception and rule to this in its self-conscious exploration of the male monster's need to shift responsibility for her victimization to the woman. For *Peeping Tom* exposes the male aggressor's need to believe that his female victims are terrified by their own distorted image. It thus reveals the process by which films themselves ask women to believe that they have asked for it.

Much more typical are *Psycho*, *Dressed to Kill* and a host of vastly inferior exploitation films—what Roger Ebert calls the new brand of "woman-in-danger" films—including *He Knows You're Alone, Prom Night, Terror Train, Friday the 13th*.[23] Ebert points out that in these films we rarely see the psychopathic murderer whose point of view the audience nevertheless adopts. This "non-specific male killing force" thus displaces what was once the subjective point of view of the female victim onto an audience that is now asked to view the body of the woman victim as the only visible monster in the film. In other words, in these films the recognition and affinity between woman and monster of the classic horror film gives way to pure identity: she *is* the monster, her mutilated body is the only visible horror.

These films are capitalizations—and vulgarizations—of currently popular formulae begun with *Psycho* and *Peeping Tom*. There are, of course, obvious differences of technical and aesthetic quality between these exploitative women-in-danger films and a film like *Dressed to Kill*. Ebert suggests that the distinction lies in the "artistry. . . and inventive directional point-of-view" of such films as *Halloween, Dressed to Kill, The Texas Chainsaw Massacre* over *Friday the 13th* and the rest. The former films endow their villains with characters, while in the exploitative films they are faceless non-characters whose point of view the audience is forced to adopt.[24]

Although we must be deeply indebted to Ebert for identifying and condemning the onslaught of these offensive films (and for doing so on public television), the argument that the greater artistry and characterization of the more "artistic" films exonerate them from the charge of gratuitously punishing their female heroines rings false. The real issue (to continue the argument in Ebert's terms of false or non-existent characterization) is that the *women* in these films are non-existent fantasies. *Dressed to Kill* is a male horror fantasy in drag; the film attributes a whole slew of inauthentic fantasies to an ostensible female subject who is never really there in the first place. While supposedly about Bobbie's desire to castrate her male half, what the film actually shows is not this mutilation but another: the slow motion slashing of Kate's body as substitute for the castration Bobbie cannot yet perform on Elliot. In this light, Bobbie's vengeance on Kate can be viewed not as the act of a jealous woman eliminating her rival, but as acting out the *male* fantasy that woman is castrated, mutilated, "what men would be if they had no penises—bereft of sexuality, helpless, incapable."[25] Thus the mutilation of Kate should be properly viewed as a form of symbolic castration on a body that is frightening to the male precisely because it cannot be castrated, has none of his own vulnerability. The problem, in other words, is that she is not castrated; the fantasy solution of the male psychopath and the film itself is symbolically to prove that she is.

It is crucial for women spectators to realize the important change that is taking place before our very eyes, but which habits of viewing, not to mention habits of *not* viewing, of closing our eyes to violence and horror in general, may keep us from seeing. We are so used to sympathizing, in traditional cringing ways, with the female victims of horror that we are likely not to notice the change, to assume that films such as these have maintained this sympathy while simply escalating the doses of violence and sex. What we need to see is that in fact the sexual "freedom" of such films, the titillating attention given to the expression of women's desires, is directly proportional to the violence perpetrated against women. The horror film may be a rare example of a genre that permits the expression of women's sexual potency and desire, and which associates this desire with the autonomous act of looking, but it does so in these more recent examples only to punish her for this very act, only to demonstrate how monstrous female desire can be.

NOTES

1. Laura Mulvey, "Visual Pleasure and Narrative Cinema," *Screen*, vol. 16, no. 3 (Autumn 1975), pp. 6-18. See also John Berger's description of the different "social presence" of the woman in western painting and advertisement, in *Ways of Seeing* (London: Penguin Books, 1978), pp. 46-47. Berger argues that where the man in such works simply "surveys" the woman before acting towards her, the woman is split into a "surveyor" and a "surveyed." In other words, she is constantly aware of being looked at, even as she herself looks. Mary Ann Doane similarly notes the woman's status as spectacle rather than spectator and goes on to make a useful distinction between primary and secondary identifications within these structures of seeing in "Misrecognition and Identity," *Ciné-Tracts*, vol. 3, no. 3 (Fall 1980), pp. 25-31.

2. The pathetic blind heroine is a cliché of melodrama from D.W. Griffith's *Orphans of the Storm* to Chaplin's *City Lights* to Guy Green's *A Patch of Blue*.

3. Mulvey, "Visual Pleasure." Also Christian Metz, "The Imaginary Signifier," *Screen*, vol. 16, no. 2 (Summer 1975), pp. 14-76.

4. *Enoch Arden* (1911) is a two-reel remake of Griffith's earlier one-reeler entitled *After Many Years* (1908). Both are adaptations of Tennyson's 1864 poem "Enoch Arden." The earlier version is often cited as Griffith's first integrative use of the close-up and as his first radical use of spatial discontinuity. The 1911 version is usually cited as his first expansion into the two-reel length. Lewis Jacobs, *The Rise of the American Film* (New York: Teachers College Press, 1967), pp. 103-104.

5. The intertitle is quoted verbatim from Tennyson's poem.

6. In Tennyson's poem Annie Lee fails to catch even this last sight of Enoch. Enoch had assured her that she could prolong their farewell by looking at him through a spyglass—the same spyglass that Griffith uses to emphasize her inability to see in subsequent scenes. In the poem Annie fails to operate the glass properly and thus misses her last look at Enoch.

7. It could very well be that the tradition of the fair-haired virgin and the dark-haired vamp rests more upon this difference in the lightness or darkness of the eyes than in hair color. The uncanny light eyes of many of Griffith's most affecting heroines—Mae Marsh, Lillian Gish and even his wife Linda Arvidson, who plays Annie Lee—contribute to an effect of innocent blindness in many of his films. Light eyes seem transparent, unfocused, easy to penetrate, incapable of penetration themselves, while dark eyes are quite the reverse.

8. Mae West is, of course, one "master" of such reversals.

9. Mary Ann Doane, "The 'Woman's Film': Possession and Address" (see this volume, pp. 67-82).

10. Ibid., p. 72.

11. Miriam White points out that the film's visuals suggest that Nina is really awaiting the Count, not her husband, even though the film's intertitles construe Nina's behavior only in relation to her husband: "Narrative Semantic Deviation: Duck-Rabbit Texts of Weimar Cinema." (Paper delivered at the University of Wisconsin-Milwaukee, Center for Twentieth Century Studies conference on Cinema and Language, March 1979.)

12. I am indebted to Bruce Kawin for pointing out to me the way in which the audience receives the first shock of this look at the Phantom.

13. Leslie Fiedler refers to this passage in *Freaks: Myths and Images of the Secret Self* (New York: Simon and Schuster, 1978), p. 17.

14. Mulvey, pp. 10-16.

15. Stephen Heath, "Difference," *Screen*, vol. 19, no. 3 (Autumn 1978), p. 92.

16. Susan Lurie, "Pornography and the Dread of Woman," in *Take Back the Night*, ed. Laura Lederer (New York: William Morrow, 1980), pp. 159-173. Melanie Klein, in *Psycho-Analysis of Children* (London: Hogarth Press, 1932), has written extensively of the child's terror of being devoured, torn up, and destroyed by the mother, although for Klein these fears derive from a pre-oedipal stage and apply to both male and female infants.

17. According to Stan Brakhage the word "nosferatu" itself means "splashed with milk" in Transylvanian. A Rumanian legend tells how a servant woman frightened by Count Dracula spilled a pitcher of milk on him. Brakhage thus suggests that the word connotes a homosexual allusion of "sucking for milk." (*Film Biographies* [Berkeley, CA: Turtle Island, 1977], p. 256.)

18. *The Book of the Vampires*, as quoted in Murnau's *Nosferatu*, states that only a woman "pure in heart," who will keep the vampire by her side until the first cock crows, can break his spell.

19. Henry Herrings' as yet unpublished comparison of these two films, "The Endurance of Misogyny: *Psycho* and *Dressed to Kill*," points out the way in which the woman is both cause and perpetrator of the violence against her in both films.

20. Andrew Sarris, one of the few critics to call the film on this issue, writes: "In De Palma's perhaps wishful world, women do not just ask for it, they are willing to run track meets for it." (*Village Voice*, 17 September 1980, p. 44.)

21. This is another of De Palma's Hitchcock allusions—this one to *Vertigo*—in which the Kim Novak character sits pretending to be entranced before the portrait of her supposedly dead former self. Sarris correctly points out with respect to such borrowings that De Palma "steals Hitchcock's most privileged moments without performing the drudgery of building up to these moments as thoroughly earned climaxes." (Ibid.)

22. Heath, p. 92.

23. Roger Ebert, "Why Movie Audiences Aren't Safe Any More," *American Film*, vol. 6, no. 5 (March 1981), pp. 54-56.

24. Ibid., p. 56.

25. Lurie, p. 166.

From Repressive Tolerance to Erotic Liberation: *Maedchen in Uniform*

B. Ruby Rich

> *What in God's name does one call this sensibility if it be not love? This extraordinary heightening of all one's impressions; this intensification of sensitiveness; this complete identification of feeling?. . .I was Manuela, as she is Manuela, and everything that has happened to her has in essence, and other circumstances, happened to me. This incredible feeling of sisterhood.*[1]
>
> —Dorothy Thompson, upon meeting Christa Winsloe

There are moments when one historical period seems to beckon to another, offering the semblance of lessons to be learned or errors to be avoided. Certainly, that is true today for those of us reviewing the fate of progressive political organizations in the Weimar period preceding Adolph Hitler's coming to power in the inflation-torn and authority-hungry Germany of 1933. In particular, the history of women's-rights groups and homosexual-emancipation organizations is one that needs to be better known and analyzed. It is a testimony to our ignorance of the period that Leontine Sagan's film, *Maedchen in Uniform* (1931), is generally assumed to be an anomaly, a film without a context, or else a metaphor, a coded tale about something *else*, something other than what appears on screen. If we are to understand *Maedchen in Uniform* fully, then it is important to keep in view the society within which it was made: the celebrated milieu of Berlin *avant-la-guerre*, the Berlin with dozens of gay and lesbian bars and journals, the Berlin of a social tolerance so widespread that it nearly camouflaged the underlying legal restraints (which were to grow, rapidly, into massive repression). I would stop short of claiming an outlandish Rosetta Stone status for the film, no matter how tempting, lest the reader lose faith. Yet, it might be emphasized, *Maedchen in Uniform is* an exemplary work, not only for what it presents to us on the screen but also for the timely issues that its analysis must confront. It is the film revival most central to establishing a history of lesbian cinema.

Maedchen in Uniform was filmed by Leontine Sagan in Germany in 1931, based upon the play, *Yesterday and Today,* by Christa Winsloe (alias the Baroness von Hatvany) and republished as a novel, *The Child Manuela,* also by Winsloe. The film, like the play, enjoyed a tremendous initial popularity, both within Germany and internationally; yet it has been nearly invisible in the past few decades within the academic study of German cinema. The film has frequently fallen into a seeming limbo between the silent German Expressionist cinema and the notorious products of the Third Reich studios. Despite its remarkable sound quality (praised by Lotte Eisner as the work in which "the prewar German sound film reached its highest level")[2] and in spite of its evocative cinematography (which Kracauer cited as transmitting "the symbolic power of light"),[3] *Maedchen in Uniform* faded from the text books, the revival houses, and even eventually from distribution entirely. During the early 70s, however, Sagan's classic was resoundingly redeemed by the cycle of women's film festivals, gathering a solid following and the critical attention it had long lacked. The result, today, is that the film is back in distribution in a beautifully reconstructed print (in contrast to the butchered, mistitled print that made the rounds of the early festivals) and is accorded a secure spot in the history of pre-Reich cinema.

In part, the film's reputation rests upon unusual stylistic components. Sagan's montage-inflected structure manages to break away from the usually stagey and claustrophobic *mise-en-scène* of early sound films. Her montages, no doubt Soviet-influenced, establish a persuasive counterpoint to the more theatrical scenes and mold them into a cinematic rhythm. Dramatically, her use of a large cast of nonprofessional actresses lends the film a fresh and documentarylike tone, while the performances of the lead actresses won widespread praise.

Sagan was a pioneer in her use of sound, not only as a functional synchronous accompaniment, but also as a thematic element in its own right. However, most important to the film's reputation through the years has been its significance as an antiauthoritarian and prophetically antifascist film. And, to be sure, the film has suitable credentials for such a claim. Any film so opposed to militarism, so anti-Prussian, so much in support of the emotional freedom of women, must be an antifascist film. Furthermore, it was made through the Deutsche Film Gemeinschaft, a cooperative production company specifically organized for this project—and was the first German commercial film to be made collectively. Add to such factors the fact that the film was made on the very eve of Hitler's rise to power, just prior to the annexation of the film industry into Goebbel's cultural program, and the legend of Sagan's proto-subversive movie is secure. In emphasizing the film's progressive stance in relation to the Nazi assumption of power, however, film historians have tended to overlook, minimize or trivialize the film's central concern with love between women.

Today, we must take issue with the largely unexamined critical assumption that the relations between women in the film are essentially a metaphor for the real power relations of which it treats, i.e., the struggle against fascism. I would suggest that *Maedchen in Uniform* is not only antifascist, but also antipatriarchal in its politics. Such a reading need not depend upon metaphor, but can be more forcefully demonstrated by a close attention to the film text. As I propose to read it, *Maedchen in Uniform* is a film about sexual repression in the name of social harmony; absent patriarchy and its forms of presence; bonds between women which represent attraction instead of repulsion; and the release of powers that can accompany the identification of a lesbian sexuality. The film is a dual coming-out story: that of Manuela, the adolescent who voices "the love that dares not speak its name" and who, in distinguishing between fantasy and desire, dares to act upon the latter; and that of Fräulein von Bernburg, the teacher who repudiates her own role as an agent of suppression and wins her own freedom by accepting her attraction to another woman. In this reading, the film remains a profoundly antifascist drama, but now its political significance becomes a direct consequence of the film's properly central subject, lesbianism, rather than a covert message wrapped in an attractive but irrelevant metaphor. If *Maedchen in Uniform* is the first truly radical lesbian film, it is also a fairly typical product of late Weimar society, a society in which "homosexuality...became a form of fashionable behavior" linked to "the Weimar idea of making a complete break with the staid and bankrupt past of one's parents' generation."[4] As such, it offers a particularly clear example of the interplay between personal and collective politics—and the revolutionary potential inherent in the conjunction of the two.

The film centers upon the relationship between two women. Manuela (Hertha Thiele) is a young student newly arrived at a Potsdam boarding school that caters to the daughters of German officers who, in the mid-20s, are largely impoverished, as is the school itself. With her mother dead, her father unable to look after her, and her aunt/guardian icily uncaring, Manuela is left craving affection. Fräulein von Bernburg (Dorothea Wieck) is the school's most adored teacher, champion of a maternalistic humanitarianism opposed to the school's Prussian codes. Harsh, ascetic, militaristic, the boarding-school environment is enforced by a totalitarian principal (Emilia Unda) dedicated to toughening up her charges.

Manuela quickly develops a passionate attachment to Fräulein von Bernburg, who simultaneously nourishes and discourages her admirer. Manuela's infatuation is even more intense than the crushes that her fellow students have upon the esteemed Bernburg. Furthermore, she carries matters to an unprecedented level by announcing her passion publicly, to all the school. The declaration occurs when Manuela, drunk and in male attire, celebrates her thespian success in the school play by offering the news of her affections as a convivial toast. For such a transgression, Manuela is confined to solitary in the infirmary by the school principal, who forbids students and faculty alike from so much as speaking to her.

The mounting crisis impels Fräulein von Bernburg to confront the principal and challenge her authority, a climax which coincides with the desperate Manuela's own decision to solve the problem by committing suicide. Distraught at having to give up her beloved teacher, Manuela climbs the school's forbidding staircase (a central leitmotif in the film) and is about to throw herself from its uppermost railing when her schoolgirl companions, disobeying the injunction, come to her rescue. Their arrival is paralleled by the rush of Fräulein von Bernburg to the scene, confirming her affection for Manuela and her identification with the students' action. The aversion of imminent tragedy is a triumph for the forces of love and community, signalling the coming of a new order. The event seals the fate of the evil principal, who retreats down the hall into the shadows even as Fräulein von Bernburg remains in the light, united through crosscutting with Manuela and the students grouped above her on the staircase.

As should be clear from the summary, the action of *Maedchen in Uniform* transpires entirely within an all-woman environment and, indeed, a thoroughly "feminine" atmosphere. However, the very first establishing shots of the film serve to inform us of the real power of absent patriarchy and remind us that an all-woman school in no way represents a woman-defined space. The montage of visual icons in the first few frames establishes an exterior world of military preparedness, steeples and archways, bugle calls and the marching rhythm of soldiery. And this world of regimentation extends to the neat rows of students who, two by two, file past the gateway into the domain of the school. The link between the exterior authority and the interior order is explicitly visualized only once, but it informs our reading of the entire film (particularly as represented by the emblematic use of off-screen sounds and on-screen symbols, like the staircase).

On her first day of school, Manuela listens to the principal's speech outlining her required duty and identity: "You are all soldiers' daughters and, God willing, you will all be soldiers' mothers." The girls are there to be taught the Prussian values in order that they might transmit the "correct line" to their future progeny. They are destined to be the transmitters of a culture, not its inheritors. The learning is not for them as women in their own right, but for their function as reproducers of bodies and ideologies. The extent to which the absent patriarchy (which at no point in the film takes the shape of actual men on screen) dominates the women's world is a theme constantly reiterated by Sagan in her many visualizations of classically Romantic leitmotifs. Barred shadows cross the women's paths, a sternly overbearing staircase encloses their every movement, a frantic montage marshals their steps into a militaristic gait, and even the school songs reinforce the authority of a demanding fatherland with a handful of schoolgirls in its grasp. The film's very title underlines this theme, with its play of meanings on the word "uniform" meaning (as a noun) the clothing of a regimented educational/military/professional institution, or (as an adjective) the regulated, all-alike behavior of uniformity dictated by the rules of the patriarchal order.

The ultimate incarnation of the absent but controlling patriarchy is the school principal. Her identity as the "phallic woman" is suggested by her reliance on an everpresent cane with which she measures her steps and signals her authority, and by the phallocentric codes of *Kinder, Kirche, Küche*, which she is dedicated to instilling. Her mandates and bearing call to mind a vision of Frederick the Great, to whom she has been compared. Perhaps coincidentally, her jowly face and disassociated affect are equally reminiscent of that other prophetic cinematic persona of demented authority, Doctor Caligari. Like the mad Doctor, this principal is accompanied by an obedient assistant, a dark hunchbacked figure who carries out her orders. Unlike Caligari's missions of murder, the principal's agenda is more properly "feminine" in its details of manipulation and reconnaissance. The henchwoman is a warped figure; like the principal shuffling with her cane, the assistant presents an image of womanhood carrying out patriarchal dirty work and physically warped by her complicity. Her hands huddled close to her chest, her eyes pinched and shoulders stooped, the assistant becomes a physical marker of emotional damage. In *The Cabinet of Dr. Caligari* madness and hypnotism were held responsible for complicity in murder; Sagan is willing to pinpoint a more precise cause in the dogma of an authoritarian ideology. Just as nuns have long provided an easy example of a woman's order subject to entirely male authority (in the form of priest, Pope, or God the Father, Son, the heavenly bridegroom), so, too, the institution of the woman's boarding school is shaped to the mold of the militaristic patriarchal society, poured like molten liquid into its empty spaces to keep it whole.

How, then, does the power structure within the school itself function? Specifically, what are the roles assumed by the beloved Fräulein von Bernburg, champion of the emotions, and the hated Principal, enforcer of discipline? Traditionally, critical readings of the film have identified Fräulein von Bernburg as a sort of freedom fighter, a humanitarian standing up to the forces of repression, and have targeted the Principal much as I have described her, a tyrant ruling over a regime of denial. I would take issue with this romanticized view and trade its simplistic hero/villain dichotomy for a different model, i.e., a system of repression based instead on the "good cop, bad cop" pattern, with the Principal as the "bad cop" and Fräulein von Bernburg as the "good cop."

To comprehend the logic of such a system in the case of the boarding school, it is necessary to return to the point made earlier in the Principal's opening speech. As she made clear, the young women are being bred ("educated") as transmitters of the patriarchal German culture everpresent in encoded form within the world of the school. In order to ensure this training, preserve the young women's "honor" and most effectively carry out their special socialization, it is necessary for society to shape women within an all-female setting; in fact, prior to feminist movements, this was no doubt the primary reason for "separatist" institutions. What, however, is the danger to the patriarchal society presented by such an institution? It is a sexual danger: the threat that the heterosexuality required of these women may, in the cloistered pressure-cooker atmosphere of the boarding school, become derailed into a focus upon their own sex. The possibility that heterosexuality on the part of women may become transferred ("warped" as the father might say) into homosexuality presents a powerful threat to a system geared for procreation and the rearing of male offspring. "Gender is not only an identification with one sex; it also entails that sexual desire be directed toward the other sex."[5] The danger of the boarding school is that a concentration on the former entails a corresponding relaxation of the latter. Perhaps it is because the women's boarding school is the Achilles' heel of patriarchy that it figures in so much lesbian literature and cinema.

In *Maedchen in Uniform*, the code name for this sexual threat is "emotionalism." When Fräulein von Bernburg early in the film catches two schoolgirls exchanging a love letter, she confiscates the paper and, to their relief and delight, rips it up without reading a word; smiling but strict, she warns them to desist in the exchange of such letters because they can lead to "emotionalism." Again, later in the film, the student ringleader, Ilse, uses the same expression with the same negative message. She is engaged in declaiming a series of mock toasts during the post-play banquet, all phrased in the language of the school's official ideology, and thus she reprimands Manuela for the acting style of her male impersonation: "Remember, next time, less emotionalism."

In line with the model of repression that I suggest, Fräulein von Bernburg's task as the "good cop" seems to be to keep "emotionalism" in check and to make her charges more comfortable in their oppression. She acts as a pressure valve and as the focus of dissident energies in order that the overall system will not be endangered. Fräulein von Bernburg has two guises, then, for coping with the social and sexual schisms. Socially, she polices the heart, i.e., the emotional life of her students. As she puts it at one point to Manuela, "You mustn't persuade yourself it isn't nice here." It is her presence in the school's cabinet of power that keeps the girls from rebelling against an order that would otherwise be totally abhorrent. Likewise, it is her presence as a confidante that permits her to discern and block any tentative moves in the direction of revolt, as, for example, when she persuades the headstrong Ilse not to run away from the school. Thus she functions as mediator between the top and bottom of the school hierarchy.

It is made clear, however, that the methods by which Fräulein von Bernburg exercises her functions are sexual. For instance, she succeeds in persuading Ilse to stay by slapping her on the ass and speaking to her seductively. This is her second guise: she capitalizes upon the standard form of transference that leads adolescent girls to develop crushes on their teachers. Her positioning of herself as the exclusive object of schoolgirl affection may be seen as a tactic of repressive tolerance carried out in the arena of sexuality. Under the camouflage of her tolerance is the reality of repression. If the girls focus their sexual desires upon her—where they can never be realized—then the danger of such desires being refocused upon each other (where they *could* be realized) is averted. The figure of the teacher remains ever more powerful, more attractive, more worthy of adoration, than any mere fellow student. It is, in fact, very nearly a relationship of adoration in the religious sense, with forms of expression that are thoroughly ritualized and contained, as, for example, the evening bedtime scene makes clear.

The scene is set in the dormitory on Manuela's first night in the school. It is filmed with the soft focus and radiant light of a Romantic painting, for example, a Friedrich. The lights are dimmed by Fräulein von Bernburg to make the scene more seductive. All the girls are poised on the edge of their beds, kneeling in identical white gowns, heads upraised to receive the communion of her lips touching their foreheads, which she holds firmly as she administers each ritualistic kiss. This extreme fetishizing of the kiss by the nature of the teacher's gestures and the film's style is emblematic of the unspoken codes of repressive tolerance. The kiss is permitted, to each alike, but it is at once the given and the boundary. Nothing more may be allowed or even suggested, although the tension of that which is withheld suffuses the scene with eroticism and grants the teacher her very power. The kiss is both minimum and maximum, a state of grace and a state of stasis. The entire equilibrium is founded upon this extreme tension, which is snapped when Manuela, overwhelmed by the atmosphere and her feelings, breaks the rules. She throws her arms around Fräulein von Bernburg's body in a tight embrace and receives not a punishment but a kiss—a kiss, not merely on the forehead, but full on the lips.

Of course the school's system of sexual repression does not crumble from this one transgression; it is much too securely established. Less so is Fräulein von Bernburg, whose situation is a difficult one. It is apparent that the sexual repression she forces upon the students she also forces upon herself. Yet Manuela causes a surplus of feeling which she cannot control. Sagan carefully presents Fräulein von Bernburg almost entirely in terms of Manuela. The first time she appears in the film, she is looking at the newly-arrived Manuela on the stairway. The extent to which she begins to identify her own desires and sensitivities with Manuela's takes the shape of a literal superimposition. When Sagan presents a scene of Manuela as student in Fräulein von Bernburg's classroom, it is the anguish of the conflicted pair that she portrays through an extraordinary dissolve that predates the more widespread (and more pernicious) use of the motif by Ingmar Bergman in *Persona*.[6] In the scene while struggling vainly to retrieve a memorized passage from a mind gone blank in the beloved teacher's presence, Manuela's vision begins to blur. Fräulein von Bernburg's sight, subjectively rendered, blurs as well, as her face becomes superimposed and fused with Manuela's staring back at her. It is she, as teacher, who breaks the locked gaze, averts her eyes, and reprimands Manuela with a "not prepared again," thus reasserting her authority and utilizing her rank to shield her emotions.

The next meeting of the two takes place in Fräulein von Bernburg's office soon after, where she has called Manuela in order to give her one of her chemises (in response to an attendant's expressed pity for the young girl's lack of undergarments, due to her lack of a caring mother). By giving Manuela one of her own chemises, she attempts to channel her concern and affection into the quasi-permissible form of a maternal gift which, however, is clearly an erotic token. The conversation that transpires between the two provides further evidence of the code of repressive tolerance exercised toward the students' incipient homosexuality. From the start, it is clear that "emotionalism" rules the encounter, as Fräulein von Bernburg begins by reprimanding Manuela, who has burst into tears at the gift of the chemise: "What an excitable child you are." Manuela confesses she isn't crying out of unhappiness, and finally is coaxed to explain by the teacher's concern: "Is there a reason you can't confide to me?" It is the loneliness of the nights that plagues her, the moments after the goodnight kiss: "I stare at your door and would like to get up and go to you, but I'm not allowed....I like you so awfully much." She is tortured by the passage of time: "I think of when I get older, and have to leave the school, and you'll kiss other children." Her expression of love, desire and jealousy is quite explicitly phrased (although, in the older prints of the film, it was largely unsubtitled). Unprepared for such a declaration and unwilling to face the consequences of receiving such information, Fräulein von Bernburg lays down the law of the land: "I think of you, too, Manuela.... But you know I can't make exceptions. The others would be jealous."

Her response is telling. She doesn't say that she does not share the girl's feelings of attraction; if anything, she implies that she does. She does not invent a boyfriend to assert a defensive heterosexual identity. She asserts only that she is under obligation to love all the girls equally in order to maintain her position as object of their affection; therefore, she cannot break that egalitarianism in order to reciprocate Manuela's passion. The system which she must serve—as its token humanitarian—represses her own sexuality as well as that of the students. She is as much the victim as the promulgator of its repression, unlike the Principal, whose phallic identity cancels out any homo-eroticism. However, despite her struggle to repress her own emotions, Fräulein von Bernburg does act. The gift of the chemise is a turning point: it leads to the crisis of the school play, which is the central moment of the film, the moment which changes its direction from repressive tolerance to one of erotic liberation, the choice taken by Manuela throughout and by Fräulein von Bernburg, more complexly, at the film's end.

The school play, a favorite device of the boarding school genre, necessitates the pleasurable moment of cross-dressing in male attire. Manuela plays the lead role of Don Carlos in the 1787 play of the same name by Friedrich Schiller, scion of the *Sturm und Drang* school that brought to culmination the ideals of the Weimar classicism movement led by Schiller and Goethe.

The choice of this play by Sagan and Winsloe to be the play-within-the-film is particularly significant.[7] *Don Carlos* is identified with the youthful Schiller, in that it represents the peak of his early idealistic period (indeed, after it, Schiller went into a period of doubt and reevaluation that kept him from writing plays again for a full decade). *Sturm und Drang* was a literary movement that presaged German Romanticism in its emphasis upon the individual in conflict with a rationalist, unjust order. Both Schiller and Goethe stressed emotional harmony and a community of sympathy as the basic social values to put forward in opposition to the oppressive rationalism of the Enlightenment; *Don Carlos* is considered the very embodiment of that theme. Based upon the life of Don Carlos, son of the Spanish King Philip II, the play counterposes the son's liberal idealism with the brutal tyranny of his father's reign. In the play, Don Carlos forms an alliance with the older-and-wiser Marquis Posa, who conspires with him to advance a humane order and overthrow the ruler. In Schiller's play, the Marquis—learning that their plans are suspected—saves the prince by drawing all guilt upon himself, consequently suffering execution by the king's decree in order to save the prince. The play ends tragically, with Don Carlos refusing to relish his fatally-bought freedom, showing his true face to the king, and thus suffering a similar death at the hands of the bloodthirsty Inquisition.

Thus far, then, *Don Carlos* would seem the perfect corollary to the film's much-advanced theme of humanitarian idealism counterposed against a fascist reign. In such an interpretation, Manuela would essentially play herself, while the Marquis Posa would represent the Fräulein von Bernburg role and the King would represent the Principal. Schiller, like Winsloe/Sagan, thus assumes the mantle of proto-antifascist for his eloquent, romantic opposition to the maddened illogic of absolute order. The Principal's invited guests seem prone to this same interpretation, for they cluck disapprovingly over their tea that "Schiller sometimes writes very freely."

However, the subsequent scenes following this admonition, as well as the choice of the scene from *Don Carlos*, suggest the same sort of alternate reading that I have been suggesting for *Maedchen in Uniform* as a whole. The scene immediately following the tea-talk is one of the schoolgirls, giddy from a dose of spiked punch, dancing in each others' arms, disobeying the rules, and generally enacting their guardians' worst fears. The scene chosen from *Don Carlos* is not one dealing in political matters, but rather, the rarified scene in which Don Carlos at last wins an audience with the Queen and declares his forbidden love to her. Reprimanded for his rashness in compromising them both by coming to see her, Don Carlos tells the Queen that "Even if it means death, I shall not go from here: One moment lived in Paradise is not too dearly bought with death." These are the lines spoken by Manuela (as Don Carlos) in the scene we see of the school play. A significant key to the narrative of *Don Carlos* is the fact that the Prince's beloved is his father's newly-acquired wife: she is, literally, his mother, which makes their love forbidden as, in the words of Schiller's play, "the world and nature and the laws of Rome condemn such passions." Sagan clearly annexes this sentiment by choosing the scene in which Don Carlos proclaims his love for Elizabeth, the name both of the Queen Mother and of Fräulein von Bernburg. With Manuela cross-dressed as the passionate suitor (in a performance heralded by all for its remarkable sincerity!), the sequence represents the central theme of forbidden love encoded within the sanctity of German high culture.

Drunk with punch and the euphoria of her success, Manuela decides to extend her role into real life: she rises to deliver an impassioned toast in which she declares her love for Fräulein von Bernburg and announces the gift of her chemise as proof of its reciprocation. She abandons caution to proclaim "I know she likes me." She echoes and surpasses Don Carlos in her insistence on sharing the news: "Nothing else matters. . . . I'm not afraid of anything . . . . Yes, everyone should know." In a coming out that is the opposite of Don Carlos' vow of silence, she concludes with a celebratory generosity: "Long live Fräulein von Bernburg, beloved by all."

Despite the school's aura of eroticism, it is this act of pronouncement which constitutes the unpardonable transgression. It is the *naming* of that which may well be known, this claiming of what is felt by the public speaking of its name, that is expressly forbidden.[8] For her speech, which is witnessed by the dread Principal, Manuela is immediately imprisoned, significantly enough within the confines of the infirmary—in a reference to the pseudo-scientific view of homosexuality as a species of mental imbalance, a disease, but one that nevertheless can be punished as a crime. Indeed, the first view of Manuela in the hospital traces her position in bed below heavy bars of light emblazoned on the shadowed wall above her head. The immediate wish of the Principal is to blot out history, to expunge the traces of the "scandal" and pretend that nothing ever happened. It is a wish that is initially reflected in Manuela's own coming to consciousness, as she emerges from her hangover with the complaint that she cannot remember what has happened or what she has done. So powerful is the taboo that amnesia is the consequence of its transgression.

The public speech, in fact, can be seen as an extremely powerful transgression, one which, unlike the private actions between Manuela and Fräulein von Bernburg, publicly disrupts and subverts the prevailing order of the school. The Principal's regime could tolerate the widely-acknowledged schoolgirl crushes and libidinous undercurrents as long as they remained marginalized and subservient to the dominant ideology. The homoeroticism had been portrayed graphically ever since the time of Manuela's arrival: Ilse told her how envious other girls were, asking if it were true that "the Golden One" really "kisses you good night, oh god, oh god . . ."; the laundrywoman explained the heart and initials on her school uniform, "E.V.B.", by laughing that "the girl who wore this dress must have been infatuated with Fräulein Elizabeth von Bernburg, thus the initials"; and pairs of girls were repeatedly shown holding hands, embracing by windows, or passing love notes. An unendorsed *de facto* eroticism could be contained within the reigning patriarchal order, but a double challenge could not be abided: the challenge of Manuela's public naming of that eroticism and the challenge of Fräulein von Bernburg's material action in presenting the chemise over and above the limits of egalitarianism. For this reason, amnesia was a possibility only for Manuela. Everyone else remembered quite well what had occurred.

Unable to turn back the clock, the Principal opts for quarantine: Manuela is sentenced to solitary confinement, as though homosexuality were a communicable disease spread by social contact. As Manuela becomes distraught in the final phase of the film, Fräulein von Bernburg struggles, more consciously than her young student, to come to terms with her sexuality and acknowledge her feelings for her own sex. In her final meeting with Manuela, held clandestinely in defiance of the Principal's prohibition, she tries to tell the girl the exact nature of a "crime" she seems unable to understand: "you must be cured...of liking me so much." At the same time, she makes a telling complaint about Manuela's speech. She does not reproach Manuela for what she has brought upon herself, as we might expect, but instead says: "What you have done to me, you know." There is more meaning to the statement than the fact of Manuela's speech, which to be sure has damaged her standing at the school but yet is not wholly different from countless other private declarations she no doubt has withstood. Rather, Fräulein von Bernburg may well be referring to the terrible inner conflict into which Manuela's speech has thrown her. It is a conflict not unlike that felt by so many in-the-closet homosexuals of both sexes in this country following the opening-up of sexual boundaries during the Stonewall eruption and the succeeding gay liberation movement of the late 60s and early 70s. This period carried for many an undesired pressure to identify a previously privatized sexuality (in Fräulein von Bernburg's case, to make that identification not only to others, but to herself as well). From the moment of this reproach, the teacher's struggle to "come out" and emerge from the raging conflict within her becomes the central theme of the film. It is a theme concerned with finding the courage to oppose an unjust authority, a courage shared, finally, with the other students of the school.

Fräulein von Bernburg's inner struggle reaches its peak immediately after this meeting with Manuela, which has concluded badly, with the girl rushing out of the room in desperation and the teacher's race to call her back blocked by the arrival of the Principal. In fact, her confrontations with the Principal have been escalating ever since the "theatrical" incident. She has begun assuming more radical stances in opposition to the Principal's edict. Earlier, arguing over her permissiveness toward Manuela, she had declared: "What you call sin, I call love, which has a thousand forms." She was speaking in general terms of her philosophy of maternal nurturance versus the Principal's punitive discipline, but the more explicit meaning of the statement also holds true. Intent on subjugating the teacher to her authority, the Principal now threatens her: "I will not permit revolutionary ideas." Fräulein von Bernburg then breaks rank in the only truly decisive way possible, responding: "I resign." Herewith, she makes her choice to reject her role as the "good cop" and seek a genuine humanitarianism *outside* the corrupt system of the school, which in turn means seeking also her genuine sexuality as she has come to recognize it.

As the teacher and the Principal enact their battle of will and authority, Manuela prepares to throw herself over the stairwell. It is at this point that the film's second superimposition of the faces of Manuela and Fräulein von Bernburg takes place. Again, it is Fräulein von Bernburg who "experiences" the blurred vision and "sees" Manuela's face projected through her own image. This time, however, having made her choice to break with the patriarchal order, she does not avert her gaze or try to separate herself from the vision. Instead, she recognizes this "vision" as a psychic signal of her bond with Manuela.

What does the superimposition mean in this context? The Principal had earlier warned the teacher to "dissolve" her contact with Manuela, suggesting the nature of this shot. The blurring of definition and melding of identities has usually had a negative impact when applied to women in cinema. In Ingmar Bergman's *Persona*, for example, the loss of individual identity is the threat which haunts women's intimacy like a destructive spectre: getting too close to another woman means losing oneself. In addition, there is always the companion myth of narcissism. The superimposition shots here may also be a tacit recognition by Sagan of the myth of homosexuality as a narcissistic doubling, an attempt to solidify one's identity by the addition of its likeness in another. Rather than balking at the vision, however, Fräulein von Bernburg recognizes the merged faces as a signal of power by combination. She does not read the superimposition as erasure (the patriarchal warning) or negative bonding (the mirror phase prolonged), but rather as a positive depiction of the strength exercised by such a *redoubling* of energy and identity. She trusts the sign and acts on it. Shouting Manuela's name, she rushes from her office (and the startled Principal) to the stairwell, intent on rescuing Manuela, where of course she discovers that the schoolgirls have arrived ahead of her and saved the day.

There are only these two superimpositions in the entire film, and significantly they are both assigned to Fräulein von Bernburg at times in which Manuela is in distress. It is Fräulein von Bernburg, and the force she has come to represent, who prevails in the film's final scene: the rescued Manuela is cradled by the schoolgirls as the defeated Principal, bereft of her authority, slowly retreats down the long, gloomy hall. The darkness of the hall deepens in her wake, her cane taps faintly on the floor, the sound of bells and finally bugles can be heard in the distance. As the bugle calls signify, it is a provisional victory, and yet the patriarchal order *has* been ruptured within the school by the liberation of eros among the women.

In terms of the interpretation which I have been suggesting, as well as the more traditional interpretation of antifascism, the ending of the film is extremely important. Yet the nature of the ending has been frequently obscured in cinema histories. Many reports of the film have cited a supposed "other" ending in which Manuela successfully commits suicide, and some critics have even cited the existence of a "Nazi" suicide ending and an "export" version like this one. Yet as several German sources testify, such was not the case.[9] However, the original play *did* have Manuela kill herself and ended with the Principal setting a cover-up in motion at play's end; but this is one of many differences between the play and the film which I will discuss later. In point of fact, the film *Maedchen in Uniform* concludes with an ending of rescue. What does this ending signify? Such an ending confers a unity upon the film's two themes—the widely acknowledged one of anti-authoritarianism as well as the previously ignored one of erotic liberation—and shapes them into a consistent and harmonious whole.

It has frequently been argued that the preferred ending for a proto-Nazi film was suicide, i.e., the ultimate abandonment of hope that leads the individual to throw herself/himself into the depth of oblivion or, conversely, into the hands of a superhuman savior. That was the scenario against which a film like *Kuhle Wampe* (by Slatan Dudow with script by Bertolt Brecht) rebelled, by refusing to end on a note of despair and insisting instead on the persistence of faith in the future. So, too, Sagan. Her anti-Naziism is nowhere more apparent than in the ending, which posits not only the maintenance of hope but also the vindication of resistance as a very different "triumph of the will" from Leni Riefenstahl's brand. In Riefenstahl's film of the same period, *The Blue Light* (1934), the heroine (played by Riefenstahl) finally throws herself from a cliff, despairing, isolated from others of her kind, done in by an unsympathetic society. Not so Manuela: the schoolgirls of the boarding school integrate her sensibility into their own consciousness; instead of closing ranks against her, they come to her (and, by extension, their own) rescue. The cliffhanger ending is at once a powerful statement of political resistance, both individual and collective, and a validation of lesbianism as a personal and public right.

The Principal earlier condemned Fräulein von Bernburg's feelings and actions as "revolutionary," and so they may indeed be. In a patriarchal society which depends upon women for the reward and procreation of its (his) own kind, a break in the link is disastrous: "What would happen if our hypothetical woman not only refused the man to whom she was promised, but asked for a woman instead? If a single refusal were disruptive, a double refusal would be insurrectionary."[10] The ending of the film serves to validate Fräulein von Bernburg's difficult development from humanitarian disciplinarian to a free, stronger, and woman-identified woman. The progression of the scenario depends upon her inner struggle and final evolution in response to the catalyst of Manuela's passion. At the film's end, Fräulein von Bernburg stands triumphant with the schoolgirls witnessing the Principal's melancholy retreat. She wins this position *not* by maintaining her power in the hierarchy but by rejecting it, *not* by tightening the reins of her repression but by casting them down, *not* by cooption but by refusal. Her place on the staircase at the end may be seen, then, as a reward for her "coming out" and acknowledging her sexuality, just as Manuela's rescue at the end represents a social legitimation of her passion. *Maedchen in Uniform* presents a positive vision of lesbianism that has been largely disregarded for years, a film victim of a subtle, critical homophobia that has insisted upon perceiving the literal as the merely metaphoric.

An analysis of the film today clarifies the meaning and can easily annex Sagan's work to our contemporary tradition of lesbian culture. But historical differences nevertheless persist between the perspectives of Sagan making a film cooperatively in Berlin on the eve of the Third Reich and most of us today. Differences are apparent even in the shifts of meaning between Christa Winsloe's original play and its metamorphosis into *Maedchen in Uniform*. Yet most surprising, perhaps, are the similarities that slowly become recognizable upon reexamining both the film and its period—similarities which in some cases are crucial for us to recognize as we proceed into the 80s.

Sagan's movie is in many respects a more radical work of lesbian celebration than Winsloe's play, while at the same time it focuses far more on the codes of patriarchal power than the stage production. The stage play (both the original, *Yesterday and Today*, and the international version, *Girls in Uniform*, which was widely performed after the film's release)[11] actually fits quite tidily the model of the "lesbian fairy tale" which Elaine Marks traces to its Sapphic origins in her important essay on lesbian literature:

> Although there is no evidence in Sappho's poems to corroborate the notion that she did indeed have a school, religious or secular, for young women, the gynaeceum, ruled by the seductive or seducing teacher has become, since the eighteenth century, the preferred locus for most fictions about women loving women. . . . The younger woman, whose point of view usually dominates, is always passionate and innocent. If, as is usually the case when the author of the text is a woman, it is the younger woman who falls in love, the narrative is structured so as to insist on this love as an awakening. The older woman as object of the younger woman's desire is restrained and admirable, beautiful and cultivated . . . the exchanges between the older and the younger woman are reminiscent of a mother-daughter relationship. The mother of the younger woman is either dead or in some explicit way inadequate. Her absence is implied in the young woman's insistent need for a goodnight kiss. The gynaeceum, particularly when it is represented by a school, also controls time. Time limits are set by the school calendar whose inexorable end announces the fatal separation, which may involve a death. Temporal structures reiterate the almost universally acccepted notion that a schoolgirl crush is but a phase in the emotional development of the young woman, something that will pass. The dénouement in these lesbian fairy tales is often brought about by a public event during which private passions explode.[12]

If the contours of Marks' paradigm bear a striking resemblance to the film (which in fact was viewed as an adolescent tale far more than a lesbian one), its elements fit the play even more so. For example, in the play a subplot involves Manuela's pursuit by a diligent, if unwanted, male suitor: her equestrian instructor, no less. In the play, Fräulein von Bernburg is not unmotivated in her feelings for the girls: she secretly wants to be the head of the school herself. She does not resign in the final confrontation with the Principal, but merely tries to increase her power base through the face-off; and Manuela throws herself out a window before anyone has had the chance to rescue her. Since the play can end with only Manuela having stepped out of line and dead for her actions, it is far more easily recuperable into the tradition of lesbianism as tragic, powerless, passive, and in particular, fatal to its adherent. As Marks emphasizes, the "constraints" of the genre signify the "marginal status of lesbians and lesbianism."[13]

While incorporating the classic elements of the "fairy tale" in *Maedchen in Uniform*, Sagan goes further. She changes a few areas of the story line and utilizes the visual and editing codes particular to cinema in order to extend the meaning of the original text.[14] One of the film's strongest features is its success in making palpable the functioning of patriarchal codes despite the absence of any male or militaristic figures. The use of the central staircase is one such case, with a symbolism both visual (its barred railings and threatening abyss) and philosophical (its use by the girls prohibited from using the formal front staircase). The stairwell suggests a confining enclosure, carceral in its grates of iron and shadow, as well as the functional confinement of virtually all the girls' activities. At one point, the schoolgirls drop an object from the top in order to test a formula for calculating the time a falling body takes to reach bottom. The staircase is thus both a representation of the prevailing order and its power of organization, and also a portent of tragedy in its depth and shadows. The camera frequently views the marching of the girls through the iron forms, further emphasizing their molding into Prussian "women of iron." And, of course, the very first meeting between Manuela and Fräulein von Bernburg occurs on the staircase, their bodies positioned midway between forbidding shadows at screen left and a bright window screen right.

In addition to such visual compositions, Sagan inserts a series of montages that provide a bridge between the fairly theatrical scenes involving the central characters and the documentary-style observations of schoolgirl behavior. The large cast of schoolgirls—all nonprofessional actresses—functions as an alternate discourse to set against the patriarchal regimentation. The students horse around, express homesickness, carry on multiple intrigues with each other, play jokes, dress and undress, and relate to each other in a tone that shifts between childishness and eroticism.[15] At one point, a locker room scene of bedtime activities is immediately followed by a montage which marshals the disorganized activities into a marching order of mouths in extreme close-up barking orders, feet hurrying to obey, identical lines of students filing past, and so on. The montage ends with a shift to the famous dormitory scene of Fräulein von Bernburg's goodnight kisses, a scene which is itself ambiguous in its resolution of eroticism with regimentation.

Most significant are the montage sequences which frame the encounters between Manuela and Fräulein von Bernburg, and indeed, frame our entire encounter with the film. The montage which opens the film communicates a view of the exterior towers of Potsdam; the old stone putti and statue which resembles a tiny soldier and the sounds of church bells and bugles portray an atmosphere of patriarchal readiness within which the school building itself is located. Traces of the same montage appear as narrative interruptions at key moments in the evolution of Manuela and Fräulein von Bernburg's relationship. For example, just after Manuela has thrown her arms around the teacher in the goodnight scene, Sagan inserts a rapid cut to the towers and statues. Later, when Fräulein von Bernburg gives the student her chemise, Sagan similarly terminates the scene with a cut to the stone towers and the sound of bells tolling. The montages appear to be cautionary, clues to the audience that emotions between women are never free of the shadow of patriarchal aggression. Their intrusion into the film is an antidote to viewing this all-female space as a "free zone" within a patriarchal society which can be seen to dominate not only in the concrete form of the staircase or Principal, but in the equally threatening form of external authority which waits just outside the school gates.

Even at the film's end when the two women and their student supporters seem most victorious, the ominous sound of the bugles reappears to accompany the Principal's retreat. While Siegfried Kracauer contends that the prominence of the motif at the end of the film proves that "the principle of authority has not been shaken" within the school,[16] I would suggest otherwise: the motif reminds the audience just how provisional the victory is, and just how powerful are the patriarchal forces with which any new order within the school must contend. It is a warning that separation from the dominant order does not automatically grant freedom from its dominance. It should have been a warning to lesbians then living in Germany that the time for strong collective action was upon them, as the forces of fascism gathered outside the windows. Instead, the Third Reich indeed came to power, and most of those responsible for *Maedchen in Uniform* left the country.

Who were they? Little has been written and little known about the women behind this work. Their sexuality has been as thoroughly veiled as the lesbian theme of the film itself. Rumors, anecdotes and bits of stories form the customary trail of unofficial history. Blanche Wiesen Cook is instructive regarding what *not* to look for. Commenting upon *Maedchen in Uniform*,

Ann Elisabet Weirach's *The Scorpion*, and other works of this period and genre, Cook warns against accepting the tragic tales of unrequited love and tragic abandonment as autobiographical fictions: "The truth is that these passionate little girls were not always abused and abandoned. They did not commit suicide. They wrote books about passionate little girls, death, and abandonment."[17] Not infrequently the lives of the authors and their models display a depth and breadth of options not readily visible in their constructed tales—when, that is, their lives are recoverable at all.

Leontine Sagan was born in Austria in 1889 and was married at some point to a doctor from Vienna. She trained as a stage director and actress and worked with such directors as Bernofskey and Max Reinhardt, teaching for a time at Reinhardt's drama school. As an actress, she appeared alongside Salka Viertel in an early production of the Ibsen play *John Gabriel Borkman*, and also in a rare production of Franz Blei's *The Wave*. The circumstances of her taking on the direction of *Maedchen in Uniform* are not now available, although she was certainly a popular figure in the Berlin theater scene. She left Germany soon after and went to England, where Alexander Korda sought to capitalize on her success by engaging her to direct *Men of Tomorrow*, a sort of "boys in uniform" film about Oxford; not surprisingly, the success was not repeated. Judging by the published script and cast list for a production of *Maedchen in Uniform*, Sagan also worked in theater in London. The play, retitled *Children in Uniform*, is listed as being "produced by Leontine Sagan" at The Duchess Theatre, London, opening October 7, 1932. Soon after, Sagan left England. She moved to the United States for several years and thence to South Africa, where she cofounded the National Theater. She died in 1974 in Johannesburg. As far as is known, she never made another film.

The two leading actresses of *Maedchen in Uniform*, Hertha Thiele and Dorothea Wieck, starred together in another film shortly afterward. Directed by Frank Wysbar in 1933, *Anna and Elisabeth* returned to the traditional view of intimate attachments between women as debilitating and demonic: Hertha Thiele played a young girl with miraculous powers who drove Dorothea Wieck to attempt suicide because Thiele failed to resurrect her husband! The women are portrayed as having an unnaturally close, almost supernatural, relationship; lesbianism is explicit only as the power of darkness. Both actresses are still alive today, and much additional material should be forthcoming from Karola Gramann, the *Frauen und Film* editor who has been interviewing Thiele.[18]

Christa Winsloe is the best remembered of the *Maedchen in Uniform* women, perhaps simply because her intimates wrote memoirs. Erika Mann, who herself played one of the schoolgirls in the film, remembered Winsloe (the Baroness von Hatvany) in her memoirs of 1939 in a fashion that would please Blanche Cook. Smiling and confident, dressed in white shirt and tie,

Christa Winsloe looks out at us from a photograph captioned "once a maedchen in uniform." Erika Mann recalls Christa's life as a "beautiful and amusing society woman" who ran an expensive household in Munich, and hosted salons in Budapest and Vienna as the wife of Baron Ludwig Hatvany, a Hungarian writer and "grand seigneur." She made animal sculptures and held exquisite dinner parties, at one of which Mann remembers her announcing her plan to write a play about her own childhood boarding-school experiences. Trying to explain the play's phenomenal success, Mann suggests:

> How was it?...Because Christa Hatvany had guarded in her heart, and now rediscovered, a simple, strong and genuine feeling, and because she could so express it that hundreds of thousands of people [sic] recognized the pain and ecstasy of their own childhood, their own first love, which had, in their own hearts, been overlaid, but never stifled. The poignant feeling of recognition...[19]

If Mann holds to the favorite view of lesbianism as a phase through which "hundreds of thousands" of women pass during adolescence, she at least manages to hold out a phrase of reservation regarding the impulse which is yet "never stifled."

Certainly it was never stifled in Christa. Nor in Dorothy Thompson, the U.S. journalist who was married to Sinclair Lewis when, in 1932, at her own ten-day Christmas party, she fell in love with Christa, who was then on the verge of getting a divorce from the Baron. Dorothy Thompson's diaries of the time reveal her struggle to name her experience, to try to understand how she can be "happily married, and yet wanting that curious tenderness. That pervading warm tenderness—there are no words for it..."[20] When the party guests had left, Dorothy followed Christa to Budapest. In March, the two met in Italy, where they shared a villa at Portofino for several months. Upon leaving the villa, Dorothy brought Christa back to the U.S. with her. In August, the two women traveled back to Austria together. When apart, they wrote constantly. In early 1934, Sinclair Lewis had to be out of town for several months and Dorothy stayed in New York with Christa. "They were a couple," said their friend John Farrar. "If you asked Dorothy for dinner, you asked Christa too."[21]

After two years, however, relations between the two began to break down, with Dorothy answering one of Christa's letters: "I feel that something between us has broken....I had a strange dream last night. I dreamed I was putting out into a very rough sea in a frail ship, and the crew were all women. I was afraid, and woke up, sweating...."[22] By this time, Thompson was persona non grata in Germany, having been expelled on her last trip by Adolph Hitler himself because of an uncomplimentary interview (and, no doubt, her habit of laughing at Bund rallies). Christa couldn't return to her home, so went instead in 1935 to live in southern France. Their continued intimacy was so strong that, in 1940, when the Nazi occupation of France made it impossible for Christa to withdraw money from her Munich bank, Dorothy began sending her money every month to live on.

Christa Winsloe's life had a sad end, but nothing at all like a Marks fairytale formula: she was murdered on June 10, 1944 by a common criminal named Lambert, who pretended to be operating as a member of the French resistance. His claim led to ugly speculation that Winsloe had been a Nazi spy and to an old friend's writing Dorothy Thompson at the end of the war (1946) to inform her of the death and beg help in clearing Christa Winsloe's name. The friend explained the rumors by Christa's liaison at the time with a French-Swiss girlfriend, Simone Gentet, who was alleged to be a spy:

> Christa once described her as a hysterical, dissolute morphine addict and alcoholic, but she certainly knew nothing of Simone's other activities, should the rumor be true . . . we know with such absolute certainty that Christa was the most violent enemy of National-Socialism and that she would never have made the slightest compromise. On the contrary, we were always worried that the Gestapo would grab her and we still believed this is what happened to her because she had helped many Jewish friends get out of the country.[23]

Thus, the author of *Maedchen in Uniform* was killed by a man claiming to be a resistance fighter but whom her friends believed to be a Gestapo agent, an ambiguity that lends to her death the same confusion that continues to surround the relationship between homosexuality and the Nazi era.

As an example of their conflation, Rossellini's *Rome, Open City* established an early tradition of identifying homosexuality with fascism through his narrative of hearty male resistance fighters betrayed by a lesbian morphine addict and her Gestapo lover. Bertolucci continued the tradition by consistently portraying fascists as suffering from sexual repressions or "perversions" in his films (with time out in *The Conformist* for a lesbian resistance fighter in the person of Dominique Sanda, although he did equip her with a male mentor and suggest that her attraction to women was her weakness). The connections have not depended upon cinema, either Italian or German, for promulgation. The stereotype of Nazi campiness, of SS regalia as s-&-m toys, of the Gestapo as a leather-boy thrill, of the big bull dyke as concentration camp boss, etc., all seem to have a firm hold in our culture's fantasy life and historical mythology—this despite the facts of the Third Reich's large-scale massacre of homosexuals as pollutants of Aryan blood and a stain on the future master race. Hitler apparently agreed with Manuela's boarding-school Principal in seeing homosexuality and lesbianism as "revolutionary." He did not hesitate to purge his own ranks, as on the infamous "night of the long knives" of June, 1934, when Ernst Röhm (the SA chief of staff and a well-known homosexual) and his followers were murdered to make the SA, as Hitler put it, "a pure and cleanly institution."

Why the Nazis wanted to eliminate homosexuals along with Jews, communists and various national minorities is a question that seems fairly well answered and understood now in the light of Nazi ideology and the "final solutions" it proposed for the united, fascistic, patriarchal Aryan race. Why gay men or any women should have joined the Nazi party at all is quite another question. What circumstances led to the existence of a Röhm? What sort of outlook could have lent credence to Christa Winsloe's murder as an act of Resistance, or alternately, as an act of Nazi vengeance? What sort of lesbian community inhabited Berlin during the Weimar Republic and the rise of the Third Reich? What sort of women's movement was there to combat the Nazi ideology of woman's place? What were social and legal attitudes toward homosexuality? Who liked *Maedchen in Uniform*, and why? To answer these questions fully lies outside the possibilities of this article, but to address them at least in part is crucial to our understanding of the film and to our recognizing just how exemplary was Leontine Sagan's combination of personal liberation and collective action.[24]

Germany had a radical women's movement in the early years of the century, beginning with the country's first large rally for women's suffrage in 1894. The movement for women's rights was part of a larger movement for overall reform known as the *Lebensreformbewegung* (the Life Reform Movement) which encompassed groups working on behalf of women and homosexuals as well as youth, natural health, clothing reform and nudity. There do not seem to have been lesbian political organizations as such, but many lesbians were active in women's suffrage and feminist groups (notably Anita Augspurg and Lida Gustava Heymann, who fought for suffrage and opposed World War I as "a men's war fought between men's states"), and many others worked with the Scientific-Humanitarian Committee founded by Magnus Hirschfeld (the key figure in homosexual rights struggles). As early as 1904, Anna Ruling had addressed the Committee at a meeting on the common struggles of women's and homosexuals' rights groups, complaining that women's organizations were "not lifting a finger...doing nothing, absolutely nothing" in support of homosexual emancipation.

In 1909, however, a bill was proposed to criminalize lesbianism, which up until then had not been subject to the Paragraph 175 laws against male homosexuality. Seeing the bill as a clear retaliation against the gains of the women's movement, Dr. Helene Stocker (who in 1905 had founded the League for the Protection of Maternity and Sexual Reform) spoke at a meeting held jointly with the Committee to support its petition drive against the proposed bill and to denounce the criminalization of lesbianism as "a grave error." The arguments on behalf of both women and homosexuality were diverse and at times contradictory, with variations in ideology so wide that some elements could be supportive of the new Russian Revolution as a model while other elements drifted into support of National Socialism.

Stocker's argument for keeping lesbianism legal rested on the defense of "individual freedom in the most private part of private life—love life"; Hirschfeld rested his arguments on scientific theories of human sexuality/ psychology and upon a human-rights-type plea for tolerance; certain other groups based their homosexuality upon theories of male supremacy and past models of soldiery and lovers-in-arms leading to an early Nazi identification; while other groups initially supportive of sexual freedoms for women, like those in the "sexual hygiene" movement, turned antiabortionist for racial reasons and ended up merging with the proto-Nazi "racial hygiene" groups.

Varying definitions of private and public life—and private versus public rights—are key to the differences. Hirschfeld, unlike many others, threw all his energies into effecting social education and legal changes (although with a tone of apology and tolerance-begging foreign to our styles today). The years of the Weimar Republic witnessed a flowering of women's rights and of struggles for homosexual emancipation, as well as a bursting forth of a large lesbian and gay subculture quartered largely in Berlin. And the sexual theories of the time are fascinating. In 1919, Hirschfeld opened the doors of his Institute of Sexual Science and won substantial support for the theory of "a third sex" that was neither male nor female: he called homosexuals "Uranians" and based much of his strategy upon this notion of a literally alien species.

The move to criminalize lesbianism had been dropped with the advent of the Republic and the end of World War I, which had seen women move so totally out of the former spheres as to make such a bill ineffective as a stay-at-home device. Therefore, much of Hirschfeld's Committee's efforts went toward the repeal of Paragraph 175 (prohibiting male homosexual practice). The Coalition for Reform of the Sexual Crimes Code (founded in 1925) worked to legalize acts between "consenting adults." The German Communist Party, following the lead established by revolutionary Soviet laws in support of homosexual rights, had a strong presence on the Reichstag committee for penal code reform—which succeeded in recommending for approval the repeal of Paragraph 175 (but unfortunately, its approval came on October 16, 1929, when the crash of the U.S. stock market changed the whole nature of the political scene in Germany, leading to the tabling of the resolution and the quick rise of the Nazi forces). As anti-Semitism, misogyny and homophobia grew alongside the move to the right in Germany, Hirschfeld became an ever more popular target. Attacked in 1920, his skull fractured in 1921, fired upon in 1923, attacked verbally by a Nazi delegate to the Reichstag in 1927, he had the dubious honor of seeing the library of his Institute become one of the first victims of book-burning on May 10, 1933, just four months after Hitler became chancellor.[25]

The cycle of free expression followed by total persecution experienced by Magnus Hirschfeld was symptomatic of the treatment of the larger gay population and culture he had come to symbolize. Jim Steakley provides a partial answer to the obvious reaction (how could such a thing happen?), pinpointing the Weimar contradiction "between personal and collective liberation"—a contradiction manifested in the simultaneous existence of a widespread social tolerance of homosexuality (including the flourishing of gay culture, the growth of bars, and de facto police acquiescence, at least in Berlin) alongside repressive laws and the frequent failure of most legal actions on behalf of lesbians or gay men.[26] The history of Berlin's gay male subculture is fairly well known today; according to Steakley, there were some forty gay bars and between one and two thousand prostitutes in the city by 1914, as well as perhaps thirty homosexual journals published during the course of the Weimar years. However, the same "invisibility" that granted lesbians immunity from the criminal laws has also granted the Weimar lesbians a less welcome immunity from the history books.

Recent research has begun to yield materials that can outline for us the contours of the lesbian community that was so lively during the same period, especially in the larger cities of Berlin and Munich. Louise Brooks (who starred as Lulu in G.W. Pabst's *Pandora's Box*, which offered a glimpse of Berlin's decadent ways) has reminisced about the mood of Berlin, recalling for example a lesbian bar, the Maly, where "there was a choice of feminine or collar-and-tie lesbians."[27] Alex de Jonge provides a more embroidered account in a male visitor's account of the Silhouette, which was "one of Berlin's most fashionable night spots." He, too, describes the scene of role-dressed couples on a night out, but makes an important point: "You could see women well known in German literature, society, the theater and politics. . . . There was no suggestion of vice about the place. It was a usual phenomenon in German life."[28] While the Silhouette admitted men if accompanied by a lesbian regular, other women's bars did not; de Jonge mentions Die Grotte and Entre Nous as two of the "more exclusive" places, about which he therefore can provide no information.

Ilse Kokula has provided one of the most complete accounts of the period in her brief but tantalizing summary, "The Uranian Ladies Often Meet in Patisseries."[29] She expands upon the meaning of "uranian" by tracing its root as an epithet of Aphrodite taken to mean "celestial" or spiritual, and she reiterates Hirschfeld's popular theory of "a third sex." The estimate of homosexuality in Weimar Berlin is placed at fifty thousand out of a population of two and a half million (although the methodology behind the statistics is not specified). While bars, hotels and saunas serviced gay men, there were also, more surprisingly, various services for lesbians seeking to meet each other. For example, there were *Vermittlungsbüros*, or agencies that fixed up single lesbians. There were personals columns in which lesbians advertised for partners. One such ad from the period listed the following: "Fräulein, decent, 24 years old, looking for pretty Fräulein as a girlfriend." There were also a number of social clubs for lesbians that met in cafes and *Konditoreien* (patisseries), such as one group of "Israelite" (Jewish) lesbians who met from 4:00 to 6:00 in the afternoon to talk and play chess. Balls were held regularly, run by and for lesbian women. There was a general attitude of self-recognition, with many lesbian couples eager to convince the world how well-adjusted they were and to combat the stereotypes of depravity and tragedy.

From 1918 on, lesbian journals were part of the culture, usually presenting a perspective that was part political and part educational; they had such titles as *Frauenliebe* (womanlove), *Ledige Frauen* (unmarried women), and *Die Freundin: Weekly Journal for Ideal Friendship Between Women*. *Die Freundin* was published continuously during 1923-32 by the *Damenklub* (women's club, or bar) "Violetta"—itself a coded name, as violets were considered a sign of lesbianism at the time. Some of Ilse Kokula's information is evidently derived from first-hand sources, as she is able to comment that many older lesbians still remember the cafes "with great pleasure," and that one such woman, Kati R., remembers that the secret lesbian balls continued into the 1950s and 60s, with as many as two hundred women attending. What emerges, then, is a picture of lesbian life as a widespread phenomenon, surprisingly aboveground and organized around its own publications, clubs and rituals. This is reflected in virtually none of the films or official histories of the time.

Despite such a spirit of freedom and such an ambience of lesbian permissiveness, at no point, either in its own time or in ours, has *Maedchen in Uniform* been critically (i.e., publicly) discussed as a lesbian text. And yet the histories specify its initial *succès de scandale*, implying an at least unofficial recognition of the film's true meaning. Why has this meaning been so hidden, so difficult to retrieve? The extent of the obstacles in the path of the gay historian seeking to reinterpret film texts has been emphasized recently by Vito Russo's uncovering of the original New York State censor's notes on the American release of *Maedchen in Uniform*.[30] Almost line for line, scene for scene, the shots and subtitles that I have specified as revolutionary and most fundamentally lesbian were the sections of the film that the censors wanted to cut. Initially condemned, the film was approved by the censors for release in August 1932 only after all evidence of lesbianism had been cut. Their notes were specific; for example, "Reel Four: Eliminate all views of Manuela's face as she looks at Miss Von Bernburg in the classroom." The censors at least understood the power of the superimpositions! But, in a cruel irony of manipulation, the contemporary critics reviewed the butchered film positively, using its now antiseptic contents to ridicule all who had been holding the film up as an example of "neuroticism. . . a celluloid *Well of Loneliness*."

Ever since, most critics have been eager to harness its tale of schoolgirl struggle to an assumed "universal" of humankind's fight against fascism, rather than some perverse championing of inverted emotions. With hindsight, however, we can equally read the film as a celebration of and warning for its most sympathetic audience: the lesbian population in Germany in 1931. Like Manuela and Fräulein von Bernburg, the lesbian community was proud and outspoken, romantic and idealistic, equally opposed to a bourgeois morality as well as to outdated models of woman's proper place. The schoolgirls may have been stand-ins for the lesbian women they could grow up to become (if they passed through Erica Mann's famous "phase" intact). If the boarding school was chosen as a literary and cinematic motif because it was more socially acceptable than the grown-up reality, then how ironic that it is all that remains for us. We need more research into our history. We need more information on films of the period that have been almost entirely forgotten, like *Anna and Elizabeth* or *Different from the Others*.[31] We need to heed carefully Blanche Cook's warning not to judge the authors entirely by their texts, lest literary conventions of the time blind us to the unexpected. We need to recognize *Maedchen in Uniform* not only as a beloved fairy tale but also as a powerful expression of its own time—an individual record of a collective aspiration.

Maedchen in Uniform has been extremely influential for other writers and films as well as for lesbian viewers down to the present day. Colette herself wrote the text for the subtitles of the French release print.[32] None other than Hollywood mogul Irving Thalberg was a fan of the film. He quizzed Salka Viertel, as she worked on the screenplay of *Queen Christina*, as to whether she'd seen Sagan's film. "Does not Christina's affection for her lady-in-waiting indicate something like that?" he asked, and urged her "to keep it in mind" because, "if handled with taste it would give us very interesting scenes."[33]

Stephen Spender came to New York in February of 1982 to speak about "Experiencing the Cinema In Berlin."[34] The film he most vividly remembered was *Maedchen in Uniform*, which he and Christopher Isherwood had gone to see during their 1931-32 residence in Berlin. Spender recalled that they had slipped away from some other event to see what he decribed as "the most remarkable film we'd ever seen," due in large measure to the "extraordinary impression" made upon them by Hertha Thiele; indeed, he went so far as to decribe the film as "full of extraordinary images based on this girl's face." Of special relevance to us is Spender's description of a Berlin caught up in a cinematic fever inspired by the Soviet films that showed two or three times a week. "Unlike futurist art," said Spender, the Soviet and progressive Weimar films "really did make you think they would change your life." With a certain nostalgia for a time *before* everyone became "suspicious about photography,"

Spender pinpointed the importance for him of *Maedchen in Uniform* and the progressive films with which he identified it: "The great thing about photography in this period was that it seemed an expression of freedom." It is only in today's historical considerations that this film and others like it have come to be graded on formal qualities disassociated from any political meaning. Spender's remarks are useful in reminding today's viewers (and scholars) that Sagan was working at a time when "the camera was linked to the idea of a revolution that was still possible."

Like Spender, we can acknowledge what Colette, Thalberg, Viertel and Garbo all seem to have known: that *Maedchen in Uniform* was a film about women's love for each other. And what Louise Brooks knew: that such love was no rarity in Weimar Berlin. And what Alex de Jonge knew: that it was no vice. And today we can also begin to consider what Jim Steakley knew: that there was a disturbing gap at the time between "personal" and "collective" liberation.

Maedchen in Uniform emerges from such a review of Weimar's lesbian subculture not any longer as an anomaly, but as a survivor. The film assumes a new importance when seen not as a curiosity but rather as a clue, an archaeological relic pointing back to an obliterated people and pointing ahead, for us, to a much-needed perspective on our current situation.

The first lesson of *Maedchen in Uniform* is that lesbianism has a much larger and finer history than we often suspect, that the film indicates as much, and that we need to do more work on reconstructing the image of lesbian culture that has been so painfully erased. The second lesson is that in looking backward and inward we cannot afford to stop looking forward and outward. The bells and bugles that sound periodically throughout the film, casting a prophetic pall upon the love of Manuela and Fräulein von Bernburg, are waiting just outside the gates for us as well. As I have suggested, the ending of the film can be interpreted as a warning to heed the forces mounting outside our narrow zones of victory and liberation. Such an interpretation, if it was perceived at the time, went unheeded by the film's lesbian audience in 1931. Today, the work in building a lesbian culture cannot afford to ignore the context of such labor in a society veering so strongly in the opposite direction.

Today, we must begin to consider the contemporary gap between "personal" (or lifestyle) freedoms and "collective" (or legal political) rights. We must begin to examine what the links and coalitions are, in our own time, between lesbian, gay male, and feminist organizations. We must learn strategy and remember that when the pre-Weimar misogynist, F. Eberhard, wanted to attack the women's movement, he accused the emancipated women of being lesbians and, therefore, depraved. The women's groups of the late Weimar period exhibited a distressing willingness to take such attacks to heart and try to accommodate themselves accordingly. Polite cooptation sapped the strength of the groups. Too late, many lesbians must have learned that patisseries do not grant asylum.

Struggle was postponed to a fatally late date due to false perceptions of homosexuality as a "private" issue that was being adequately handled and of lesbians/gay men as somehow more protected than others because of the history of social tolerance. The celebrants of the staircase must listen hard to the rallying cries outside the school and take heed. Today, we can not afford to ignore history, nor to repeat it. While lesbianism and feminism are certainly "revolutionary" (to quote the Principal yet again), the history of Weimar politics demonstrates that they are not *inherently* so unless linked to a pragmatic political strategy and set of principles. In the 80s our struggles for sexual freedom and gender flexibility must be integrated with the ongoing fights against economic injustices, racism, growing militarism, and all such forces that have an impact on every individual in our society. We have to do better.

NOTES

1. Jonathan Katz, *Gay American History* (New York: Avon Books, 1976), p. 843. Acknowledgement is due here to two people who contributed the very heart of this article: Karola Gramann, who has written me extensively from Frankfurt and shared her own knowledge and research on *Maedchen in Uniform*; and Bill Horrigan, who brought numerous sources to my attention and even located copies of rare materials like the original playbill and published play script—his materials improved my work immeasurably. In addition, I owe thanks to Ramona Curry, who provided encouragement and translations, and to Rennie Harrigan, who offered background information and suggested avenues of research. The section of this article which deals with specific textual analysis of the film was originally presented as a paper at the 4th Annual Purdue Film Conference, March 1979, on a panel devoted to early German cinema. Thanks to Jim Franklin for his encouragement at that time. This article was first published in *Jump Cut*, no. 24/25 (March 1981), pp. 44-50, as part of a special section on Lesbians & Film; without the context and spirit of that special section and my co-editors on it, this article could not have been written. A shorter version was published in *Radical America*, vol. 15, no. 6 (1982).

2. Lotte H. Eisner, *The Haunted Screen* (Berkeley, CA: University of California Press, 1969), p. 326.

3. Siegfried Kracauer, *From Caligari to Hitler* (Princeton, NJ: Princeton University Press, 1947), p. 227.

4. Alex de Jonge, *The Weimar Chronicle: Prelude to Hitler* (London: Paddington Press, 1978), p. 138.

5. Gayle Rubin, "The Traffic in Women: Notes On the 'Political Economy' of Sex," in *Toward An Anthropology of Women*, ed. Rayna R. Reiter (New York: Monthly Review Press, 1975), p. 180.

6. The comparison with *Persona* is pointed out by Nancy Scholar as well, in an article which marks the 70s revival of the film. See her *"Maedchen in Uniform,"* in *Sexual Stratagems: The World of Women in Film*, ed. Patricia Erens (New York: Horizon Press, 1979), pp. 219-223.

7. It should be noted that *Don Carlos* appears to be yet another innovation of the film, as opposed to a borrowing from the play. In the published play script of *Girls in Uniform*, the production (which takes place entirely off-stage) is described as a light French drama of courtly love with Manuela featured as a knight in armor. Apart from the clearly delineated statements on forbidden love that I outline in the text, the choice of *Don Carlos* also serves to throw into relief the differing consequences for the outlaw lovers of both periods. In the Schiller drama, death by *auto-da-fé* awaited heretics of the reigning order. By the time of *Maedchen*, however, the lover marked by the heresy of lesbianism already faced a modern narrative expectation: in the absence of a functioning Inquisition, she is expected to perform her own execution via suicide. The quotation recited by Manuela about death as the payment for Paradise thus accrues additional meaning.

8. For a fuller discussion of this issue, see my article on "The Crisis Of Naming in Feminist Film Criticism," *Jump Cut*, no. 19 (December 1978) and a considerably revised verison, "In The Name Of Feminist Film Criticism," *Heresies* 9 (Spring 1980).

9. Variations on the theme of a double ending have been repeated by a number of critics, including Nancy Scholar and Sharon Smith in *Women Who Make Movies* (New York: Hopkinson and Blake, 1975); Caroline Sheldon in "Lesbians and Film: Some Thoughts" (in *Gays and Film*, ed. Richard Dyer [London: British Film Institute, 1977]); and Parker Tyler in *Screening the Sexes* (New York: Holt, Rinehart and Winston, 1972). While American and English critics display a striking unanimity on this point, the German critics of the period of the film's release make no such acknowledgement. Both Eisner and Kracauer specify the averted suicide at the end of the film they are discussing, while neither makes reference to any such "home market" alternate ending. In private correspondence, Karola Gramann wrote me that she was unable to find anyone in Germany who had seen the alleged suicide ending. However, in a recent interview with the still-lively Hertha Thiele (living in East Berlin and still active in theater), Gramann discovered that a suicide ending was indeed filmed—but never included in the final film, for the reason that the scene was too pathetic-looking to the filmmakers. As best as can be determined, no one in Germany ever saw the film with such an ending.

10. Rubin, p. 183.

11. Quotations and data are derived from personal copies of the original playbill, Blackstone Theatre, Chicago, "beginning Sunday Night, March 11, 1934," and the published play: Christa Winsloe, *Girls in Uniform: A Play in Three Acts* (Boston, MA: Little, Brown & Co., 1933).

12. Elaine Marks, "Lesbian Intertextuality," in *Homosexualities and French Literature*, ed. George Stambolian and Elaine Marks (Ithaca, NY: Cornell University Press, 1979), pp. 357-358.

13. Ibid, p. 357.

14. I refer here to Leontine Sagan alone, but that is inaccurate. Carl Froelich is listed as "supervisor," but other sources of the period make claims for co-director or even director status for Froelich, although there is no firm evidence to support such a claim. It should be noted that Froelich stayed in Germany after Hitler's ascendancy and directed films that met the standards of the Third Reich. In addition, there is a fascinating detail for speculation. According to Erwin Leiser's *Nazi Cinema* (New York: Macmillan Co., 1974), Carl Froelich directed a film about Frederick the Great, *The Hymn of Leuthen*, which showed for the first time on February 3, 1933, four days after Hitler became Chancellor of the Reich—suggesting that the intelligence that created *Maedchen* must have belonged to Sagan and not to Froelich. Given the analogy of the Principal to the Frederick stereotype, however, the progression is fascinating. It has been said (by none other than the Reich actor Emil Jannings) that an historical line may be drawn "from Frederick the Great to Bismarck to Hitler." Given that, here is the fascinating detail: a 1942 film on Frederick (Veit Harlan's *The Great King*) detailed the episode of the Prussian king's defeat at Kunersdorf in 1759 and in particular shows the disdain that Frederick manifested for one regiment which "preferred life to victory" and had not thrown itself into suicidal combat. Stripped of stripes and insignia for this action, the regiment's colonel commits suicide. The name of the colonel and his regiment? Bernburg. Such a detail makes one wonder what Froelich's contribution could have been, as Sagan seems so clearly to have had her way thematically.

15. At one point, in the first locker room scene, the model of heterosexuality comes under discussion and, obliquely, attack. There is a photo of a male actor in Ilse's locker, a male pinup some girls are giggling over, and finally, highlighted, an illustration in Manuela's book that depicts a woman being rapaciously carried off by a swashbuckling man on horseback—a rather dark statement on the power principles of heterosexual fantasy and reality.

16. Kracauer, p. 229.

17. Blanche Wiesen Cook, " 'Women Alone Stir My Imagination': Lesbianism and the Cultural Tradition," *Signs*, vol. 4, no. 4 (1979), p. 722.

18. Information on *Anna and Elizabeth* is taken from David Stewart Hull, *Film in the Third Reich* (Berkeley, CA: University of California Press, 1969), pp. 37-38, and also from private correspondence with Karola Gramann.

19. Erika and Klaus Mann, *Escape to Life* (Boston, MA: Houghton Mifflin Co., 1939), pp. 50-51.

20. Katz, p. 841.

21. Marion K. Sanders, *Dorothy Thompson: A Legend in Her Time* (Boston, MA: Houghton Mifflin Co., 1973), p. 190.

22. Ibid., p. 193.

23. Ibid.

24. The three basic texts to consult on issues of feminism and homosexuality in Weimar Germany are: Richard Evans, *The Feminist Movement in Germany 1894-1933* (Beverly Hills, CA: Sage Publications, 1976); Lillian Faderman and Brigitte Eriksson, *Lesbian-Feminism in Turn-of-the-Century Germany* (Tallahassee, FL: Naiad Press, 1979); and James D. Steakley, *The Homosexual Emancipation Movement in Germany* (New York: Arno Press, 1975). Relevant information in this article is culled almost entirely from these sources. For a superior review and perspective piece, see Carol Anne Douglas, "German Feminists and the Right: Can It Happen Here?" in *off our backs*, vol. 10, no. 11 (December 1980). She discusses at length the political crosscurrents I have barely managed to summarize here.

25. Interestingly enough, Hirschfeld appeared in a film he must have taken a part in producing. *Different From the Others* (directed by Richard Oswald in 1919) starred Conrad Veidt as a homosexual blackmail victim who is "saved" by the intervention of a philanthropic doctor played by Hirschfeld himself. It was widely banned, but evidently more for reasons of anti-Semitism (directed against Hirschfeld) than homophobia, if such a distinction can indeed be made. The film was remade in 1927 as *Laws of Love*, again starring Veidt, but minus Hirschfeld, whose absence in this version led to Veidt's character's suicide.

26. Steakley, pp. 78-79.

27. Louise Brooks, "On Making Pabst's *Lulu*," in *Women and the Cinema*, ed. Karyn Kay and Gerald Peary (New York: E.P. Dutton, 1977), p. 81.

28. de Jonge, p. 140.

29. Ilse Kokula, "Die urnischen Damen treffen sich vielfach in Konditoreien," *Courage*, no. 7 (Berlin: July 1980); copy courtesy of Karola Gramann.

30. Vito Russo, *The Celluloid Closet: Homosexuality in the Movies* (New York: Harper and Row/Colophon Books, 1981), pp. 56-59. Russo's book came out after this article's initial publishing. It is an important work, beautifully researched and filled with primary data, but unfortunately marred by a bitchy misogyny. Nevertheless, the photograph of a very butch Dorothy Arzner arm-in-arm with Joan Crawford on the 1937 set of *The Bride Wore Red* is itself worth the price of the book.

31. See note 25. A print of *Different From the Others* survives in an East German archive. A print of *Anna and Elizabeth* survives in an archive at Koblenz. A special form of *Different From the Others* was made for screenings in Montreal and New York City in 1982; *Anna and Elizabeth* has yet to be seen here.

32. The French subtitles and a preface explaining Colette's role in writing them can be found in *Colette au cinéma*, ed. Alain and Odette Virmaux (Paris: Librairie Ernest Flammarion, 1975). Unfortunately, the entire *Maedchen in Uniform* section has been omitted from the English-language edition (trans. Sarah W.R. Smith [New York: Frederick Ungar, 1980]).

33. Salka Viertel, *The Kindness of Strangers* (New York: Holt, Rinehart and Winston, 1969), p. 175. Viertel's memoirs are discreetly restrained on virtually all topics of sexuality and therefore shed no light on the nature of her relationship with Greta Garbo. Viertel wrote the screen treatments for Garbo's films and was her frequent companion. In his dirt-digging *Hollywood Babylon* (San Francisco, CA: Straight Arrow Books, 1975), Kenneth Anger wrote that: "Garbo's genuine reserve held the gossips at bay for the most part. There was, however, occasional speculation about how close her friendship really was with writer Salka Viertel." (p. 172.)

34. The event was the International Center of Photography's symposium, "Avant-Garde German Photography: 1919-1939," held at the Guggenheim Museum. Quotations are based on notes.

(*Maedchen in Uniform* is available through Films Incorporated, 733 Green Bay Road, Wilmette, Illinois 60091, as well as through Films Incorporated offices in New York, Hollywood and Atlanta.)

Dis-Embodying the Female Voice

Kaja Silverman

It is by now axiomatic that the female subject is the object rather than the subject of the gaze in mainstream narrative cinema. She is excluded from authoritative vision not only at the level of the enunciation, but at that of the fiction. At the same time she functions as an organizing spectacle, as the lack which structures the symbolic order and sustains the relay of male glances.[1]

It is equally axiomatic that the female subject as she has been constructed by Hollywood cinema is denied any active role in discourse. The mechanisms of that exclusion are much more complex than those which deny her access to authoritative vision, though, and they warrant a very careful formulation.

Like the male subject, the female subject emerges only within discourse; she knows herself from the place of language, and once inside the symbolic order she has no more access to her biological real than does her masculine counterpart. Both are spoken by discourses and desires which exceed them. However, whereas the male subject has privileges conferred upon him by his relationship to discourse, the female subject is defined as insufficient through hers.

A corollary of this very important difference (and it is at this level that sexual difference must be conceptualized) is that the male subject is granted access to what Foucault calls "discursive fellowships," is permitted to participate in the unfolding of discourse.[2] In other words, he is allowed to occupy the position of the speaking subject—in fiction, and even to some degree in fact. Within dominant narrative cinema the male subject enjoys not only specular but linguistic authority.

The female subject, on the contrary, is associated with unreliable, thwarted, or acquiescent speech. She talks a great deal; it would be a serious mistake to characterize her as silent, since it is in large part through her prattle, her bitchiness, her sweet murmurings, her maternal admonitions and her verbal cunning that we know her. But her linguistic status is analogous to that of a recorded tape, which endlessly plays back what was spoken in some anterior moment, and from a radically external vantage. The participation of the male subject in the production of discourse may be limited, and contingent upon his "willingness" to identify with the existing cultural order, but the participation of the female subject in the production of discourse is nonexistent.[3]

Classical cinema projects these differences at the formal as well as the thematic level. Not only does the male subject occupy positions of authority within the diegesis, but occasionally he also speaks extra-diegetically, from the privileged place of the Other. The female subject, on the contrary, is excluded from positions of discursive authority both inside and outside the diegesis; she is confined not only to safe places *within* the story (to positions, that is, which come within the eventual range of male vision or audition), but to the safe place *of* the story.[4] Synchronization provides the means of that confinement.

> *Prisoner of a sensible appearance, doubly mastered by the camera lens and the gaze of the spectator, the [female] voice is subject to the most rapid of critiques, that of the eye.*
>
> **—Pascal Bonitzer**[5]

Synchronization functions as a virtual imperative within fiction film. Although the male voice is occasionally permitted to transcend that imperative altogether, and the female voice is from time to time allowed a qualified respite from its rigors, it organizes all sound/image relationships. It is the norm to which those relationships either adhere, or from which they deviate. Since within dominant cinema the image track is cut to the measure of the human form, and the sound track to the measure of the human voice, the rule of synchronization must be understood as referring above all to the smooth alignment of the human form with the human voice—i.e., to the representation of a homogeneous thinking subject whose exteriority is congruent with its interiority. The "marriage" of sound and image is thus performed in the name of homo-centricity, and under Cartesian auspices.

However, the union is less harmonious than it seems. It is based not so much on mutual respect as on mutual antagonism: body and voice are played off against each other in a way calculated narrowly to circumscribe their signifying potential. Both Heath and Bettetini speak of the voice as a device for mastering the body ("Everything that the image shows of its own accord becomes specifically indicated by the words that accompany it and restrict its sense to one or more meanings"),[6] while Bonitzer describes the body as a mechanism for restraining the voice—for diminishing "its resonance, its amplitude, its tendency to stray, its power and its restlessness."[7] Synchronization plays a major part in the production not only of a homo-centric but an ideologically consistent cinema; by insisting that the body be read through the voice, and the voice through the body, it drastically curtails the capacity of each for introducing into the narrative something heterogeneous or disruptive (it minimizes, that is, the number and kinds of connotations which can be activated).

Like the shot/reverse shot and other elements within the system of suture, synchronization helps to stitch together the fabric of the fiction over the apparatus.[8] It asserts the primacy of the diegetic over the extra-diegetic, creating the illusion that speech arises spontaneously from bodies, and that narrative proceeds from the desires and movements of self-present actants. The promptness with which sounds follow images—their seeming simultaneity—makes the former seem immanent within the latter, rather than the product of a complex enunciation. Script, dialogue coach, the voices of the actors, sound engineer, recording and mixing equipment all fade into oblivion before the impression of "direct" speech.

By deepening the diegesis and concealing the apparatus, synchronization also maintains the viewing/listening subject in a protective darkness and silence. Metz has discussed at length the connections between voyeurism and film viewing ("the obscurity surrounding the onlooker, the aperture of the screen with its inevitable keyhole effect...the spectator's solitude...the segregation of spaces").[9] However, not only does the moviegoer see without being seen; he or she listens without being heard. As Mary Ann Doane observes, "in the fiction film, the use of synchronous dialogue and the voice-off presuppose a spectator who overhears and, overhearing, is unheard and unseen himself."[10] (The synchronic instance is here, as elsewhere, to be distinguished from the voice-over, which not only assumes a listener, but addresses the listener directly, over the "heads" of the characters.)

What has not yet been remarked is that the rule of synchronization is imposed much more strictly on the female than on the male voice within dominant cinema. Although the latter, like the former, is largely limited to diegetic appearances (i.e., to speaking parts which remain "inside" the narrative, even when they are "outside" the frame), and although most of these appearances take the form of synchronous dialogue, it does on occasion manifest itself in both dis-embodied and extra-diegetic ways. In other words, from time to time the male voice speaks from an anonymous and transcendental vantage, "over" the narrative.

Apart from the documentary, where it is almost an institution, the dis-embodied male voice-over occurs most frequently in police thrillers and prison dramas of the "B" variety. The foregrounding of criminality in these films, as well as their rather low production values, would seem to necessitate a kind of "voice on high," whose superior knowledge and diegetic detachment promise eventual justice, despite the vitality of the robbers, the impotence of the cops, and the sleaziness of the *mise-en-scène*. As Bonitzer observes, this voice is a pure distillate of the law; not only does it "forbid questions about its enunciation, its place and its time," but it speaks with an unqualified authority:

> ... the voice-over represents a power, that of disposing of the image and of that which it reflects from a place which is absolutely other. Absolutely other and absolutely indeterminable. In this sense, transcendent. . . . In so far as it arises from the field of the Other, the voice-off is assumed to know: such is the essence of its power.[11]

The capacity of the male subject to be cinematically represented in this disembodied form aligns him with transcendence, authoritative knowledge, potency and the law—in short, with the symbolic father. Since these are the qualities to which he most aspires at the narrative level, but which he never altogether approximates, we could say that the male subject finds his most ideal realization when he is heard but not seen; when the body (what Lacan would call the "pound of flesh" which must be mortgaged in man's relationship to the signifier)[12] drops away, leaving the phallus in unchallenged possession of the scene. Thus, despite its rather rare occurrence in the fiction film, the dis-embodied voice-over can be seen as "exemplary" for male subjectivity, attesting to an achieved invisibility, omniscience and discursive power.

It would be schematically gratifying to say that the female subject finds *her* most ideal representation when she is seen but not heard. However, as I indicated above, the female voice plays an important part in classical cinema, serving as the means by which she is established as occupying the positions of mother, siren, patient, innocent, etc. Mark Rutland, for instance, does not attempt to silence Marnie in the film of the same title; on the contrary, he extorts speech from her, using it first as a tool of diagnosis, and then as a device for inserting her into a more orthodox subject-position. The female voice serves a similar function in *Snake Pit* and *A Woman's Face*. The first of these, which dramatizes the rehabilitation of a female inmate in a mental institution, contains the memorable line: "Oh, you've talked—you're going to get well now, I know you will." The second, which is structured around a courtroom scene in which a woman is on trial for murder, concludes happily when that woman speaks the desires which she has previously escaped ("I've always wanted to get married...I want a home and children, to go to the market and cheat the butcher...I want to belong to the human race").

Lola Montes, most writerly of "woman's films," suggests that it would be more correct to say that ideally the female subject is both *over-seen* and *over-heard*, and that as a consequence of this system of double surveillance she is spoken even when she seems to be in control of her own speech. Lola pays for her notorious past, in which she exercised power rather than submitting to it, by playing not only to the eye but to the ear of an all-male circus audience. The story which she tells "in her own inimitable words" belongs to Mammoth Circus, "copyright reserved"; when she forgets her lines the ringmaster prompts her, bending her voice to the contours of the confession he has scripted for her. He even determines which of the audience's questions she is to answer. Lola is the prototype of the female subject within dominant narrative film, an extension both of male vision and male discourse.

Both constituents of the surveillance system—visual and auditory—must be in effect in order for it to be successful. To permit the female subject to be seen without being heard would be to activate the hermeneutic and cultural codes which define woman as a "dark continent," inaccessible to definitive male interpretation. To allow her to be heard without being seen would be even more dangerous, since it would disrupt the specular regime upon which mainstream cinema relies; it would put her beyond the control of the male gaze, and release her voice from the signifying obligations which that gaze sustains. It would be to open the possibility of woman participating in a phallic discourse, and so escaping the interrogation about her place, her time and her desires which constantly re-secures her. (See Teresa de Lauretis' article on *Bad Timing* in this volume.) Indeed, to dis-embody the female subject in this way would be to challenge every conception by means of which we have previously known her, since it is precisely *as body* that she is constructed.

If, as I proposed a moment ago, male subjectivity is most fully realized when it is most invisible—when it approaches a kind of theological threshold—female subjectivity is most fully achieved when it is most visible. Through a kind of paradox, the male subject, with his "strikingly visible" organ, is defined primarily in terms of abstract and immaterial qualities (potency, power, knowledge, etc.) whereas the female subject, whose organ does not appeal to the gaze, becomes almost synonymous with the corporeal and the specular.

It is of course precisely what is invisible to a symbolic order which is organized around the phallus—that which the symbolic order can only perceive as an absence or lack—which threatens to escape its structuration, and to return as heterogeneity or a foreclosed real. Hence the fascination with the female body, the concern to construct it in ways which are accessible to the gaze and to hear it attest in a familiar language to dominant values.

Thus (with the exception of music) there are no instances within mainstream cinema where the female voice is not matched up in some way, even if only retrospectively, with the female body. For the most part woman's speech is synchronized with her image, and even when it is transmitted as a voice-off the divorce is only temporary; the body connected to the female voice is understood to be in the next room, just out of frame, at the other end of a telephone line. In short, it is always fully recoverable.

The female voice almost never functions as a voice-over, and when it does it enjoys a comparable status to the male voice-over in film noir—i.e., it is autobiographical, evoking in a reminiscent fashion the diegesis which constitutes the film's "present," a diegesis within which the speaker figures centrally. Lisa's narration in *Letter From an Unknown Woman*, which provides one of the most extended voice-overs in classical cinema, is a case in point. Not only is it at every point anchored to a specific female body, but the temporal interval which separates it from that body constantly diminishes as the film unfolds. Moreover, Lisa speaks to a male auditor (Stephan) whose willingness to read her letter activates its discourse. In a sense what we *hear* is what he *overhears*; her voice is his mental construction. (In the same way, what we see is what he imagines, as the final, montage flashback makes clear.) Lisa's narration is obedient to Stephan's desires, to his ear.

Not surprisingly, feminist cinema has focused an enormous amount of attention on the female voice. Three examples from New German Cinema suggest that this is true not only of experimental work, but also of documentary and even more conventionally narrative films. Helga Reidemeister's documentary, *Apropos of Fate*, is in large part the deployment of cinema by the female members of a family for the express purpose of talking through their relationships to each other, men, work and the social order. The director participates in this conversation, but her dis-embodied status—the fact that she remains "pure" voice—indicates the irreducible distance which separates her, both as an effect of the apparatus and as someone external to the family, from the pro-filmic event. Helke Sander's *All-Round Reduced Personality* utilizes an anonymous female voice-over to situate the work and personal problems of a woman photographer (Etta) within the context of West Berlin politics and culture, a device which emphasizes the general fragmentation to which the central character is subjected (since that voice remains so close to Etta, we are encouraged to think of it as something of her own from which she has become alienated).

Jutta Bruckner introduces *Hunger Years* with an autobiographical voice-over which enjoys an unusual relationship with the image track: the film's narrative concludes with the apparent suicide of its female protagonist, a suicide prompted by her inability either to tolerate or to break with the maternal legacy—with the legacy, that is, of classical female subjectivity forcibly bequeathed to her by her mother. However, both the profound pessimism of the larger text and the finality of the act of self-destruction with which it concludes, are qualified by the introductory voice-over, which speaks about survival, transformation, escape. That voice converts the images of a highly ritualized suicide into metaphors of rupture and change—in short, it de-literalizes them.

It is in feminist avant-garde practice, though, that the female voice has been most exhaustively interrogated and most innovatively deployed. A statement by Laura Mulvey in an interview about *Riddles of the Sphinx* can be taken as an epigraph to this practice:

> . . . there is an important theme: the difficulties of women being articulate and putting emotion or thought into words. In *Riddles*, I think, I felt the time had come not to deal with that kind of silence which so many in the women's movement had felt and talked about, a kind of cultural silence essentially. Having taken that as a fact, one had to go ahead and try to fill in the gaps and think of what ways one would give voice to female desires.[13]

However, whereas *Riddles of the Sphinx* attempts to exhume a female voice which has been repressed by patriarchy, but which has nevertheless remained intact for thousands of years at some unconscious level, the films about which I would like to talk for the remainder of this essay function more as a series of responses to cultural "givens" about female subjectivity. In other words, rather than searching for a pre-symbolic female language, they confine themselves to an examination of the place of the female voice within the existing discursive field.

In each case that examination involves the dislocation of the sound from the image track. Indeed, all of these films—*Misconception, Film About a Woman Who, Dora, News From Home, Empty Suitcases* and *Journeys From Berlin/71*—resort in one way or another to the principle of non-synchronization, devising various strategies for divorcing the female voice from the female body. *Journeys From Berlin/71* makes clearer than any of the other films precisely what is at stake in this disassociation of sound and image: the freeing-up of the female voice from its obsessive and indeed exclusive reference to the female body, a reference which turns woman—in representation and in fact—back upon herself, in a negative and finally self-consuming narcissism.

Perhaps the simplest strategy for challenging the imperative of synchronization, especially insofar as it provides the support for sexual difference, is the alignment of the female voice with a male body, or that of a male voice with a female body. This is the strategy employed by Marjorie Keller at a key moment of *Misconception*, a film which is devoted to the exploration of the three-way relationship between the male voice, the female voice and the female body.

Misconception, which records the birth of the filmmaker's niece, uses heavily edited documentary footage to dispel the myth that childbirth is not only painless but a kind of *jouissance*. Shots from the delivery room are intercut with both interior and exterior shots of the wife, the husband and their son taken at an earlier moment in the pregnancy. The sounds from one context are often connected with the images from the other, but no extra-diegetic information is introduced.

The film's complex ironies are produced primarily through the juxtaposition of the mother's voice and image with the voices of the husband and doctor. Indeed, the pregnant woman's voice is edited more at the level of the documentary "fiction" than at that of the enunciation, by the verbal pressure of those two men. She is encouraged to emit only those sounds—linguistic and pre-linguistic—which belong to the sanctioned discourse of motherhood. The cries of childbirth enjoy a particularly prominent place here, as does a telephone conversation immediately after delivery in which the mother expresses her pleasure that "it's a girl." Contradictory statements are usually interrupted or corrected. When she confesses, for instance, that if she had it to do over again, she wouldn't have become a mother, her husband firmly responds that she is forgetting the "joys" of her position.

The chief expositor of these joys is the doctor, who, after the successful delivery of the second child, speaks almost orphically about the agents of childbirth:

> Those who feel they've done perfectly, they'll feel godlike. They might feel actual ecstasy and look back on it as having transcended. If they are critical the worst that happens is that they recognize they are human beings, that they feel pain, may react other than perfectly, in their own eyes that is, to pain.

But the image track belies this mystical interpretation of childbirth, showing us blood, tissue, the umbilical cord, the afterbirth: signifiers of suffering and toil. It also dramatizes the failure of the spectatorial paradigm by means of which the doctor defines motherhood—a paradigm which demands of the female subject that she "look" at her body and its response to labor in order to determine whether or not she is "perfect."

The failure of that paradigm is anticipated earlier in the film, when the voice of the pregnant woman takes exception to an article in *Esquire* addressed to the topic of childbirth: "I think there is a lot of difference between men's view of having a baby and a woman's. . . . A woman's view is that I just want to make it as easy as possible. . . and a man's view is that it shouldn't hurt to begin with." Non-synchronization thus occurs within the diegetic as well as the extra-diegetic discourse; not only do the images in the delivery room not correspond to the doctor's voice-off, but the female subject refuses to look at herself from the place which is prescribed for her, insisting instead on the disequivalence between her own self-image and that projected for her by the discourse of motherhood.

In an interview with the *Camera Obscura* Collective, Yvonne Rainer suggests that one of the central projects of *Film About a Woman Who* is the establishment of a dialectical relationship between sound and image, the replacement of synchronization with counterpoint:

> ...I was...concerned with interweaving psychological and formal content, i.e. with images being 'filled up' or 'emptied' by readings or their absence, with text and speech being 'illustrated' to varying degrees by images. This made for a situation where the story came and went, sometimes disappearing altogether as in the extreme prolongation of certain soundless images....I was trying to make a silent film—with occasional sound.[14]

These remarks are indicative not so much of an impulse to privilege image over sound as the desire to interrupt their conventional and mutually impoverishing marriage, to establish different lines of communication between them. The female subject is seen as having a particular stake in the reconceptualization of the relationship between cinema's two tracks.

Film About a Woman Who resorts to a number of devices for dislodging the female voice from the female image. One of these devices, which is taken even further in *Kristina Talking Pictures*, is the delineation of more than one female body to which story and speech can be "pinned." The automatic signifying transfer from a particular female voice to a particular female image is thus frustrated; the semic code is rendered inoperative by the absence of a proper name, a stable visual representation, and a predictable cluster of attributes.

The film's reliance upon voice-over and intertitles further denaturalizes the female voice, also contributing to the jamming of the semic code. The episode entitled "Emotional Accretion in 48 Steps" utilizes both of these strategies, as well as periods of complete silence. It also makes startlingly evident what is at issue for woman in the avoidance of synchronized sound.

In this episode a man and a woman lie in bed together, sometimes turning towards each other and sometimes away. Each movement or gesture is separated by a number introducing a new "step," some of which include intertitles and others of which do not. The intertitles narrate rather than offering direct dialogue, substituting the pronouns "he" and "she" for "you" and "I."

The intrusion of a fragmented but nonetheless intensely psychological narrative into a cinematic system which provides none of the usual supports for viewer identification results in a good deal of free-floating anxiety. The woman who tosses and turns on the bed, and who is described as first wanting to tell the man to go and then deciding to demand his attention, seems to be constrained by a discourse (the discourse of the "affair") within which she is not entirely comfortable, and to which moreover she does not entirely accede. The use of the pronoun "she," and of an indirect rather than a direct construction, indicates her unwillingness fully to activate her own subjectivity within that discourse, an event which, as Benveniste tells us, requires the articulation of the first-person pronoun.[15]

The climactic moment in this episode involves precisely such an articulation. In the only use of synchronized sound in any of the 48 steps, the woman asks: "Would you hold me?" The contradiction between the discourse to which she here accedes and her own desires is indicated in steps 43 through 48, where we read:

> She arrives home. She is very angry. She knows the crucial moment was when she said "hold me." Somehow she had betrayed herself. She hadn't wanted to be held. (Do you think she could figure her way out of a paper bag?) She had wanted to bash his fucking face in.[16]

The convergence of synchronization and the first-person pronoun ("me") is highly significant, emphasizing the part played by the former in the production of a coherent, stable and "manageable" subject. *Film About a Woman Who* shows the alignment of image and sound to be an agency of entrapment, one of the means by which the female subject emerges within a discourse contrary to her desires, submits at least temporarily to a fixed identity.

Weinstock, Pajaczkowska, Tyndall and McCall's film, *Sigmund Freud's Dora*, does not at any juncture actually disengage the female voice from the female image. Indeed, it employs synchronized sound throughout. However, by overtly and literally appropriating the text of Freud's case study, and by introducing footage from "adult" movies and television advertisements, it creates a space between its female voices and the words they speak, a space which shows those words to proceed from a source external to them. In short, the film foregrounds a number of discourses by means of which female subjectivity is presently constituted.

It also suggests—and this may be its most important contribution—that the female voice plays a vital (albeit passive) role in at least two of these discourses: psychoanalysis and advertising. It indicates, that is, that these two discourses require a female subject who speaks about herself in rigorously codified ways, who implicates her body at every turn of phrase. *Sigmund Freud's Dora* thus demonstrates that for psychoanalysis and advertising, as for cinema, the ideal female subject is one who permits herself to be heard as well as seen, who participates in the discursive alignment of her body with male desire (that of the father, Herr K, Freud), commodities (liquid Tylenol, F.D.S. deodorant), and the scopic drive, always testifying to the excellence of the "fit."

The concluding section of the film adds a voice which has been conspicuously absent from its earlier sections, as from Freud's case study—that of the mother. Once again the female voice is oddly disassociated from the words it utters; in fact, this sequence indicates more clearly than any of the others that the female voice is, within the existing social order, a reading voice, one which repeats what has always already been written or spoken elsewhere. However, a series of disruptions at the discursive level effectively frees the female voice from any signifying relationship to the words she articulates. The mother, whose image remains stable but whose identity is put into extreme flux towards the end of the film (she could be the psychotic housewife, the grandmother, the woman both Herr K and Dora's father "got nothing out of," the image of the madonna, the mother Dora sought in her brother, the real or the symbolic mother) reads aloud from a group of postcards written by a daughter whose own identity remains equally indeterminate. Although that daughter is also called Dora, she is not always—as Jane Weinstock observes—a resident of the same century:

> ...the postcards could not have the same return address. The early letters seem to be sent by a 19th century daughter, very much like Freud's Dora, and the later ones by a 1970's feminist, also named Dora. Moreover, the 19th century Dora's postcards of twentieth century pornography set up a literal contradiction. The spectator, already uprooted by a shifting address, is now split between centuries....[17]

The proper name thus no longer serves as the locus for a relatively stable cluster of attributes, but is itself the site of an extreme temporal and discursive division.

Chantal Akerman uses the letter-reading device as a means for introducing an even more radically split subjectivity into one of her films. She inscribes both a mother and a daughter into *News From Home* through a voice which at no juncture meshes with the images we see, images of New York City. That voice reads aloud letters sent to New York from a mother who remains in Belgium, and it is defined only as the receiving point for this maternal address.

Its formal status is also extremely ambiguous. Because it is dis-embodied it is technically a voice-over of the transcendental variety, but it has none of the authority or appeal to superior knowledge which are the usual attributes of that device. In fact, it is often drowned out by the noises of the city, and because of the monotony of its message we only periodically attend to it. Moreover, it at no point connects with the image track, either as diegetic complement or metalanguage. Whereas the former depicts a sultry Manhattan, the latter dwells persistently on the domestic situation back "home," in Belgium.

Finally, we are asked to distinguish between the voice itself and the words it utters, a distinction which the classic text would work hard to erase. To begin with, this voice has a very definite flavor or grain, in contrast to the carefully standardized voice used in documentaries and police thrillers. To its qualities of youthfulness and softness the English version of *News From Home* adds foreignness, for it speaks with a strong Belgian accent. Dis-embodied though it is, Barthes would say that this voice engages the flesh

("The 'grain' is that: the materiality of the body speaking its mother tongue").[18]

Secondly, the words "belong" to the mother, and the voice to the daughter, which is another way of saying that they represent very diverse points of view. In her own gloss on the largely autobiographical *News From Home* Akerman emphasizes that diversity; she describes her mother, source of the film's words, as an uneducated woman who has never been to America, and whose entire existence revolves around her tightly integrated family. Each detail underscores the daughter's distance from the home front:

> My mother wrote me love-letters, and that was marvelous. With her own words. . . . My mother didn't learn to write, she quit school at 11, and then there was the war. She writes as she can, she formulates her feelings in an unsophisticated way, they really reflect her. If she were more sophisticated, she wouldn't have dared to ask me all the time 'When are you coming back? You know very well that we love you, you know that we miss you.' She wouldn't have dared, she would have said it by a thousand 'detours.' But she's not sophisticated, she used the words she had, so she had a more direct relationship.[19]

The film indicates the same thing through its non-continuous sound and image tracks: the claustral and repetitive quality of the mother's phrases contrasts markedly with the detachment and open-endedness of the cinematography and editing, which are here signifiers of the daughter's "outlook" on the world.

There is never, however, any implied hierarchy between these two points of view. Nor is there any implied hierarchy between the New York we see, and the Belgium we hear. Fundamentally, the letters which the daughter reads and the city which she visits belong to two different discourses, neither of which is capable of "containing" her. We hear her voice reading one, and we participate in her vision of the other, but she remains on the edges of each. Significantly, all of the film's shots, with the exception of those inside the subway system, are exterior, and the final one leaves us stranded in the New York harbor, neither "here" nor "there."

The dis-embodied voice of *News From Home* anticipates what might be called the "traveling" voice of *Empty Suitcases*. This film, like *Kristina Talking Pictures* and *Film About a Woman Who*, frustrates the spectator's attempts to connect the sound and image tracks by projecting a diversity of female bodies, any one of which could be the "heroine." However, the real mobility of the film—not just the shift from one female representation to another, but the movement from one city to another, and one discourse to another—is an effect of the sound track.

Near the beginning of *Empty Suitcases* we journey back and forth from New York to Chicago dozens of times in the space of five minutes, as a female voice reads aloud from a stack of postcards, some of which are addressed from one of those cities, and some from the other. Even more spectacular are the transits from one melodramatic mode to another—from the subject-position of the suffering artist to that of the rejected professor, the angry mistress, the terrorist, the teller of oedipal dreams. Filmmaker Bette Gordon negotiates these constant relocations through a multiplicity of female voices and discursive strategies, including not only the voice-over but the voice-off, synchronized dialogue and monologue, and musical lyrics.

It is through the last of these aural modes that *Empty Suitcases* makes both its wittiest and perhaps its most important statement about the female voice. In the episode in question a woman lies on a bed lip-synching the words to the Billie Holiday song, "All of me." Although there is a perfect match of the movements of the woman's lips with the lyrics we hear, it is belied by the complete disequivalence between her facial expression and the affect of the music; she remains completely impassive as Holiday's voice reaches ever new crescendos of masochistic ardor. The song is ostensibly about a woman's complete surrender of herself to her lover, but it takes the form of a series of auto-references. Holiday's voice offers up her body piece by piece, in an elaborate dismemberment ("Take my lips...take my arms...you took my heart, so why not take all of me?").

This sequence points to the intimate connection between the synchronization of the female voice with the female image in classical cinema, and the semiotics of self-reference which it habitually promotes in its women viewers and listeners. That semiotics, which obliges the female voice to signify the female body, and the female body to signify lack, isolates the female subject from effective political action, prevents her from making investments in a new social order, and guarantees that she will remain in the same place.

These issues are treated at much greater length in what is unquestionably the most remarkable deployment of female voices within the feminist avant-garde, if not within the whole of experimental cinema: Yvonne Rainer's *Journeys From Berlin/71*. Two of its many voices—those of the "patient," also called Annette, and that belonging to Rainer herself—are synchronized with the image track, while a third—that of the female analyst—connects up with a woman's back. Two other female voices remain completely dis-embodied, although the persona represented by each is evoked with extraordinary vividness. These voices "belong" to an adolescent girl, and to an adult woman who is engaged simultaneously in a conversation about political violence and the preparations for a meal.

One other voice must be included in this list, although it derives from a man. This last voice could best be characterized as a dirty phone-caller, but during his longest and most persistent intrusion he delivers one of the film's most important female monologues:

> My daddy called me Cookie. I'm really a good girl. I'll go along with anything as long as you'll like me a little. I'll even promise not to bring up all that business about being such a low element, such primeval slime, such an amoeba, such an edible *thing*. I'm not one for fussing. Not like those movie women: Katy Hepburn facing the dawn in her posh pad with stiff upper chin. Merle Oberon facing the Nazi night with hair billowing in the electric breeze. Roz Russell sockin' the words 'n' the whiskey to the best of them. Rita Hayworth getting shot in the mirror and getting her man. Jane Wyman smiling through tears. I never faced the music, much less the dawn; I stayed in bed. I never socked anything to anybody; why rock the boat? I never set out to get my man, even in the mirror; they all got me. I never smiled through my tears; I choked down my terror. I never had to face the Nazis, much less their night. Not for me that succumbing in the great task because it must be done; not for me the heart beating in incomprehensible joy; not for me the vicissitudes of class struggle; not for me the uncertainties of political thought. . . . [20]

The dirty phone-caller speaks from the position of the traditional female viewer; "her" voice registers the subjectivity conferred upon women by classical cinema—a subjectivity which is the effect of a masochistic misrecognition. Rita Hayworth, Katharine Hepburn, Merle Oberon, Rosalind Russell and Jane Wyman (both as stars and as characters) provide some of the ideal representations by means of which that misrecognition occurs, propelling the female viewer into a negative narcissism. [21]

Images of the kind cited above both structure and exceed the female viewer; indeed, they structure largely through excess, through the elaboration of hyperbolic spectacle. The felt inadequacy of the female subject in the face of these ideal images induces in her an intense self-loathing. At the same time it is impossible for her simply to turn away from them, to retreat into herself, since she has only a relational identity, knows herself only through representation. Her inability either to approximate or transcend the mirror in which she sees herself as the dim reflection of a luminous original locks her into a deadly narcissism, one more conducive of self-hatred than self-love. It must further be noted that each of the movie citations enumerated by the dirty phone-caller constitues a masochistic inscription. Each glamorizes pain, renunciation, death. Classical cinema thus overdetermines the production of a docile and suffering female subject.

Journeys From Berlin/71 explores the relationship of subjectivity to the existing symbolic order not only through the voice of the dirty phone-caller but through those of the adolescent girl, the patient, the cooking woman and the director herself. Each is located within a context in which women have traditionally been encouraged to talk, contexts which structure and circumscribe their subjectivity. Thus the adolescent girl addresses her diary, the patient her analyst, the cooking woman the man with whom she presumably lives, and Rainer her mother. Each of these discourses is characterized by a high degree of reflexivity; although they all probe the relationship between the personal and the social, the accent falls increasingly on the first of those terms. Toward the end of the film the four voices converge more and more, until they finally seem to be participating in the same narcissistic speech.

The diary entries read aloud by the voice of the adolescent girl range across a wide variety of topics. However, the self is a constant point of reference. The first entry describes a number of events whose common denominator is that they induce in the writer what she calls the "chills" or the "shivers." Subsequent entries return obsessively to the feelings evoked in the adolescent girl by other people and things. The one dated Friday, September 28 is symptomatic:

> The tears are here again. Brush them away. Something just happened. Mama just finished listening to one of those one-hour dramas, a real tragedy. She said, "I shouldn't listen to those stories, they really move me too much. But I don't know what else to do with my time." And the tears came. Sometimes I feel an overwhelming tenderness for her. I don't know if it's love. Right now I am being strangely moved by my feeling for her.

The object is virtually eclipsed in this libidinal economy, whose extensions are all circular.[22]

Events in the external world function as signifiers of the self in much the same way in the patient's discourse. Vietnam provides material for masturbatory fantasies, Samuel Beckett finds his way into a story about shopping in Bloomingdale's and the defeat of the patient's hard-won independence, and statistics about political prisoners lead to the seemingly unconnected observation that "rejection and disappointment are the two things that I've always found impossible to take." The most breathtaking assimilation of the public into the private is effected during a reverie about the body:

> Some people don't seem to notice their own body changes. . . . I can predict exactly where new pressures of clothing will occur the next day—buttocks, thighs, belly, breasts—what new topography will appear on my face: creases and barrows as conspicuous as the scars slashed by two world wars into the soil of Europe.

Here all of twentieth-century history and a large portion of the world's geography yield metaphoric precedence to a woman's face and figure, and to the self-loathing of which they are the distillate. The patient's voice is synchronized to her image in more ways than one.

The voice associated with kitchen noises speaks about virtually nothing but women anarchists and revolutionaries, reading at length from their letters. However, when asked whether she has read the political writings of Emma Goldman, she responds: "No, I have a collection of her essays, but all I've read is her autobiography." Moreover, towards the end of the film this voice talks a good deal about the difficulty she has always experienced in empathizing with oppressed groups. Instead, she gravitates toward radical "stars," ideal representations which frustrate rather than assist her desire to transcend traditional female subjectivity. Like classical cinema's exemplary woman viewer, she both identifies with the suffering of these ideal representations, and defines herself as lacking through them (thus whereas the figures she most admires all heroically subordinate the personal to the political, she herself despairs of even achieving "correct social behavior"). *Journeys From Berlin/71* draws attention to the similarities between these two sets of images when it shows the female analyst looking through a stack of photographs in which Jane Wyman and Rita Hayworth coexist with Vera Figner, Ulrike Meinhof and Vera Zasulich.

Finally, there is the voice—and the image—of Yvonne Rainer, speaking from Europe to her mother about a movie she has just seen, a movie filmed in Berlin before the war. Rainer talks about how affected she and the other viewers were by the shots of a city which no longer exists. Again the emphasis falls on the feelings evoked in the female subject by external occurrences, on sentiment rather than history or the social order. The auto-referentiality of all these voices is periodically accentuated by the appearance against a black background of rolling white titles providing facts and figures about West German postwar politics, i.e., by a discourse traditionally associated with values of "objectivity" and "neutrality," as well as by the interpolation at the level of the sound track of other, more strident political statements and accounts (here excerpts from a letter written by Ulrike Meinhof to Hannah Krabbe about the necessity of resisting prison psychiatrification).

In the general conversation about narcissism to which all of the female voices contribute during the last third of the film, a conversation which often occurs simultaneously on several registers, the adolescent girl confesses:

> Everything I've written has been put down for the benefit of some potential reader. It is a titanic task to be frank with myself. I fear my own censure. Even my thoughts sometimes appear to my consciousness in a certain form for the benefit of an imaginary mind-reader. And strangely enough, *I* am that reader of these pages; *I* am that reader of this mind. I have very strong impressions of my childhood "acting." Up to a few years ago, whenever I was alone I would "perform." I didn't think I did anything unusual or dramatic at these times, but the things I did do I did with the thought in mind that I was being watched. Now this reaction is becoming more and more unconscious, having been transmitted to my actions, speech, writing, and my thoughts. This last is the most unfortunate of all.

What this female voice records is the internalization of the specular and auditory regime upon which classical cinema relies, and which it helps to perpetuate within the larger cultural order. The notion of performance is of course an important one in all of Rainer's films, but in *Journeys From Berlin/ 71* it gains new resonance.[23] It becomes a metaphor for female subjectivity, for the interiorization of discursive demands which must be met at every moment of psychic existence, and which carry out the functions of over-seeing and over-hearing the ego even in the most solitary of situations. The rigors of that performance are so severe that they leave the female subject with no capacity for struggle on any other front, and result in extreme cases in suicide.

Journeys From Berlin/71 engages in a relentness expose not only of the female voice, but of the psychic mechanisms which operate it, and the symbolic field of which they are an extension. It suggests that by taking into herself the power-relations which organize the existing cultural order the female subject can never be anything but smoothly aligned with it—that her speech and her image will always be perfectly synchronized not only with each other, but with those discourses which are dominant at any given moment. The invocation by the woman analyst of Freud's *Mourning and Melancholia* is not coincidental, since it is there that we find the most chilling account of a condition which may be pathological for the male subject, but represents the norm for the female subject—that condition of negative narcissism which blights her relations both with herself and her culture:

> The patient represents [her] ego to us as worthless, incapable of any achievement and morally despicable; [she] reproaches [herself], vilifies [herself] and expects to be cast out and punished. [She] abases [herself] before everyone and commiserates [her] own relatives for being con-nected with anyone so unworthy...[she] declares that [she] was never any better.[24]

Journeys From Berlin/71 does more than deconstruct this closed theater of female subjectivity; it also points beyond. Not only does it detach voice from body, interrupting in the process the coherence upon which the performance relies, and revealing the degree to which the former has been obliged to talk about and regulate the latter, but in its final moments it involves its female speakers in a choric repudiation of ideal images and self-hatred. It also broaches, in a tentative and fragmentary manner, the possibility of moving beyond masochism toward externally directed action—the possibility, that is, of political struggle: "one might conceivably take greater risks. . .in using one's power. . .for the benefit of others. . .resisting inequities close at hand."

NOTES

1. See in particular Laura Mulvey, "Visual Pleasure and Narrative Cinema," *Screen* vol. 16, no. 3 (Autumn 1975), pp. 6-18; Linda Williams, "Film Body: An Implantation of Perversions," *Ciné-Tracts*, vol. 3, no. 4 (Winter 1981), pp. 19-34, and "When the Woman Looks" (in this volume, pp. 83-99); Teresa de Lauretis, "Through the Looking Glass," in *The Cinematic Apparatus*, ed. Teresa de Lauretis and Stephen Heath (New York: St. Martin's Press, 1980), pp. 187-202; and Sandy Flitterman, "Woman, Desire and the Look: Feminism and the Enunciative Apparatus in Cinema," *Ciné-Tracts*, vol. 2, no. 1 (Spring 1978), pp. 63-68.

2. In *The Archaeology of Knowledge and the Discourse on Language*, trans. A.M. Sheridan-Smith (London: Tavistock, 1972), Foucault speaks of " 'fellowships' of discourse, whose function is to preserve or to reproduce discourse, but in order that it should circulate within a closed community, according to strict regulation, without those in possession being dispossessed by this very distribution." (p. 225.)

3. For a more extended discussion of the connections between sexual difference and discourse, see my *"Histoire d'O*: The Story of a Disciplined and Punished Body," *Enclitic*, vol. 7, no. 2 (1983).

4. Stephen Heath describes the insertion of the voice into the diegesis as its preservation within a "safe place," and adds that this place is carefully maintained in the fiction film (see "Narrative Space," *Screen*, vol. 17, no. 3 [Autumn 1976], p. 100).

5. Pascal Bonitzer, *Le Regard et la voix* (Paris: Union Générale d'Editions, 1976), p. 30.

6. In "Body, Voice," (in *Questions of Cinema* [Bloomington, IN: Indiana University Press, 1981]) Stephen Heath writes "the sound cinema is the development of a powerful standard of the body and of the voice as hold of the body in image, the voice literally ordered and delimited as speech for an intelligibility of the body..." (p. 191); Gianfranco Bettetini, *The Language and Technique of the Film*, ed. Thomas A. Sebeok (The Hague: Mouton, 1973), p. 161.

7. Bonitzer, p. 30.

8. "Suture" designates any cinematic element which encourages the viewer/listener's identification with fictional characters and narrative progression. The shot/reverse shot formation has been seen by many theoreticians as virtually synonymous with the system of suture, functioning as it often does to align a character who looks with the supposed object of that character's gaze. Such an alignment organizes the spectator's point of view around character, and inspires in him or her the desire for the next shot, i.e., for more narrative. For a fuller treatment of the system of suture, see Chapter 5 of my *The Subject of Semiotics* (New York: Oxford University Press, 1983).

9. Christian Metz, "The Imaginary Signifier," trans. Ben Brewster, *Screen*, vol. 16, no. 2 (Summer 1975), p. 64.

10. Mary Ann Doane, "The Voice in Cinema: The Articulation of Body and Space," *Yale French Studies*, no. 60 (1980), p. 43. See also "Ideology and the Practice of Sound Editing and Mixing," in *The Cinematic Apparatus*, pp. 47-56.

11. Bonitzer, p. 33.

12. Jacques Lacan, "Desire and the Interpretation of Desire in *Hamlet*," trans. James Hulbert, *Yale French Studies*, no. 55/56 (1977), p. 28.

13. "An Interview with Laura Mulvey and Peter Wollen on *Riddles of the Sphinx*," *Millennium Film Journal*, no. 4/5 (1979), p. 24.

14. "Yvonne Rainer: Interview," *Camera Obscura*, vol. 1, no. 1 (Fall 1976), p. 89.

15. In *Problems in General Linguistics*, trans. Mary Meek (Coral Gables, FL: University of Miami Press, 1971) Emile Benveniste writes that "Language is... the possibility of subjectivity because it always contains the linguistic forms appropriate to the expression of subjectivity and discourse provokes the emergence of subjectivity because it consists of discrete instances. In some way language puts forth 'empty' forms which each speaker, in the exercise of discourse, appropriates to his 'person,' at the same time defining himself as *I* and a partner as *you*. The instance of discourse is thus constitutive of all coordinates that define the subject, and of which we have briefly pointed out only the most obvious (i.e., pronouns, verb forms, etc.)." (p. 227.)

16. See *October* 2 (1976), pp. 39-67 for the script of *Film About a Woman Who*.

17. Jane Weinstock, "Sigmund Freud's Dora?" *Screen*, vol. 22, no. 2 (1981), p. 73.

18. Roland Barthes, "The Grain of the Voice," in *Image—Music—Text*, trans. Stephen Heath (New York: Hill and Wang, 1977), p. 182.

19. Christina Creveling, "Chantal Akerman," *Camera Obscura*, vol. 2, no. 2 (1977), p. 137.

20. All quotations from *Journeys From Berlin/71* are taken from the complete, unpublished script.

21. For a fuller and somewhat different discussion of this condition, see my "*Hamlet* and the Common Theme of Fathers," *Enclitic*, vol. 3, no. 2 (1979), pp. 106-121.

22. A passage quoted in *Journeys From Berlin/71* from Sigmund Freud's "Mourning and Melancholia" suggests that melancholia (or negative narcissism, as I prefer to call it) always involves the loss of any external object: "The analysis of melancholia now shows that the ego can kill itself only if, owing to the return of the object-cathexis, it can treat itself as an object—if it is able to direct against itself the hostility which relates to an object and which represents the ego's original reaction to objects in the external world.... In the two opposed situations of being most intensely in love and of suicide the ego is overwhelmed by the object, though in totally different ways." (In *The Standard Edition of the Complete Psychological Works of Sigmund Freud*, trans. James Strachey [London: Hogarth Press, 1953], Vol. XIV, p. 252.)

23. B. Ruby Rich treats this metaphor at some length in *Yvonne Rainer* (Minneapolis, MN: Walker Art Center, 1981).

24. Freud, p. 246.

Now and Nowhere: Roeg's *Bad Timing*

Teresa de Lauretis

> —*You said you loved me!*
> —*I said I'd arrest you.*
> —*You know it means the same thing.*
> —Angie Dickinson as Feathers to John Wayne as Sheriff
> John T. Chance in *Rio Bravo* (Howard Hawks, 1959).

The now aging debate within avant-garde and independent cinema on the ideological effects and political effectivity of representational, "illusionist" or "anthropomorphic" film versus abstract or structural-materialist film may have found new oxygen in the writings of Michel Foucault, particularly in his notion of the social as a "practical field" in which technologies and discourses are deployed.

Whether cinema is considered to be an art or a mass industry, experiment or entertainment, a language-system or a subjective, fantasmatic production, cinema depends on technology, or better, is implicated with it. The particular advantage of Foucault's historical methodology is that, in opposing the bourgeois tradition of a history of ideas in favor of the analytical transcription of "empirical knowledge," it bypasses the base-superstructure model. Within that model, technology is usually assigned to the base—as the ensemble of purely technical, instrumental means—while ideas are assigned to the superstructure. Redefined as a set of regulated procedures, mechanisms and techniques of reality-control deployed by power, the notion of technology is thus expanded to include the production of social subjects, practices and knowledges; consequently, ideas themselves assume a practical, pragmatic character in their articulation with power relations.

Were one to adopt Foucault's method of historical analysis and to adapt it to cinema, one would have to shift the terms of the question "cinema" away from the ideas of cinema as art, documentation or mass communication, and from the idea of cinema history as the history of those ideas; away from auteur theory as well as from the project of an economic history of cinema *per se*; away from the presumption that a film expresses the filmmaker's individual creativity, her/his "visionary" draw on the bank of a collective unconscious; and away from the assumption that historical research is done by collecting and assembling "data." This would also mean abandoning—theoretically, that is—the concept of an autonomous or internal development of cinema's "technological means," whether mechanical, chemical or electronic, the techniques supposed to derive from them, and even the expressive styles elaborated against or in spite of them; would mean abandoning, too, the idea of cinema as a device to capture phenomena and guarantee their reality and historical occurrence, their taking or having taken place. In short, one would have to abandon the idea of cinema as a self-contained system, semiotic or economic, imaginary or visionary.

Some of this shifting has already begun in film theory and practice.[1] This is why there is a growing interest in Foucault's work and, perhaps ironically, on the part not of film historians but of those concerned with current film practice and with the practical field in which is deployed the cinematic discourse—its film texts, the elaboration of genres and techniques, the development of audiences through tactical distribution and exhibition, the ideological effects it produces (or seeks to produce) in spectatorship.[2] In this context, and not as an "application" of Foucault's proposals but in the attempt to engage them from a feminist critical position, the following reading of Nicolas Roeg's *Bad Timing* is offered.

But first we must ask: What is the practical field in which technologies, cinema for example, are deployed? It is the social in general, understood as a crisscrossing of specific practices, involving relations of power and pleasure, with individuals and groups assuming variable positions or positionalities; as power is exercised "from below," says Foucault, "from innumerable points, in the interplay of non-egalitarian and mobile relations," so are resistances. The existence of power relations depends on "a multiplicity of points of resistance...present everywhere in the power network." Both power relations and points of resistance invest or pass through "apparatuses and institutions, without being exactly localized in them," traverse or spread across "social stratifications and individual unities."[3] This map of the social as a field of forces (discourses, and the institutions which anchor and guarantee them, are for Foucault—much like signs are for Eco—social forces) where individuals, groups or classes move about assuming variable positions, exercising at once power and resistance from innumerable points, defined by constantly shifting relations, is a very appealing, almost optimistic vision of an unlimited political semiosis. Everyone really has a chance to resist. Pleasures are practically guaranteed.

This, parenthetically, may not be the least reason why Foucault's writings, eminently quotable in themselves, seem to be more and more often quoted in relation to cinema: technology, power and pleasure, sexuality and the body, the family and other forms of confinement, prisons and hospitals, psychoanalysis—what other historian or philosopher has put together and spoken of things that so directly concern cinema? Who can resist, for instance, applying his notion of sexuality as a "technology of sex" to cinema: a set of regulated procedures which produce sex and the desire for sex as their end result, sex as not just the object of desire but at the same time its very support? Cinema—in its "sixty years of seduction," as ABC has recently reminded us—both exemplifies and employs, even perfects, that technology of sex. It exemplifies the deployment of sexuality by its endless investigations and confessions, its revealing and concealing, its search for vision and truth; and it perfects its technology by "implanting" images and patterns of meaning in the spectators' body, in perception and cognition, implanting the very terms of its imaging, its mechanisms of capture and seduction, confrontation and mutual reinforcement.[4] Few can resist it. Yet perhaps we should. It's almost too easy, too congruent, too pleasurable, almost numbing.

I close the parenthesis and go back to my sentence: this map of the social as a field of force relations is an appealing vision of unlimited political semiosis, of the political as a continuous production of meanings, positionalities and struggles in an open range of practices and discourses. Groups form and dissolve, relations of power are nonegalitarian but multiple and mobile, never fixed. One is almost reminded here of Bloch's argument in *Das Prinzip Hoffnung* that all utopias "have socialism in mind," since they express the expectant tendency in human history, a tendency which at certain points becomes concrete (as in the French revolution, the Paris commune, the October revolution, etc.), when the "objective-real possibilities are acted out," and "existing actuality is surrounded with tremendous latency, the times when the 'potency of human hope' links up with the potentialities within the world."[5]

There may be some danger in accepting Foucault's representation as a description of the social (which one may be led to do by virtue of its rhetorical strategy, the fact that it presents itself as historical writing instead of, say, philosophical or literary writing). While it is not divergent, epistemologically, from several neo-Marxist conceptions of the public sphere—from Negt and Kluge to Eco's view of sign production—unlike them it tends to account for everything, every phenomenon and event, leaving nothing outside the reach of its discursive order, of its power of explanation, its knowledge/power. For Bloch, the utopian tendency was to find concrete expression only in Marxism, which alone "disclosed the real possibilities":

> Marxism also reveals totality again—which is the method and the subject matter of all authentic philosophy. But, for the first time this

totality appears not as a static, as a finished principle of the whole, but rather as utopian, or more precisely, as a concrete utopian totality, as the process latency of a still unfinished world.[6]

Whereas the utopian-teleological drift appears to be absent from Foucault's "histories," where the world is always both finished and in process, his conception of history as discontinuity does not dispel the sense of totality, of a totalizing power of discourse, which is very much there in his writing and which, according to Bloch, characterizes "all authentic philosophy."

But if one more modestly asks: What does cinema do? What films shall we make or exhibit? Should women filmmakers bother to go to Hollywood? Should black students study filmmaking? etc., Foucault assures us that power is exercised from below, and that the "points of resistance are present everywhere in the power network"; they are not superstructural, or "in a position of exteriority in relation to power"—a great single Power with the capital P—and "by definition, they can only exist in the strategic field of power relations." Thus, according to him, the question should be: How do we seek out "the most immediate, the most local power relations at work"? How do we analyze them? How do we weigh "the effects of resistance and counterinvestments"?[7] The critical tools for this kind of history, this "microanalytics" of cinema, are yet to be developed. But therein lies, I think, the usefulness of Foucault's work for current film theory and practice.

An example of this difficulty in weighing the effects of resistance and counterinvestments is provided by the reception of Nicolas Roeg's *Bad Timing: A Sensual Obsession*, a film which seems to have caused more displeasure than pleasure to practically everyone: general audiences (it was not a box office success), official media critics, and women's groups involved in the antipornography campaign. The film has been found boring and confusing, overreaching and pretentious, "technically good," and offensive to women. The X-rating and pattern of exhibition (art cinemas in first run, then immediately the revival circuit), plus the director's cult reputation (based on *Performance, Don't Look Now, Walkabout, The Man Who Fell to Earth*) place *Bad Timing* in a special category of commercially distributed, nonmainstream films such as Oshima's *In the Realm of the Senses*, Cavani's *The Night Porter*, Pasolini's *Salò*, or, to a lesser degree, Godard's *Every Man for Himself* and, lesser still, Bertolucci's *Last Tango in Paris*.

All these films deliberately seek to articulate the sexual, the political and the cinematic through a sustained questioning of vision and power; and though not "independently" produced (thus undeserving of the moral commendations extended to low-budget movies, the ethical rewards of poor cinema), they urge us to reconsider the current definitions of cinema no less forcefully than do other, more explicitly and programmatically "alternative" practices: avant-garde filmmaking and political film, or what Solanas and

Getino in 1970 called "third cinema"— to distinguish it from European art cinema on one side and Hollywood on the other.[8] Today we do not speak of only three kinds of cinema; categories have multiplied, discourses and practices intersect and overlap (*The Love Boat* remakes Busby Berkeley, Michael Snow makes a travelogue—*Presents*, Bruce Beresford's *Breaker Morant* finally shows that socialist realism can be effectively beautiful, and more effective than Marlon Brando as anti-war protest).

Still there are films that do not seem to fit anywhere, and *Bad Timing* is one such film. That it does not belong to the "great artist's film" slot with *City of Women* (the latest Fellini-Mastroianni hoopla) and *The Last Metro* (Truffaut), or in a package of "new foreign cinema"—German, French, Australian, whatever—or with "independent," social-issue-oriented films like John Sayles' *The Return of the Secaucus Seven* or Connie Fields' *The Life and Times of Rosie the Riveter*, is one more reason for its arousal of displeasure. Then there is the question of genre; neither a thriller nor a love story, though the opening and closing songs pay homage to both; not an appeal to the political mythology of Nazi-Fascism; not a remake of a James Cain novel, nor a metacinematic remake of *Psycho* or *8½*—*Bad Timing* has a well chosen title indeed. Yet Harvey Keitel is everyone's favorite actor, Theresa Russell is very beautiful, the sound wonderful, the cinematography impressive as always in Roeg's films, and the editing is almost as stunning as Thelma Schoonmaker's in *Raging Bull*.

Its problem, I think, is not displeasure but *unpleasure*: its preventing spectating pleasure by undercutting spectator identification in terms of both vision (literally, a difficulty in seeing) and narrative (a difficulty in understanding events and their succession, their timing), thus problematizing our "time" in the film, its vision for us. Of Oshima's film, Stephen Heath has written:

> *In the Realm of the Senses* produces and breaks the apparatus of look and identification; it does so by describing—in the geometrical acceptation of the word: by *marking out*—the problematic of that apparatus; hence its drama is not merely 'of vision' but, undercutting that classic narrative transposition, of the relations of cinema's vision and of the demonstration of the terms—including, above all, the woman—of those relations.[9]

While the question of the nexus of look and identification is central to Roeg's film as well (with its thematics of voyeurism twice relayed through the generic pattern of the police investigation in which is encased the "confessional" investigation of sexuality) the work of the film is less with vision than with narrative—or better, less on the problem of seeing as such than on the problem of *seeing as understanding* events, behaviors and motivations. A common viewer response to *Bad Timing*'s "love story" is: Why does Milena stay with him, why is she attracted to him, what does she *see* in him (that I don't)? He—Art Garfunkel as Dr. Alex Linden, an American research psychoanalyst who teaches at the University of Vienna, photos of Freud looming large behind his office desk and couch, on which Milena twice lies down and where once Alex joins her—he, for most viewers, is not a particularly attractive character, with his tweed suits, humorless conversation, low-key voice and overall dull, noncommanding personality. Nor is Art Garfunkel a star, glamorous by association with previous roles or gossip columns, but an ex-60s songwriter whose image simply has not kept up with the times, and who never had the bisexual versatility of a Mick Jagger or a David Bowie (primarily responsible for the box office success of Roeg's prior film, *The Man Who Fell to Earth*), nor, for that matter, the beauty of Oshima's actor, Fuji Tatsuya. If beauty is by no means considered essential to the sexiness of male characters and stars (or even important, as witness the appeal of Harvey Keitel as Inspector Netusil to both men and women), Garfunkel/Alex Linden seems to have none of the qualities that allow viewers to like him or to identify with him.

Thus the point of entry into the film's narrative, the path of access to its inscription of desire, is through the character of Milena/Theresa Russell and what she sees in him (that we don't). That for many this path is not viable, we know from recent role-reversal films like Jane Wagner's *Moment by Moment*, and, of course, from the history of unpleasure that has kept Dorothy Arzner's movies confined to the morgue of film archives. Here too, much in the same way, access to narrative pleasure is blocked by the film's generic contiguity with several familiar genres and their preconstructed patterning of expectations; the love story *cum* investigation spreads across a generic spectrum that goes from the psychological thriller (*Marnie, Vertigo*) and film noir (*The Big Sleep, Double Indemnity*) up to the "woman's film" (*Rebecca, Letter From an Unknown Woman*), only the latter genre allowing some measure of identification with the female protagonist and thus access, through her, to the narrative trajectory of (oedipal) desire. In *Bad Timing*, however, the remembering of the events of the relationship, presented in flashback, cannot be attributed to Milena who, in terms of the diegetic present, is unconscious for all but the very last scene.

Literally, Milena is the "object" of Alex's desire; she is most desirable when unconscious, body without speech, look or will, in the infamous "ravishment" scene, which we see but which Alex never confesses to Inspector Netusil. That he does not "confess" is very important: it establishes ravishment not as an individual aberration, a deviation from "normal" sexuality, a perversion to be punished or cured (Netusil has no interest in the law as such, Alex is not a practicing but a "research" analyst), or avowed and most of all confessed ("Confess. Please, Dr. Linden, as a personal favor," begs Netusil; "What is detection, if not confession?...between us, it might help...I can help you, Dr. Linden. Confess, between us, tell me what you dare not"); and, once confessed, then to be attributed to, and serve to characterize, a certain type of deviant personality.[10] On the contrary, if not admitted, if disavowed, ravishment remains a sado-fetishistic fantasy inherent in the masculine structure of desire and perfectly congruent with the power relations sustained by other social discourses and practices which the film engages—juridical, politico-diplomatic, psychoanalytic, legal-medical and surgical. The security check (a psychological "profile") that Alex runs for NATO on Milena's file (stored in a locked vault like a body in the morgue) conveys the chilled passion of necrophilia; Netusil's investigation is conducted, much like Quinlan's in *Touch of Evil*, from the "hunch" that the real crime is not suicide or murder but rape or ravishment; the vaginal examination performed on Milena's unconscious body, ordered by Netusil, is intercut with shots of her sexual intercourse with Alex; even the emergency room efforts to revive her, to make her expel the ingested amphetamines, show doctors inserting several objects into her throat—matched to a soundtrack of thumping, gulping and bedroom sounds—before finally cutting her trachea. Nor is psychoanalysis exempt from this imagery as Milena, stretched out on the couch in Alex's office, asks: "Well, Doctor, is there hope for us?"

In the terms of Foucault's argument, Alex's refusal to confess, thus to collaborate with the mechanisms of the "technology of sex," could be read as a resistance to the power/knowledge paradigm; but that refusal is precisely what places him in a position of power in relation to Netusil ("My need is a confession. Would you like to confess, Dr. Linden?" pleads the inspector). For Alex knows that "through the gratification of curiosity, one acquires knowledge," as he tells his students, while backed by screen-size projections of "some famous spies" (which include "the first spy"—a male child; and "the first to be spied on"—a couple making love, the child's "primal scene"; as well as Freud, J. Edgar Hoover and Stalin—"two of whom might be called political voyeurs")—and the equation knowledge/power could not be clearer. "I prefer to label myself an observer," lectures Dr. Linden, "The guilt-ridden voyeur is usually a political conservative." Nevertheless, that he and Netusil play by the same rules, and duplicate or implicate one another as do psychoanalysis and the law, knowledge and power, is visually and aurally established throughout the film, beginning immediately after the lecture scene, with a continuous soundtrack of classical music (Beethoven's *Fidelio* overture) over crosscut shots of the two men in their respective homes, Harvard diplomas hanging in full view in Netusil's study. The inspector is a family man, and so indeed is Alex, who wants to marry Milena and go back to America. It is her refusal to marry him, her "resistance" in Foucault's terms, that places them both in jeopardy with the law ("Husband? Relation? Boyfriend?" the police keep asking Alex, who replies reluctantly, "You can say a friend"), and makes Netusil suspect Alex of some kind of crime.

Milena's offense is against propriety, an offense not juridical but moral: her excess, the sexual, physical and domestic "disorder" that, at least in the movies, marks women who choose to be outside the family ("What a mess! Just like my sister's," says an officer of the law searching her apartment); it is an offense contemplated by the law, not even a violation, rather an "effect of the code," as Baudrillard would say.[11] Ravishment and rape, on the other hand, are crimes against property, against the legal institution of marriage as sexual ownership of the spouse's body ("You don't own me, I don't own you," protests Milena at first, declining cohabitation). By refusing to confess, and thus to acknowledge guilt, Alex resists the "politically conservative" discourse on sexuality upheld by the police inspector ("creatures who live in this sort of disorder...a sort of moral and physical sewer...they spread it around them like an infectious disease....They envy our strength, our capacity to fight, our will to master reality").[12] But Alex's resistance comes from and is made possible by the same power/knowledge apparatus as Netusil's; and Alex's politically liberal discourse wins out, with our sympathies going out to Netusil/Keitel who, though perfectly correct in his "assessment of the truth" and in the logic of his detection—operating as he is from the very same emotional and conceptual paradigm—has been outsmarted and outdone.

This kind of resistance, located within the terms of diverse but congruent practices and discourses, may either succeed and become power (as it does for Alex) or fail and end up in confinement, the morgue or the archive (as it does for Milena and for Arzner's films). The fact that in matters sexual and cinematic, those who line up with power are men and those who end up in confinement women, is not particularly new or surprising. But it should be kept in mind when reading Foucault's conclusion, which fairly well sums up Alex's tactical position in the film.

> We must not think that by saying yes to sex, one says no to power.... It is the agency of sex that we must break away from, if we aim—through a tactical reversal of the various mechanisms of sexuality—to counter the grips of power with the claims of bodies, pleasures, and knowledges, in their multiplicity and their possibility of resistance. The rallying point for the counterattack against the deployment of sexuality ought not to be sex-desire, but bodies and pleasures.[13]

Foucault's rallying point, bodies and pleasures, which in a way is represented in the character of Milena, turns out to be good and useful for Alex, and very clearly bad, in fact impossible, for Milena.

Bad Timing, however, poses the possibility of another kind of resistance, and does so thematically as well as formally, working through the problematic of temporality, narrative and montage. It suggests a resistance, in the film and within the practice of cinema, to be understood as radical difference, an absolute negativity which resists integration into the discourses of power/knowledge/vision. Actually, this other kind of resistance is also sketched out by Foucault (and thus must now be discussed), but its relation to power is much more ambiguous; in fact, Foucault does not distinguish between the two, and in *The History of Sexuality* leaves the notion of resistance underdeveloped so that, if anything, it seems to be a subsidiary of power. He writes:

> Resistances do not derive from a few heterogeneous principles; but neither are they a lure or a promise that is of necessity betrayed. They are the odd term in relations of power; they are inscribed in the latter as an irreducible opposite.[14]

For me, irreducible and opposite do not go together, an "opposite" is already "reduced," led back into a logic of unity, a dialectic or a dialogue. Elsewhere, however, it should be noted, he speaks of a pure negativity, an indeterminate force capable of escaping or dodging all controls and constrictions, all processes of normalization and determination. This negativity appears to be less a resistance, a force that can be set against power, than a non-force, an absolute difference with respect to power. For the latter, far from being a negative element of repression, is the positive condition of knowledge, the only productive force; in other words, it is power, not negativity or resistance, which spreads across the social body as a productive network of discourses, forms of knowledge and subjectivity. Foucault's examples of this pure negativity—Pierre Rivière, popular justice as a form of judiciary guerrilla, the quasi-mystical idea of a "non-proletarianised common people" (*plèbe non proletarisée*) remain indeterminate in his discourse.[15]

Again, one is drawn to a comparison with the notion of a proletarian or plebeian public sphere elaborated by Negt and Kluge's *Oeffentlichkeit und Erfahrung* in opposition to and as a development of Habermas' analysis of the bourgeois public sphere.[16] However, despite the similarities, Foucault's plebeian resistance is precisely *not* proletarianized, does not mediate toward political praxis. Hence the impression of "paradoxical conservatism" it has generated, "a sort of mysticism of indetermination."[17] Foucault's non-proletarianized masses appear somehow free of ideology: when they perceive someone to be their enemy and decide to punish or to reeducate this enemy, the masses, he argues, "do not rely on an abstract universal idea of justice [but rather] on their own experience, that of the injuries they have suffered, that of the way in which they have been wronged, in which they have been oppressed"; thus their justice is not an "authoritative [one] backed up by a state apparatus which has the power to enforce their decisons; they *purely and simply* carry them out."[18] Purely and simply? He speaks as if these plebeian masses, these sexually or otherwise undifferentiated "common people" were untouched by "abstract" ideas, exempt from symbolic processes, mythical production, patriarchal structures—in short, as if they were immune from ideology, that is to say, outside culture. Later on in the discussion, pressed on by the "Maoists" (who object that popular justice during the French Resistance missed its real target and enemy by going after the women who had slept with Germans and shaving their heads [cf. Emmanuelle Riva in *Hiroshima, Mon Amour*], instead of punishing the real collaborators), Foucault elegantly contradicts himself: "This does not mean that the non-proletarianized plebs have remained unsullied. . . . [The bourgeois] ideological effects on the plebs have been uncontestable and profound."[19] Nevertheless, the pure and simple masses must be kept unsullied for the sake of his argument:

> If people went rushing after women to shave their heads it was because the collaborators. . . against whom they should have exercised popular justice, were presented to the masses as being too difficult to deal with in that way: it was said, "Oh, those people's crimes are too great, we'll bring them before a court". . . . In this case the courts were just used as an excuse for dealing with things other than by acts of popular justice.[20]

"Paradoxical conservatism" is a very appropriate phrase for a major theoretician of social history who writes of power and resistance, bodies and pleasures and sexuality as if the ideological structures and effects of patriarchy and sexual differentiation had nothing to do with history, indeed as if they had no discursive status or political implications. The rape and sexual extortion performed on little girls by young and adult males is a "bit of theater," a petty "everyday occurrence in the life of village sexuality," purely "inconsequential bucolic pleasures."[21] What really matters to the historian is the power of institutions, the mechanisms by which these "bits of theater" become, presumably, pleasurable for the individuals involved—the men *and* the women, former little girls, proletarianized or not—who then become complicit with those institutional apparati. Here is where, despite his elegant rhetoric and radical politics (his interventions in issues of capital punishment, prison revolts, psychiatric clinics, judiciary scandals, etc.), Foucault's efforts to define political resistance and theoretical negativity sink like a paper boat in a street puddle.

A much more convincing definition of negativity, and one which is directly pertinent to my reading of *Bad Timing*, is Julia Kristeva's, also given in an interview:

> Believing oneself 'a woman' is almost as absurd and obscurantist as believing oneself 'a man'. I say almost because there are still things to be got for women: freedom of abortion and contraception, childcare facilities, recognition of work, etc. Therefore, 'we are women' should still be kept as a slogan, for demands and publicity. But more fundamentally,

> women cannot *be*: the category woman is even that which does not fit
> into *being*. From there, women's practice can only be negative, in
> opposition to that which exists, to say that 'this is not it' and 'it is not yet'.
> What I mean by 'woman' is that which is not represented, that which is
> unspoken, that which is left out of namings and ideologies.[22]

She is referring, of course, to the Western platonic philosophical tradition
which takes man as its term of reference and simply poses woman as
everything that is other, as non-man; a history of discourses, institutions and
apparati of representation (cinema prominent among them), which the
feminist critique has begun to excavate, unearthing the ideological stratifications on which it is built.[23] This "unspoken" of femininity, this "not represented" or not representable, this negativity as the underside of discourse is
the sense in which, I will attempt to show, Roeg's film inscribes the figure of a
radical and irreducible difference.

In the last scene of the film, the only one in which Milena is shown not in
flashback but in a diegetic time subsequent to her hospitalization—thus
possibly the only "real" time for her as a character independent of the
investigative frame—Alex catches a glimpse of her getting out of a cab in
New York City. He, and we, are not sure it's her until we see the scar on her
chest. Then he calls out her name, she looks at him and remains silent; the
film cuts back to Alex looking out of the cab, then to her as she turns and
walks away, then back to Alex and follows his cab disappearing into the city
traffic. The effect of this scene (Milena's survival having been previously
reported) is something of an epilogue, or a moral in the Brechtian manner.
Her stern, silent look and changed demeanor suggest an actor who, stepping
out of the play (Alex's memory drama) confronts the audience with the play's
question. The scar that identifies her, for Alex and for us (like the snakebite
scars on the bodies of the Moroccan snake charmers, like the surgical modifi-
cations performed on the sensory apparatus of Tommy/David Bowie in *The
Man Who Fell to Earth*), is a mark at once of subjection and of resistance.
Such scars are signs of a radical difference inscribed and displayed in the body,
a resistance not congruent, not commensurable with the dialectic of the
system, as Alex's resistance is, thus not its political negation but an absolute
negativity. This resistance, the film suggests, is not located within the terms
of the productive apparati of power/knowledge, for no "truth" is produced
there about Milena's character; but neither is it located outside of those
practices and discourses which constitute the given social world. It is, quite
simply, difference. The man who fell to earth cannot go back out there
whence he came and will remain on earth indefinitely as an alien, marked by
his radical, though barely perceptible, difference. Milena, too, is neither
bound by the rules and institutions of power/knowledge nor "free" of them,
and *this* contradiction is what the scar signifies: her passion and her silence,

her experience of difference, her history—past, present—inscribed and displayed in her sexed body which, now as throughout the film's alternating images, is both there and not there, conscious and unconscious, in contradiction, in excess of those dialectical oppositions.

In *The Man Who Fell to Earth*, difference, physical and cultural, is represented primarily in spatial terms; however, it is the fact that his body does not age like the others around him which in the end, despite the surgical intervention that makes it *absolutely* impossible for him to go back to his distant planet, conclusively re-marks his radical otherness. Possibly because Tommy's expanded temporal dimension and his superior (tele)vision are elements of content accounted for by the generic code of science fiction, the film's montage plays mainly on spatial displacement and discontinuities. In *Bad Timing*, as the title insists, temporality is directly in question, and its different orders must be established symbolically, i.e., cinematically. For both Tommy and Milena, the surgical operation is but the symbolic representation of a lengthy and multiple process of cultural determination, conditioning and adaptation that has preceded it. While the destruction of Tommy's vision occurs toward the end of the film, for Milena the surgical intervention is there from the beginning, so that the only way to imagine her "before"—the only representation of woman possible in discourse—is through Alex's remembering. When we see her in "real" time, "her" time, outside of Alex's and Netusil's fantasmatic construction which coincides with narrative time, she is *already* scarred. And although the linear temporal dimension of the investigation seeks to reduce her contradiction, and to establish it as an opposition (to the law, to patriarchy, to phallic desire), the montage resists that time, makes it bad, prevents it from producing that truth. The question of time—the "bad timing" of conflicting orders of temporality and the filmic representation of non-congruent temporal registers—is the problem of the film, its work with and against narrative: how to articulate the sexual, the political and the cinematic, and "the impossibilities discovered in the process of such an articulation."[24]

There is the linear time of the investigation, with its logical succession of cause and effect, crime and punishment, guilt and reparation, its movement forward toward resolution and backward toward the original scene, the traumatic moment of an oedipal drama which narrativity endlessly reconstructs. All narrative cinema, in a sense, is the making good of Oedipus, the restoration of his vision by the film's representation (reenactment) of the drama. Linear time, with its logic of identity and non-contradiction, its predication of a definite identification of characters and events, before or "now" which is not "not now," a here where "I" am or an elsewhere where "I" am not, is a necessary condition of all investigation and of all narrative; it regulates the detection of an already certain "crime," and the making good of the film's vision for the spectators. In Roeg's film this linear time is "bad," for the sequence of events between Milena's phone call to Alex and his call for the ambulance, and the time between them, cannot be reconstructed (except in his "confession"); the "evidence" is insufficient. As Netusil's detection hangs on Alex's confession, we depend on the film's structuring of visual and aural clues, but find ourselves adrift between narrative and shot, amidst mismatching images and sounds. For example, the tape of Milena's voice on the phone is played back several times at different points of the film, suggesting the nonlogical, symptomatic processes of compulsive repetition; even the ravishment scene, placed as it is concurrently with the direct confrontation between Alex and Netusil—the moment when they come together in the scenario of voyeurism and fetishism that sustains their common "sensual obsession"—cannot furnish conclusive, factual or logical proof.

By not producing the truth, i.e., the possibility of a certain identification of events and behaviors, the film denies the legality of this temporal order and of the investigative, narrative vision. Our sympathy for Netusil is a measure of our identification with his loss. Indeed, the temporal order of loss, the second register of "bad" time in the film, is that of symptomatic repetition and primary processes, the relentless, unruly return of an image-fetish—the female body, bound, strapped down, violated, powerless, voiceless or nearly inarticulate, lifeless—signalling the dimension of obsession, its compulsive timing, and an illegality of vision.[25] Together, in a systematic opposition which by definition "projects" one onto the other (as Jakobson would say, but does not Foucault as well?), the sequential, metonymic order of the investigation and the metaphoric register of obsessive repetition define the legal and illegal times of masculine, phallic desire.[26] But a third possibility is posed in the film, questioning the first two: the possibility of a different temporality, another time of desire.

"What about *my* time?" shouts Milena in a context where time stands for desire (and significantly not in a Vienna apartment but on a sunbathed Moroccan terrace from where she watches the snake charmers in the market square below); "What about now? . . ." she asks in response to Alex's marriage proposal, which is accompanied not by a diamond ring but by a one-way ticket Casablanca-New York.[27] Alex does not reply, though in our mind's ears echoes the answer given for him by all the movies we remember, "We will always have Paris." That question, indeed, could not be answered in the film in any other way. The apparatus of cinema—both classical narrative and avant-garde cinema—has been developed in a culture founded exactly on the exclusion of all discourse in which that question could be posed.[28] Milena's "now," her "time," the time of her desire is on another register altogether, not congruent or commensurate with Alex's time, which leads forward to possession as marriage and/or backward to fetishistic possession. "If I told you I was married, you'd think it meant in your way, and it wasn't like that, so better I...I don't think it was a lie....Words...[it's] not important," explains Milena. "Not important to whom? To whom? To whom? To whom?" pounds and cajoles Alex's voice over her body, which the montage locates simultaneously on their bed and on the operating table.

Along the linear dimension of his time, in the unified trajectory of phallic desire, marriage and love can only "mean" in his way, and Milena's "now" has no place; as he tells her, again *à propos* of her marital status: "Either you're married or divorced, you can't be in between. To be in between is to be no place at all." A not atypical exchange between them, which exemplifies their mismatched, nonsynchronous registers of time and desire, occurs on the bridge over the Danube that serves as border and "neutral ground" between Vienna (where the story of Alex and Milena takes place) and Bratislava (where Milena's Czech husband, Stefan, lives).[29] This scene doubles the one, very early on in the film, when Milena and Stefan part on the same border bridge (and "It does not mean I'm going away," she says). Now, she is again returning to Vienna:

Milena: How're you doin'?
Alex: What happened?
Milena: You don't like it...the way I look...I bought it for you [a new
          dress]...
Alex: You're a day late.
Milena: I wired you, didn't I?
Alex: (as she walks back on the bridge toward Bratislava): Where are
          you going?
Milena: Nowhere.

And it is Pinter's *No Man's Land* which Yale Udoff, the author of *Bad Timing*'s screenplay and himself a playwright, has Milena read in the German translation, *Niemandsland*.

If "nowhere" and "now" are the place and time of feminine desire, that they can only be stated as negativity, as borders, is what the film finally says; and it is the most it can say. Radical difference can perhaps be thematized and represented only as an experiencing of borders: nonsequiturs in the dialogue, visual and aural split ends, a running over of the sound beyond "its" image, a bleeding of the image into another, the cuts which articulate narrative and shot, and mismatch them. Borders. Not gaps—in a story, in a chain of signifiers, in a (presumed) continuity of the drive from excitation to discharge to excitation, of history from thesis to antithesis to synthesis—but borders: between cultures, between discourses, between cinema and spectatorship, between the look of the camera and the image on the screen, neither here nor there and both here and there.

And what about identification? For it is not enough that a film describe or mark out "the problematic of the apparatus," that it demonstrate the terms "of the relations of cinema's vision...including, above all, the woman," as Heath has shown of Oshima's film, as could be shown of Michael Snow's recent *Presents*.[30] To demonstrate the functioning of "woman" as the support of masculine vision, the restoration of Oedipus' sight, or the odd term in the relations of power, is no longer the task of feminist critical practice.[31] If how to "produce and break the apparatus of look and identification" is still a real issue for a political understanding of cinema, feminist practice must start from the question: What about now? What about my time and place in the apparatus of look and identification, in the nexus of image, sound and narrative temporality?

For me, spectator, Roeg's film poses that question (which is not to say that it is a "feminist film"—a label that serves at best industrial profits), as do films like Sally Potter's *Thriller* and *Sigmund Freud's Dora* (not made by Sigmund Freud, against the rules of grammatical identification and authorial ownership, but by Anthony McCall, Claire Pajaczkowska, Andrew Tyndall and Jane Weinstock). Like those films—which I mention not as "exemplary" but as the first that come to my mind—*Bad Timing* plays on two tellings of the story, several temporal registers, and a voice somewhere, nowhere, that asks a question without answer. Two tellings of the story which, in all three cases, as Billie Holiday sings over the rolling end credits, is:

> The same old story
> of a boy and a girl in love,
> the scene, same old moonlight
> the time, same old June night
> romance's the theme. . . .
> The same old story
> it's been told much too much before
> the same old story
> but it's worth telling just once more...

In *Sigmund Freud's Dora: A Case of Mistaken Identity*, the other telling of the story is, of course, Freud's own case history, a narrative genre *par excellence* dependent as it is on the oedipal trajectory of the "family romance." *Thriller* engages opera, specifically Puccini's *La Bohème*, whose narrative appeal is closer to the sentimental novel and the "weepie" film genre than the popular spectacles of Verdi or the Mythical-Mystical total theater of Wagner. What is retold in *Bad Timing* is the story of narrative cinema, from Broken Blossoms to *Chinatown*, or vice versa. Tom Waits' "invitation to the Blues," sung over the opening credit sequence with a slurred jazz cadence which only allows a few key words (Cagney, Rita Hayworth) to be comprehended, goes like this:

> Well she's up against the register
> with an apron and a spatula
> with yesterday's deliveries
> and tickets for the bachelors.

She's a moving violation
from her conk down to her shoes
but it's just an invitation to the blues.
And you feel just like Cagney.
Looks like Rita Hayworth
at the counter of Schwab's drugstore.

Hearing this song, who does not "see" Lana Turner in *The Postman Always Rings Twice*? And that is one story proven to be "worth telling just once more" over and over again. *Bad Timing* starts out from film noir and ends by reclaiming the love story, but both genres are off-key, embarrassed by the difficulty of vision and understanding: the ambiguity of Klimt's mosaic figures, of Schiele's disturbing bodies, of Blake's lovers; the incoherence or unintelligibility of language (Waits' slurred words, like Milena's barely articulate voice on tape, the doctors' German, the Czech embassy intercom messages, the broken French of Alex and Milena hitchhiking in Morocco, the snake charmers' chant); and the disphasure of image and word, pleasure and meaning in Alex's slide lecture. Here the image that is supposed to appear on the screen in front of the students to match the lecturer's words suddenly appears on a screen behind them, but by the time the students/viewers turn their heads, the words refer to another image, which is now in front of them. And, as they turn around again, that too is gone. This short sequence, on the very theme of voyeurism, is a condensed and perfect metaphor of the entire film's work with and against narrative cinema: it frustrates the expected correspondence of look and identification, power and knowledge, while it emphasizes their historical, social and cinematic complicity.

But, as I suggested, something else takes place in *Bad Timing*, as in *Thriller* and *Sigmund Freud's Dora*: the disruption of the apparatus of look and identification (which is produced and broken at the same time) is concurrent with a dispersal of narrative, temporal, visual and aural registers. Specifically, these films construct a double temporality of events where the linear dimension of the narrative, backward and forward (they all have something of an investigation going on), is constantly punctuated, interrupted and rendered ineffectual by a "now" that mocks, screams and disturbs (the tv commercials and porno clips in *Dora*, ambulance siren and the *Tel Quel* recitation in *Thriller*). In *Bad Timing* that "now" is the constant presence of Milena's sexed body which the montage succeeds in presenting as at once conscious and unconscious, both alive and dead, there and not there: never totally unconscious, for it moves and gasps, shivers and groans— registering sensations, unknown perceptions, feelings perhaps—even in the deep coma of the emergency room and of the ravishment scene (especially then); nor ever fully conscious—in the sense of having full "presence of mind" as Alex does, full self-control or self-possession—but drunk, drugged, high, caught up in hysterical elation or depression, screaming or nearly inarticulate. And then, because of this memory of montage, the presentation of contradictory temporal registers, the scar on her chest in the last scene assumes its particular significance. It is still, to be sure, the "wound" which psychoanalysis correctly identifies as the mark of woman, the inscription of (sexual) difference in the female body, just as Milena still functions narratively in the film as "the woman," image to be looked at, body of desire. But the scar *also* assumes the value of a difference much more radical than the lack of something, be it the phallus, being, language or power: it represents difference as irreducible contradiction, the figure (not the image) of "that which is not represented, that which is unspoken, which is left out of namings and ideologies"—which is to say, woman.

It is such a figure, constructed by the montage as a memory of borders (e.g., the very last shot of the film, the river), of contradiction, here and there, now and nowhere, that addresses me as historical woman. And it is in the division of the spectator-subject between registers of time and desire, that figural and narrative identification are possible for me, that I can pose the question of my time and place in the terms of their imaging.

NOTES

1. See, for example, *The Cinematic Apparatus*, ed. Teresa de Lauretis and Stephen Heath (New York: St. Martin's Press, 1980).

2. By spectatorship I mean that particular relation of viewers to the film text and to cinema as an apparatus of representation which engages the spectators as subjects. Representation, as Stephen Heath puts it, "names the process of the engagement of subjectivity in meaning, the poles of which are the signifier and the subject but which is always a complex, specifically historical and social production.... The ideological is not in or equivalent to representation—which, precisely, is this complex process of subjectivity—but is the constant political institution of the productive terms of representation in a generalized system of positions of exchange." ("The Turn of the Subject," *Ciné-Tracts*, vol. 2, no. 3/4 [Summer/Fall 1979], pp. 44-45.)

3. Michel Foucault, *The History of Sexuality* (New York: Vintage Books, 1980), pp. 95-96.

4. See my "Imaging," *Ciné-Tracts*, vol. 3, no. 3 (Fall 1980), pp. 3-12.

5. Ernst Bloch, *On Karl Marx* (New York: Herder and Herder, 1971), p. 136. Foucault states: "And it is doubtless the strategic codification of these points of resistance that makes a revolution possible." (*The History of Sexuality*, p. 96.)

6. Bloch, p. 136.

7. Foucault, pp. 95-96, 97.

8. Fernando Solanas and Octavio Getino, "Toward a Third Cinema," *Cinéaste*, vol. 4, no. 3 (Winter 1970/71), pp. 1-11.

9. Stephen Heath, "The Question Oshima," *Wide Angle*, vol. 2, no. 1 (1977), p. 51.

10. See Foucault's analysis of "the perverse implantation" by which "unnatural" sexual behaviors were, first, medically categorized and labeled as sexual perversions, then given juridical status as individual personality types (in *The History of Sexuality*, pp. 36-49). The above excerpts from the dialogue of *Bad Timing*, and all the subsequent ones, are from the actual film soundtrack. I am deeply grateful to Yale M. Udoff for his generosity in discussing the film with me and for allowing me to see his original screenplay as well as the script, bearing the title, "Nicolas Roeg's Film *Illusions*," and dated February 27, 1979 (copyright 1978, Recorded Picture Co., London).

11. Jean Baudrillard, *The Mirror of Production*, trans. Mark Poster (St. Louis, MO: Telos Press, 1975), p. 27.

12. It is not accidental that the police(man)'s role is central in narrative cinema. Foucault speaks of *police*, in the broad sense the word had in the sixteenth and seventeenth centuries, to designate the activity or systematic intervention of public institutions, especially the state, in social life for the purpose of steering it toward an ideal order: "The house of confinement in the classical age constitutes the densest symbol of that 'police' which conceived of itself as the civil equivalent of religion for the edification of a perfect city." (*Madness and Civilization: A History of Insanity in the Age of Reason* [New York: Vintage Books, 1965], p. 63.) Insofar as such policing was

dependent upon the systematic gathering of information and thus required an organization of knowledge, Gianna Pomata suggests, Foucault's later concept of power/knowledge can be seen as "the abstract formulation of that notion of 'police': an ordering of social reality which constantly sets up for itself new areas of knowledge and control." ("Storie di 'police' e storie di vita: note sulla storiografia foucaultiana," *Aut aut* 170/171 [marzo/giugno 1979], p. 53; my translation.)

13. Foucault, *The History of Sexuality*, p. 157.

14. Ibid., p. 96.

15. See Michel Foucault, ed., *I, Pierre Rivière, having slaughtered my mother, my sister, and my brother... A Case of Parricide in the Nineteenth Century* (New York: Pantheon Books, 1975) and *Power/Knowledge: Selected Interviews and Other Writings, 1972-1977*, ed. Colin Gordon (New York: Pantheon Books, 1980).

16. "The proletarian public sphere can best be understood as a necessary form of mediating, as the center of a production process in the course of which the varied and fragmented experiences of social contradictions and social interests can be combined into a theoretically mediated consciousness and life style directed towards a transforming praxis. Thus, the concept of the 'proletarian public sphere' designates the contradictory and non-linear process of development towards class consciousness... a form of interaction which expresses the vital interests of the working class in a specific form while relating them to the entire society... mediating between social being and consciousness." (Eberhard Knoedler-Bunte, "The Proletarian Public Sphere and Political Organization: An Analysis of Oskar Negt and Alexander Kluge's *The Public Sphere and Experience*," *New German Critique* 4 [Winter 1975], p. 56. The reference is to Oskar Negt and Alexander Kluge, *Oeffentlichkeit und Erfahrung: Zur Organisationsanalyse von buergerlicher und proletarischer Oeffentlichkeit* [Frankfurt am Main: Suhrkamp, 1973].)

17. "The genealogical discourse on power appears to merge into a sort of mysticism of indetermination. Hence the impression of weakness Foucault's discourse produces, its paradoxical 'conservativism,' in spite of its apparent revolutionary charge: on the one hand it falls into a kind of anarchy; on the other, in the absence of a determinate alternative, the analysis of the mechanisms of power becomes merely a description of the universal modalities of the construction of reality." (Franco Crespi, "Foucault o il rifiuto della determinazione," *Aut aut* 170/171 [marzo/giugno 1979], p. 107; my translation.)

18. Foucault, "On Popular Justice: A Discussion with Maoists" in *Power/Knowledge*, pp. 8-9; my emphasis.

19. Ibid., p. 23.

20. Ibid., pp. 14-15.

21. Foucault, *The History of Sexuality*, pp. 31-32.

22. Julia Kristeva, "Interview—1974: Julia Kristeva and *Psychanalyse et Politique*," trans. Claire Pajaczkowska, *m/f* 5/6, (1981). p. 166. (Reprinted in *Polylogue* [Paris: Seuil, 1977].)

23. See my "Woman, Cinema and Language," *Yale Italian Studies*, no. 2 (Fall 1980), pp. 5-21, and "Through the Looking-Glass" in *The Cinematic Apparatus*, pp. 187-202.

24. Heath, "The Question Oshima," p. 48. An immediate instance of such "impossibilities" is obvious in the descriptions of Milena's character given by reviewers and casual spectators alike. For example, "a mysterious young woman... whose neurotic, demanding behavior feeds and frustrates his own anxieties" (Howard Kissel, "The Fragmented Figments of Nicholas [sic] Roeg," *W*, September 12-19, 1980, p. 20); or "the occasional wife of a retired Czech Colonel, Stefan Vognic (Denholm Elliott), many years her senior and vastly tolerant of her unfaithful, unpredictable sexuality (she leaves him whenever she feels like it, has affairs)" (Ian Penman, "*Bad Timing*, a Codifying Love Story," *Screen*, vol. 21, no. 3 [1980], p. 108). Such descriptions not only proceed from an enunciative perspective entirely congruent with Alex's and Netusil's point of view, and all but disregard the film's work to disrupt that "vision" (through montage, sound-image mismatch, the final "Brechtian" epilogue, etc.), but in their moralizing ("unfaithful, unpredictable sexuality") and easy psychologizing ("neurotic, demanding") they assume the very categories of female definition produced by classical narrative discourse, which have man (husband, lover and male spectator) as their single term of reference. In short, they assume and take for granted that which in the film is, precisely, at issue.

25. The connection between this image and its libidinal investment is made several times in the film and, most explicitly, in the nightclub scene where a female performer, naked but for a "choker" and leather straps, bounces in a net suspended above the audience.

26. For Roman Jakobson, see "Linguistics and Poetics," in *Style in Language*, ed. Thomas Sebeok (Cambridge, MA: MIT Press, 1960), p. 358. See also Jacques Lacan, *Ecrits: A Selection*, trans. Alan Sheridan (New York: W.W. Norton, 1977), pp. 147-171.

27. Alex: I say we go back, we get married, we build something solid together.
    Milena: What about now?
    Alex: What do you mean now?
    Milena: Here, right now, this minute, this second, what we are. . .
    Alex: Milena, did you miss that I just asked you to marry me?
    Milena: No!
    Alex: But what are you talking about? I'm asking you to marry me.
    Milena: I love these days. . .
    Alex: I don't get it. Weren't you happy? You had to be happy. I felt it.
    Milena: I am happy. . . I was happy. . . I am happy. When I'm with you, I'm with you. . . I love being with you.
    Alex: What does that mean with me, not with me? You have a husband you don't want, but you. . .
    Milena: My own life, my own time. You can be a part of it, the biggest part of it, you *are* the biggest part of it, I love you. . . C'mon. . . look where we are!

28. See the brief dialogue between Feathers and Sheriff Chance in *Rio Bravo* quoted at the beginning of the paper, where the man speaks as "I," and the woman as "you." Only to the extent that the logical subject of discourse is one—a unity grammatically ensured by the dialogical oppositon of I and you—and thus a masculine one, is the *dialogue* possible between them, and everything that dialogue represents: love, marriage, the happy ending, the "sense" of the story, narrative itself.

29. Perhaps every movie about "woman" should be set in Vienna. The resemblance to *Letter From an Unknown Woman* goes further than the name Stefan (Lisa's lover and son), the marital triangle, the Prater waltz heard in the background of two conversations, the diegetic time span of a few hours (from late evening to early morning) during which are revisited an entire relationship and a lifetime. As Heath has suggested of *In the Realm of the Senses*, Roeg's film is also *Letter*'s "ruinous remake": Lisa is exactly where Milena is not, squarely in the center of the oedipal trajectory, the narrative time of masculine vision and desire, her dis-embodied voice only partially outside the story, finally contained in it by the film's circular temporality; but both women are unknown, except as figures of an obsession, memory traces around which Ophuls' flowing camera constructs a full narrative space, a perfect memory, and Roeg's disjunctive montage the shadow of a doubt, a fragmentary memory of difference. And perhaps it is not pure coincidence that Cavani's *The Night Porter* is also set in Vienna, the perfect scenario of masochism. See Kaja Silverman's very interesting reading of Freud and of the film in "Masochism and Subjectivity," *Framework* 12 (n.d.), pp. 2-9.

30. See my "Snow on the Oedipal Stage," *Screen*, vol. 22, no. 3 (1981), pp. 24-40.

31. "I am tired of men arguing amongst themselves as to who is the most feminist, frustrated by an object feminism becoming the stakes in a displaced rivalry between men because of a refusal to examine the structure of the relations between themselves. . . . Insofar as this homosexuality . . . is also and primarily a history, or more precisely that consistently unspoken process by which the production of history is displaced from its discursive contradictions, it remains the issue that men must now address—that of men's sexualities, the problem of their own desire, the problem of their theory." (Claire Pajaczkowska, "The Heterosexual Presumption: A Contribution to the Debate on Pornography," *Screen*, vol. 22, no. 1 [1981], p. 92.)